Dwight David Eisenhower
and American Power

American Biographical History Series

Dwight David Eisenhower
and American Power

William B. Pickett
Rose-Hulman Institute of Technology

Harlan Davidson, Inc.
Wheeling, Illinois 60090-6000

Library of Congress Cataloging-in-Publication Data

Pickett, William B. (William Beatty), 1940–
    Dwight David Eisenhower and American power / William B.
Pickett.
      p. cm. — (American biographical history series)
    Includes bibliographical references and index.
    ISBN 0-88295-918-2
    1. Eisenhower, Dwight D. (Dwight David), 1890–1969.
2. Presidents—United States—Biography. 3. Generals—United
States—Biography. 4. United States. Army—Biography. I. Title.
II. Series.
E836.P53   1995
973.921'092—dc20
[B]
                                    94–38155
                                    CIP

Cover photo: At White House, October 14, 1956. National Park
Service photograph, courtesy Dwight D. Eisenhower Library.
Frontispiece: At Camp Kilauea, Hawaii, May 17, 1946. U.S. Army
photograph, courtesy Dwight D. Eisenhower Library.

Manufactured in the United States of America
98   97   96   95   94   1   2   3   4   5   MG

EDITORS' FOREWORD

As biographies offer access to the past, they reflect the needs of the present. Newcomers to biography and biographical history often puzzle over the plethora of books that some lives inspire. "Why do we need so many biographies of Abraham Lincoln?" they ask, as they search for the "correct" version of the sixteenth president's story. Each generation needs to revisit Lincoln because each generation has fresh questions, inspired by its own experiences. Collectively, the answers to these questions expand our understanding of Lincoln and America in the 1860s, but they also assist us to better comprehend our own time. People concerned with preserving such civil liberties as freedom of the press in time of national crisis have looked at Lincoln's approach to political opposition during and after secession. Civil rights activists concerned with racial injustice have turned to Lincoln's life to clarify unresolved social conflicts that persist more than a century after his assassination.

Useful as it is to revisit such lives, it is equally valuable to explore those often neglected by biographers. Almost always, biographies are written about prominent individuals who changed, in some measure, the world around them. But who is prominent and what constitutes noteworthy change are matters of debate. Historical beauty is definitely in the eye of the beholder. That most American biographies tell of great white males and their untainted accomplishments speaks volumes about the society that produced such uncritical paeans. More recently, women and men of various racial, religious, and economic backgrounds have expanded the range of American biography. The lives of prominent African-American leaders, Native American chieftains, and immigrant sweatshop workers who climbed the success ladder to its top now crowd onto those library shelves next to familiar figures.

In the American Biographical History Series, specialists in key areas of American History describe the lives of important men and women of many different races, religions, and ethnic backgrounds as those figures shaped and were shaped by the political, social, economic, and cultural issues of their day and the people with whom they lived. Biographical subjects and readers share a dialogue across time and space as biographers pose the questions suggested by life in modern-day America to those who lived in other eras. Each life offers a time-less reservoir of answers to questions from the present. The result is at once edifying and entertaining.

The concise biographical portrait found in each volume in this series is enriched and made especially instructive by the attention paid to generational context. Each biographer has taken pains to link his or her subject to peers and predecessors engaged in the same area of accomplishment. Even the rare individuals whose ideas or behavior transcend their age operated within a broad social context of values, attitudes, and beliefs. Iconoclastic radicals, too, whatever their era, owed a debt to earlier generations of protesters and left a legacy for those who would resist the status quo in the future.

Biographers in the series offer readers new companions, individuals of accomplishment, whose lives and works can be weighed and assessed and consulted as resources in answering the nagging questions that the thoughtful in every generation ask of the past to better comprehend the present. The makers of America—male and female, black and white and red and yellow, Christian, Moslem, Jew, atheist, agnostic, and polytheist, rich and poor and in between—all testify with their lives that the past is prologue. Anxious to share his rich experiences with those willing to listen, an elderly Eastern European immigrant living in Pittsburgh boasted, "By myself, I'm a book!" He, too, realized that an important past could be explicated through the narrative of a life, in fact, his own.

When a biographer sees his or her subject in broader context, important themes are crystallized, an era is illuminated. The single life becomes a window to a past age and its truths for succeeding generations and for you.

ALAN M. KRAUT
JON L. WAKELYN

CONTENTS

INTRODUCTION AND ACKNOWLEDGMENTS

It is rare that one man comes to symbolize an era. If the decade of the 1950s is known as the age of Eisenhower, the red, white, and blue "I Like Ike" campaign button is its emblem, its dominant image the motorcade with the famous general standing in a black limousine, arms upraised, hands waving, eyes gleaming beneath the wide forehead and thinning hair, his mouth curled upward in a broad grin.

The crowds along the curb cheer as he passes. Shoved against the police lines are Americans of all ages, incomes, ethnic groups, and avocations: men, women, and children, whites, blacks, Latinos, Poles, Greeks, Asians, Southerners, Midwesterners, blue- and white-collar workers, and farmers. Some are in uniform. Many are veterans. As his car appears they turn to watch, their eyes transfixed on the almost mythical figure until he recedes into the distance. They are comforted and hopeful. Their hero in the recent victory over Nazi Germany has accepted their call to protect them again, this time from the Soviet menace.

That Eisenhower was elected President of the United States in 1952 was nonetheless, to some observers, surprising. That four years later he was elected to a second term with the largest majority in history was to them remarkable. As a military professional he had never voted, not even declaring a party affiliation until just before becoming a presidential candidate. How, they asked, could he have been such a success both as a soldier and as a President? Few historians seemed aware of Eisenhower's unique character, education, and experience.

Part of the confusion arose both from a lack of archival research and the perspective of time. The 1950s has long been viewed as a happy time of peace, prosperity, and complacency, with increasing numbers of Americans turning to individual, often selfish pursuits—a job in a large corporation, a house in the suburbs, a new car in the

garage, children playing on a tidy lawn. With federal support, highways fanned out from congested business districts to subdivisions
where tract houses, schools, and shopping malls were under construction. The age of television dawned, and with it came a new, more
pervasive form of entertainment, image making, and marketing. After two decades of economic depression and war, life in the 1950s
was, for many Americans, a living dream. Not everyone, however,
believed that such changes were for the good. Some perceived more
pressure to conform, a loss of creativity, a covetous desire to be like
the folks next door, "the Joneses" or "organization men." The afflu-
ent society, as one writer called it, was one of materialism and indul-
gence. It was during this decade that members of Congress, especially the infamous Senator Joe McCarthy, trampled free speech and
inquiry, that African Americans enjoyed only limited civil rights, despite constitutional guarantees and federal efforts to integrate schools
and protect their access to the voting booth. As one might expect of
a professional military man whose career and interests had isolated
him from domestic politics and policy, the pundits said, President
Eisenhower delegated responsibility to his cabinet and staff and spent
much of his time fishing, playing golf, and entertaining grandchildren. As a foe of the New Deal and the friend of corporate presidents, he failed to understand the problems of the poor, the elderly,
and the many who suffered discrimination—those for whom the
American dream never came true.

More recently the epochal events of the late 1980s and early 1990s
while favorable to democracy have raised new questions about the
decades of the mid-twentieth century. The Berlin Wall has been torn
down, Germany is reunified, the Soviet Union gone. Yet these recent
events have forced questions about past U.S. policy. The costs and
dangers of the cold war were enormous; did the means used by American leaders hasten or delay its conclusion? Was there a better way?

What, then, is the truth about the man and his era? It is probable
that his detractors, while correct in some areas, failed to grasp
Eisenhower and the time in which he lived. If the 1950s seem quiet
in retrospect, this is in part a tribute to those, including Eisenhower,
who shaped that perception, because U.S. leaders of that time faced
the enormous problems of the cold war. In World War II the United
States had asserted its leadership in world affairs, but that leadership
was by no means secure in 1952. War had broken out in Korea. Unrest existed in much of the developing world, and Marxist-Leninist

regimes ruled in the Soviet Union and China—respectively the world's most expansive and populous nations. All of this and a burgeoning competition between the superpowers for influence and for ever more numerous and sophisticated weapons, made another world war possible.

Newly available sources at the United States' presidential libraries include material from the 1940s and 1950s that was classified for national security reasons but is now open to scholars. A considerable body of evidence, including discoveries in the archives of the former Soviet Union, supports the view that the United States did what it had to do, did it reasonably well, and that the American official who perhaps better than any other carried the world across the technological and strategic divide between the eras of conventional and nuclear warfare was Dwight David Eisenhower.

Eisenhower's meaningful role, his successful transformation from wartime supreme commander and hero to cold-war commander-in-chief stemmed from his approach to things, his depth of understanding, and amazing adaptability. Rather curious for a professional soldier, but part of his upbringing, was his aversion to war, the answer to which he felt was deterrence. The most important lessons of the past for democracies, he believed, were the causes of war. Post–World-War-I demobilization and failure to enact universal military training (and achieve international respectability in diplomatic forums) had led to the appeasement of the Japanese when they marched into Manchuria in 1931 and of Hitler as he annexed western Czechoslovakia in 1938. In the nuclear age the United States no longer could afford such irresponsible foreign policy. Along with sufficient numbers of troops and weapons to fight limited wars, the United States, he believed, needed a strategic arsenal to inhibit a resort to arms. In international conflict the United States must persuade potential enemies that if necessary, deterrence having failed, from his command bunker, a ship, or an aircraft, the President could and would order an overwhelming attack on the enemy's forces and population. If command in wartime entailed tours of the battlefront, parades, exhortations, courts-martial, and risking one's life, command in cold war required compassion, civility, and rationality, for one's country and culture and those of the antagonist were in grave danger. The postwar era required not a heroic mask but, rather, a quiet (even cold) resolve, vigilance, and patient persuasion. Eisenhower thus used military readiness and conciliation. He admonished Americans and their allies and enemies that by manufacturing arms governments rob the hungry. Even while ordering deployment of missiles, submarines, and bombers, he asserted that their use in combat would reveal that he (and the troops too) had failed. While urging military preparedness, Eisenhower called on his fellow Americans to protect human rights and popular institutions. He genuinely feared an "unwarranted influence of a scientific-military-industrial complex." Although the international tension resulting from the breakdown of wartime cooperation in 1945 and 1946 lasted much longer and was much more costly than he had desired, his balanced approach generally succeeded.

Eisenhower's was thus a remarkable odyssey from a small town amidst grain elevators on the golden plains of central Kansas to the Oval Office of the White House as his nation attained unprecedented global influence. He was a hard-driving and hot-tempered man with strong convictions who disciplined both himself and his fellow countrymen. Seeking a federal government that would both calm fears and allow individual initiative, he moved quietly behind the scenes to create the conditions within which the Senate censured the leader of the radical right wing of the Republican party, Senator Joseph R. McCarthy. Monitoring the economy, he pushed programs to strengthen and stabilize it. Through his Supreme Court and cabinet appointees he supported the first civil rights legislation since the nineteenth century. But even with the help of loyal lieutenants, he did not always accomplish his purposes, and there was, as will be seen, a large price to be paid on the path that he and the nation took. But Dwight D. Eisenhower's contribution was considerably more important, his era more dangerous and demanding, than people knew.

Books are collaborative enterprises. Many individuals and institutions supported this one.

A sabbatical leave from Rose-Hulman Institute of Technology enabled me to move to Abilene, Kansas, for eight months of research in 1983. Later, Rose-Hulman defrayed the costs of additional research trips, awarded me a one-quarter leave in 1992, and provided computer and secretarial support. For this I thank the faculty committee on leaves, Dean James R. Eifert, President Samuel F. Hulbert, and the Rose-Hulman Board of Managers, I am indebted to two chairmen of the Department of Humanities, Social, and Life Sciences, Peter Parshall and Thomas W. Mason. Thad Smith, Rose-Hulman

professor of political science, as part of his continuing encouragement and interest in this book, invited me to discuss Eisenhower's
military career in his seminar when he was visiting professor at the
Army War College in Carlisle Barracks, Pennsylvania. John Robson,
director of the Logan Library, and Margaret Ying, interlibrary loan
librarian, fulfilled each of my requests with helpful efficiency. Finally,
Betty Moore, a painstaking and efficient department secretary, helped
with revisions, printouts, and mailings.

The assistance of the staff at the Eisenhower Library in Abilene
were enormously helpful: John Wickman, former director, gave encouragement; archivists Kathy Struss and Jim Leyerzapf were indispensable; Dwight Strandberg, archivist-librarian, engaged me in numerous useful discussions; and Hazel Stroda provided photographs
and videos. Thanks also to Suzanne K. Forbes of the John F. Kennedy
Library.

The staff of the Abilene Public Library found material for me on
the local community, and Mr. and Mrs. Duckwall showed me Kansas
hospitality.

Maureen Gilgore Hewitt of Harlan Davidson, Inc., expressed her
interest in my research. The American Biographical History Series
editors, Jon Wakelyn of The Catholic University of America and Alan
Kraut of The American University, accepted my proposal, and they,
along with editor Andrew J. Davidson, improved the manuscript with
their suggestions.

Help also came from Stephen E. Ambrose, who at the very beginning of this endeavor provided friendly advice and encouragement;
Darlene Norman of St. Mary-of-the-Woods College gave helpful advice on the early chapters; James H. Madison of Indiana University
read the manuscript and gave useful advice. David Anderson of the
University of Indianapolis, Roger Dingman of the University of Southern California, and Fred I. Greenstein of Princeton University invited me to give presentations on Eisenhower's foreign policy at professional meetings at Georgetown University, Stanford, and Princeton,
respectively. Professor William Woolley of Ripon College and Malcolm
Muir of Austin Peay State University created similar opportunities at
meetings sponsored by the American Military Institute. The manuscripts librarian at the United States Military Academy at West Point
gave me access to Eisenhower's student records and to documents
on Eisenhower in the papers of General Omar Bradley. The West
Point summer workshop on military history, 1982, gave me instruc-

tion on the history of warfare. The Hofstra University Conference on Eisenhower was an opportunity to talk with former Eisenhower administration officials and family members. Eisenhower centennial conferences sponsored by Gettysburg College, Washburn University, and the Kansas State Historical Society in Topeka in 1990 invited me to give scholarly presentations. The manuscripts division of the Library of Congress allowed me access to the papers of General George Patton. Herbert Brownell provided useful reminiscences. General Alfred Gruenther wrote a letter about his relationship with Eisenhower. General Andrew J. Goodpaster told me about Eisenhower's years with Fox Conner, the Solarium conference, and, as personal liaison to Eisenhower, his conversations with Lyndon Baines Johnson. Especially helpful were the questions and comments of the students in my classes on recent United States history and American arms and strategy at Rose-Hulman. They included notably Jerry Rominger and Donald Jenkins, who read various chapters.

During my Fulbright year in Japan in 1989 other historians asked me to report on my research. In Tokyo I received helpful criticism from the political history study group at Keio University under the leadership of Makoto Saito of International Christian University and Takeshi Igarashi of the University of Tokyo. Ichiro Iwano and Kotoro Kanai at Nanzan University in Nagoya arranged for me to give presentations at meetings of their colleagues, as did Keiji Nakatsuji at Hiroshima University. I am also indebted to Nakatsuji sensei for our numerous discussions during our stay in Abilene in 1983. Julian Jones, director of the University of Maryland Asian Division, provided an opportunity to teach at United States military installations in Korea.

More important than any other individual to the existence of this book was Robert H. Ferrell, distinguished professor emeritus at Indiana University. He recommended the topic, read drafts with care, and provided essential guidance based on his years in the Eisenhower and Truman papers. He was, in sum, a true colleague and friend.

Finally, there was the indispensable assistance of my father, Walter Nathan Pickett, my parents-in-law, Ida and Gordon Hollingsworth, my friend William K. Johnson of Winnetka, Illinois, and the three people most affected by the many absences that a project such as this requires: my wife, Janet Elizabeth, who always was there, and our sons, Robert Matthew and Jeffrey Michael. It is to the latter two that I dedicate this book with love.

WILLIAM B. PICKETT
Terre Haute, Indiana

CHAPTER ONE

Early Years

Dwight David Eisenhower was born in the small Texas town of Denison, on October 14, 1890. Though the citizens of the United States had removed the Native Americans from the land west of the Mississippi, much of this area, a vast subcontinent, remained unsettled. The country was barely a century old. Its populace was well under one hundred million. Much needed to be done. The prediction of President Thomas Jefferson that Americans would require many generations to move into and cultivate the lands of the American West had proved correct.

Shortly after Eisenhower's birth, his father, David, moved his family to Abilene, Kansas. They had moved to Texas from near Abilene so that David could take a railroad job; times were hard, and he had needed to do it. Once back in Abilene, the Eisenhowers moved first into a small, wooden house across the Union Pacific Railroad tracks on the less-prosperous south side of town, then to a square, two-story house, also on the south side, that could barely accommodate what became a family of eight—mother, father, and six sons. It was here that the young Eisenhower grew to manhood.

During this period, religion was the foundation of most people's upbringing on the farms and in the villages of small-town America, and the Eisenhower family was of the German Brethren in Christ, a sect of the Mennonites popularly known as the River Brethren because they held river baptisms. Dwight's

1

grandfather Jacob, a minister, had taken his family and three hundred members of the sect out to Abilene from Elizabethville, Pennsylvania, in the 1870s to obtain better farm land. Along with the group went a sense of the finiteness of life, the importance of preparation, the need to work and prosper, for that was what He had intended. Prosper they did; Jacob was able to give each of his fourteen children, including his eldest son David, a 160-acre farm.

In the 1890s the small town on the Kansas prairie was a place where farmers bought equipment, sold grain and, when the time came, retired. The Eisenhowers fitted easily into this place, enjoying the closeness and support of their friends, relatives, and religious community. Though happy in their southside home, their surroundings stood in contrast to the straight, elm-shaded streets and the large Victorian houses of the wealthier neighborhood north of Abilene's business center.

The experiences of childhood connect in uncertain ways to accomplishments in adulthood. Why, one might ask, did other boys from Abilene not do as well as Dwight D. Eisenhower and his brothers? Perhaps it was because the Eisenhower boys wrestled with, rather than accepted, the commonplaces of growing up.

The source for Eisenhower of what proved to be an extremely successful approach to life was his father. To be a farmer on the windswept wheatlands of east-central Kansas meant grueling, sometimes futile work. Time spent in the fields did not necessarily determine one's reward at the end of the year. It was a lottery in which weather could drastically change the growing season and international markets determined prices. Therefore, David Eisenhower, having returned to Abilene, decided to take a job as a maintenance man in the creamery owned by the River Brotherhood to avoid the uncertainties of working the land. Years before he had wanted to be an engineer and enrolled in Lane University—no longer in existence but then located in central Kansas. It was there that he met Ida Stover. The two young people fell in love and, after a short courtship, were married.

David controlled the household. The "czar" of discipline, he used the rod freely. Dwight recalled that his mother "took care of minor infractions during the day but anything serious was passed along to father for settlement." As Dwight remembered, "Mother was the one who talked more of standards, aspirations and opportunities. Dad believed more, I think, in sheer training and discipline. He was not one to be trifled with, unless you were prepared to take the consequences." But David was more than a disciplinarian. A man whose temper could "blaze with frightening suddenness," he also was a "just man, well liked, a thinker . . . undemonstrative, quiet, modest . . . never used alcohol or tobacco." Faith, prayer, and the love of family were important to him.

David was obviously a strong influence on his sons, but in rural America it was common for the mother to have a good deal of influence too, perhaps even greater than that of the father, for she after all spent more time at home. Such seems to have been the case with Ida Eisenhower—a warm, mild-mannered woman who believed in discipline but never resorted to physical punishment harsher than a gentle slap. Slender, five feet, six inches tall, with large, attractive, blue eyes and light brown hair, she was a hard worker. She memorized large portions of the Bible and became a leader of one of the home prayer and study groups that later joined to form the Jehovah's Witnesses, and which eventually rejected the use of force in society and among nations. Belief in a merciful God, her son recalled, made her "absolutely certain that those who were honest and faithful Christians would have a perpetual life of happiness."

Mrs. Eisenhower's resolve matched that of her husband, but her manner was different. Eisenhower later wrote that her selflessness, faith, and consideration of others was "saintly." He recalled that she dealt with each son according to his personality. Because her husband worked six days a week, 6:30 A.M. until 5:00 P.M., she delegated the chores, which included kitchen duty, pruning the orchard, hoeing the corn, feeding the chickens, and milking the cows, all of which she herself did as well.

Of all the children, Dwight most resembled his mother. His eyes and smile, as well as his optimism, sense of humor, and idealism, came from her. Still, he carried traits, which would become more obvious as he grew older, of his father. These were a quick temper, frugality, courage, and a keen interest in ideas. The qualities he received from his mother concerned principles and ends; those from his father pointed toward reputation and duty. Above all, from his parents Dwight acquired a sense of self-sufficiency. "Responsibility was part of our maturing," he recalled. "And ambition without arrogance was quietly instilled in us by both parents. Part of that ambition was self-dependence."

The setting of this parental influence was, of course, Abilene. Almost without notice, winter or summer, the prairie winds would whip up and howl. Returning after a little poker playing at a camping place a mile or so south of town by the Smoky Hill River, Dwight would lie in bed, listen to the wind, and dream of the six-gun days when Abilene was the railhead of the Kansas and Pacific Railroad, the northern end of the Texas longhorn Chisholm Trail.

By the 1900s the once wide-open cow town had become a quiet place, the only real excitement provided by nature. Mud Creek, a stream no wider than a long-legged boy could leap, could become a virtual torrent after a cloudburst. Two blocks west of the business district, the flooded stream could suddenly transform Abilene's north-south thoroughfare, Buckeye Street, into a raging river. In the flood of 1903, thirteen-year-old Dwight and friends took advantage of the high water by rafting down Buckeye Street all the way to the Smoky Hill River. The boys had a grand time, but David Eisenhower was not amused; with their help he could have prevented the inundation of the family basement. He made Dwight and his friends shovel out the mud.

Still, in Abilene children enjoyed learning about the natural world. On expeditions to the Smoky Hill River with a fifty-year-old bachelor who became Dwight's friend and teacher, Bob Davies, the young Eisenhower was taught the fundamentals of catching channel catfish, trapping muskrats and minks, shooting ducks with a double-barreled shotgun, flatboating, and finding one's own way in the woods, locating north from the moss on trees.

Once in a while the Eisenhower boys got into fights, and their father expected each of them to defend themselves. Quarreling in the household could break out over some minor event, such as the arrival in the mail of the *Saturday Evening Post*. But when neighborhood children attempted to tease one of the brothers, the older boys, Arthur or Edgar, were sure to intervene. One day, however, their father saw Dwight being chased home from school by a boy his size, Arthur and Edgar nowhere in sight. David demanded to know why his son was letting that boy "run you around like that?" Dwight said he was afraid he would get a whipping if he got into a fight. "Chase that boy out of here!" was the response. Dwight turned toward his attacker, who stopped, took a step back, and fled. Dwight caught up to the boy and threw him to the ground.

It was during these years that Dwight's stormy temper became apparent, a trait that at the outset required the attention of both his parents. Now called "Ike" by family and friends, Dwight turned ten years of age in October 1900. When Halloween arrived his older brothers put on costumes to call on neighbors. Dwight wanted to go along, but his parents, believing him too young, would not let him go. Flying into a rage, Dwight pounded the trunk of an apple tree with his bare hands. His father spanked him and sent him to bed. When Ike had calmed down, his mother came to his room, sat with him, and reached over to put salve on his hands. "He that conquereth his own soul," she said, "is greater than he who taketh a city."

Meanwhile, school—first at Lincoln Elementary, just across Buckeye Street, and later at Garfield High, five blocks north— provided Dwight more challenges and, as fate would have it, the preparation for a career as a professional soldier. Dwight was not a straight "A" student and did not mind. But neither was he slow. This was, after all, a boy who had learned to read from the Bible and who, because he was a stickler for detail, was an excellent speller. He began spending "too much time" reading about the wars of ancient Greece and Rome, prompting his mother to lock up his history books. He came to idolize Hannibal the Carthaginian for his military leadership, organization, and movement of troops. "The battles of Marathon, Zama, Salamis, and Cannae became as familiar to me as the games (and battles) I enjoyed with my brothers and friends in the school yard."

Garfield High School had a classical curriculum with four years of English, three of algebra, one and a half of plane geometry, three of Latin, also Latin composition, English composition, two years of German, physical geography, ancient history, English history, American history, rhetoric, civics, economics, and physics. Eisenhower's overall average was 85 percent. His best grade was 100 percent in geometry, which "entranced" him. Classmates described him in the yearbook as their "best historian and mathematician" and predicted he would be a professor of history at Yale. This youthful fascination with the people and events of the past, noticed first by his mother and now revealed by his classmates, would be perhaps the most important of his preoccupations.

Dwight also excelled in athletics. He joined a boxing club located in the back of a downtown print shop, but he took more enjoyment from team sports—baseball and, most of all, football. During his freshman year he had been a star halfback, a "triple threat." Then he skinned his knee and contracted blood poisoning, becoming so ill that his doctor discussed amputating the wounded leg. It was Ike who persuaded his parents not to allow it.

Ike's high school years included the community activities typical of the time: church picnics, ice cream socials, and, perhaps most important to Dwight, political rallies. Dwight remembered being handed a torch to carry in a rally in 1896 for William McKinley. In 1898 he followed news accounts of Lieutenant Colonel Theodore Roosevelt and the "rough riders" in Cuba. At a political banquet during his senior year, he gave a speech on the role of the student in politics. According to a report in the Abilene newspaper the oration "clearly demonstrated the necessity of young men studying politics."

High school went by quickly. The graduation ceremony for the class of 1908 was held in the Seelye Theater, a Spanish baroque vaudeville and silent-movie hall—many years later it was the site from which Eisenhower announced his candidacy for the presidency.

The two Eisenhower graduates of 1908, Dwight and Edgar, thereafter commenced the first phase of their cooperative plan to obtain college educations. Edgar enrolled at the University of Michigan; Dwight took a job to pay Ed's tuition. After two years Ed was to take a job so that Dwight could enroll at a university. Dwight first found work as a laborer and then as a "straw boss" at a company that made steel grain bins. Then he took another job, this one at the Belle Springs Creamery, first as an iceman and then, at the other end of the temperature scale, in the furnace room where he loosened clinkers from the fire bed of the boilers, dragging them out and dousing them. It was, he recalled, like working in a "small inferno." Within a year he had become second engineer with responsibilities back in the much-preferred refrigeration plant. Twelve-hour days and seven-day weeks for less than $90 a month were not easily forgotten, coming to mind years later when he encountered people who thought that as an army officer he had never done manual labor.

Considering the tedium in support of the cooperative college plan, it was not surprising that Dwight listened to a proposition from his Abilene classmate Everett "Swede" Hazlett, the son of a local physician. Hazlett had failed the mathematics section of the entrance examination for the U.S. Naval Academy at Annapolis. While studying to retake the exam, Hazlett worked in a gas lighting store his father owned, often stopping in at the creamery to see his friend Dwight, and to play poker and raid the ice cream locker. "Honesty, candor, horse-sense, and keen sense of humor" convinced Hazlett that Dwight would be ideal at Annapolis, and he told him so. For Dwight an appointment to the Naval Academy would relieve the financial burden on his brother and perhaps be an opportunity to play football. He began studying test questions. He wrote Senator Joseph Bristow and in the weeks that followed passed the screening examination, placing number-one for Annapolis and number-two for West Point (applicants had to apply for both academies). Then he discovered he was ineligible for Annapolis. The age limit for admittance was nineteen, and he was twenty. Fortunately, West Point admitted applicants until the age of twenty-two.

When, in the summer of 1911, the day arrived for Dwight to leave home, his mother and twelve-year-old brother Milton were the only family members there to see him off. His mother was unable to say a thing, Milton remembered, "I went out on the west porch with mother as Ike started uptown, carrying his suitcase, to take the train. Mother stood there like a stone statue and I stood right by her until Ike was out of sight. Then she came in and went to her room and bawled."

And so he went to West Point. Since its founding in the early nineteenth century, the military academy had created officers dedicated to duty, honor, and country. In June 1911, the unlikely looking, slender, long-armed, sandy-haired youth from Abilene trudged up the hill from the railroad station and saw for the first time the gothic fortress of gray granite. Chapel, administration building, east academic building, riding hall, and north barracks—those were some of the buildings. The corps of cadets had reached 580. Military training no longer was mainly close-order drill; Colonel Otto T. Hein, a student of the Prussian army, had introduced mountain guns, Gatlings, and mortars. But not much else had changed from the curriculum suited to the American Civil War. Cadets groomed and saddled horses, set up camp, learned open-order drill, attack formation, guard and reconnaissance, marksmanship, record-keeping, and administration. Military art and engineering included a trip to study the battlefield at Gettysburg. The first class, or seniors, also visited forts, coastal batteries, and proving grounds.

The youth from Abilene, a young man with considerable amateur knowledge of military history and the fundamentals of diplomacy, took West Point, its military routine, academic discipline, and even the hazing, in stride. Upperclassmen called freshmen "plebes," inferior beings sent to "beast barracks" to receive hazing. For recalcitrant students the system taught obedience, but Eisenhower was not bothered by such arrangements. His first encounter with the self-important yearlings (sophomores) who snapped orders, called newcomers "Mr. Dumgard or Mr. Ducrot," and demanded that plebes do pushups on command, convinced him that he should not take such things seriously. "At times the whole performance would strike me as funny and in the semi-privacy of my room I could laugh a little at myself and at the system." He determined that he would get what he came for, a free education.

In academic performance he stood in the upper half of his class. In conduct, which counted in the standing, his marks were poor. The worst "offense" occurred during his third-class year when one Saturday night on the dance floor he whirled his partner so rapidly that her dress flew out, exposing her knees. This incaution brought demotion from sergeant to private, confinement to barracks, and punishment tours on Wednesday and Saturday afternoons. Considering his high school successes in history and geometry, it was perhaps surprising that his best grades were in English, where he placed tenth. In engineering-surveying he was twenty-fifth. In history he stood thirty-ninth. In the end he did well but not exceptionally so, 61st in a class of 164.

Time for athletics at West Point proved brief. He took football seriously, playing so well as halfback in the early games of 1912 that observers predicted he would be all-American. Midway through the season, however, he was through. He wrenched his knee in the Tufts game and had to spend several days in the hospital. The following week at cavalry drill when he had to vault over his horse, his leg gave way. Damage to cartilage and tendons required more bed rest, a cast, and an end to sports. The injured knee bothered him for the rest of his time at the academy, and only a few weeks before graduation in 1915 he learned that he might not receive a commission because of it. He obtained his commission only by agreeing not to request mounted service.

As in infantry officer, Second Lieutenant Eisenhower at the outset received the usual postings, for the United States was not at war. His first duty, with the 19th regiment at Fort Sam Houston in 1915–16, was "in the main uninteresting. Nothing much doing—and I get tired of the same old grind some times." Then he became inspector-instructor of a National Guard regiment, the 7th Illinois, mobilized in 1916 on the Mexican border to defend against the bandit Pancho Villa. During this time he developed a reputation as a winning coach of post football teams.

It was during the Fort Sam Houston year that he met Mamie Doud. On his way to guard duty one afternoon he was stopped by the wife of a fellow officer who introduced friends from Denver, Mr. and Mrs. Doud and their daughter Mamie. He blurted out an invitation to take the nineteen-year-old girl on a tour of the guard posts. This was the beginning of what proved to be a low-budget courtship, with five-cent bus rides downtown for Mexican dinners and movies. "The girl I run around with is named Miss Doud from Denver," he wrote in a letter to a high school friend, "We get along well together and I'm at her house whenever I'm off duty—whether it's morning, noon or night." Miss Doud's parents consented to marriage on the condition that Ike would wait until their daughter's twentieth birthday.

With the United States' entrance into World War I in April 1917, Eisenhower's life took on new proportions that would bring the ambitious young officer both satisfaction and the dismay of never seeing combat. He was, it seems, simply too skillful as a teacher and organizer of military instruction to receive orders to Europe in the time remaining in the conflict. At first he was a supply officer. He then received promotion to captain and orders to Fort Oglethorpe, Georgia, as an instructor of officer candidates. He then moved to Fort Leavenworth, Kansas, where he taught officers and became known both for his leadership and for the effectiveness of his training, based as it was on his study of reports coming in from France of trench warfare. He then received orders to organize the 301st Heavy Tank Battalion at Camp Meade, Maryland, and finally was assigned to be the commanding officer at Camp Colt, the army tank corps training center near Gettysburg, Pennsylvania. He remained there until the end of the war on November 11, 1918. By that time he had arranged (even turning down promotion to colonel offered to him as an incentive to stay in the United States) to be part of the next troop movement to Europe. Alas, the armistice came too soon.

The experience at Camp Colt, although frustrating for an officer who knew the professional importance of combat command, influenced Eisenhower's decision—taken at this time— to stay in the army during the peacetime years that followed. Tanks offered a new way to wage war. At Colt the twenty-eight-year-old Lieutenant Colonel Eisenhower (wartime promotions had been rapid) commanded 10,000 men and 600 officers and demonstrated a capacity to learn about tanks and to organize training. The camp became a model center. Among other activities, its commander set up a development battalion for men who otherwise would have been discharged. Indeed,

Eisenhower's tank experience made it almost inevitable that he would meet Colonel George S. Patton, Jr., who had commanded the American tank corps in France and loved nothing better than to discuss new tank designs, conversations in which the two officers, Eisenhower later wrote, talked about a weapon that could change completely the strategy and tactics of land warfare. The opportunity to meet Patton occurred at Camp Meade, where the now Captain Eisenhower (he had reverted to his peacetime rank) found himself restationed after the dismantling of Camp Colt. The end of the war had brought a rapid demobilization of the army and relegation of mechanized detachments to places like Meade, where for a short while they conducted exercises. One of these took Eisenhower on a cross-country motor tour with a convoy of army trucks. In addition to rating the vehicles, the tour was to be a test of the nation's highways. In 1919 both achieved minimal standards at best, the convoy averaging less than six miles an hour. It was something Eisenhower never forgot.

Soon thereafter came a numbing personal tragedy. Dwight and Mamie discovered in late December 1920 that their two-year-old son, Doud Dwight ("Icky"), born in 1918 while they were at Camp Colt, had contracted scarlet fever. Unable to enter the child's room because of quarantine, the anguished couple could only gaze at the youngster through a bedroom window. Years later Eisenhower wrote of the child's death as the greatest disaster in his life.

By the end of 1920, Dwight Eisenhower had come a long way from Abilene, from the austere but warm Christian family, the winds of the Kansas plains, and the moan of train whistles. The adventure of life had taken him far, seemingly toward success, only to turn downward. And yet it was not the end; Eisenhower was able, resilient, and still fascinated by life's possibilities. He sensed that much remained for him to do, most immediately at a new duty station.

Ike and Mamie arrived at Camp Gaillard, Panama, in January 1922. The passage from New York had hardly been exhilarating. Their steamer had weathered a gale off Cape Hatteras. Upon arrival their baggage seemed all right, but the couple's new automobile, of which they had been so proud, was not. The model-T Ford would not run, its carburetor and distributor having been stolen during the voyage. It also had broken loose from its lashings and "raced around the deck to the eternal detriment of its finish and shape."

Gaillard was a desolate place. From the Panama Canal Railroad station the newly promoted major and his wife carried their suitcases in the humid tropical heat across one of the lock gates and up a hill. Mamie discovered that the house they were assigned, a flimsy remnant of canal construction days, was infested with vermin and, to her utmost displeasure, bats. "Mamie hated bats with a passion," Eisenhower recalled. Furthermore the frequent rain seemed to have little trouble penetrating the house's roof, walls, and window sills. Except for dances on Friday nights, bridge on Wednesdays, and mudslides that closed the canal or blocked interior trail networks, nothing promised to break what for the Eisenhowers had become a routine existence. Then Eisenhower reported to his commanding officer, Brigadier General Fox Conner.

It is clear now that had he not met Fox, Eisenhower never would have risen in the army and eventually become the President of the United States. General Conner was from Slate Spring, Mississippi, and, after graduating from West Point, had been assistant chief of staff of operations for American Expeditionary Forces commander General John J. "Black Jack" Pershing during World War I. Conner's motto, and for Eisenhower his most memorable teaching, was "take your job seriously, never yourself." More to the point, he was a remarkable student of military history, international affairs, and human nature. Conner once wrote that "man is differentiated from the other animals primarily by his ability to study, analyze, and profit."

General Conner had convictions, remarkable in retrospect, about professionalism and what it should mean to his new executive officer. He believed that Eisenhower's duty at Gaillard was to understand his (Conner's) purposes, and he intended to bring his assistant along in a way that would make him a commander. The general had met Eisenhower the previous year at Patton's quarters. On a Sunday afternoon the Conners were the honored guests at a dinner party to which the Pattons had also invited Ike and Mamie. After the meal the officers went out to survey the post to see the tanks, of course speculating about what the new weapons might mean for the future of warfare. Conner asked many questions and found Eisenhower, who no doubt drew upon his familiarity since childhood with military history, to be enormously impressive, so much so in fact that a few months later he contacted the former commander of Camp Colt and invited him to be his assistant in Panama. Eisenhower later recalled his thrill at the opportunity this presented. During the time in Panama and in the years that followed, with Conner's help Eisenhower obtained the knowledge that prepared him for virtually any career he wanted in the service of his country.

Generously sharing his experiences with his young protégé, Conner used history to make his points, comparing the masterful delaying actions of General Erich Ludendorff in the weeks after July 1918 with those of Robert E. Lee after July 1863. Eisenhower, having never seen combat but having read about Lee, was enthralled. It was amazing for him to think that just three and a half years earlier, the graying man speaking from across the campfire from him had planned the American counterattacks that caused the German offensive to falter. As the two rode together over the jungle trails, the general taught the major how to establish positions to defend the canal. An impressive speaker, Conner was able to quote from a wide variety of sources, including Plato, Tacitus, Shakespeare, and Nietzsche. Eisenhower began studying, in his spare time, on the second-story screened-in porch of his quarters, with books borrowed from Conner's personal library. Conner spoke of the importance of proper military reconnaissance, intelligence, discipline, and especially the writing of the set-piece, five-paragraph field order—the army way of assuring that every element necessary for carrying out a unit's mission had been considered.

The general discussed the ideas of the Swiss interpreter of Napoleonic warfare Baron Antoine Henri de Jomini (until 1813 a staff officer in the French army), which stressed the importance of bases and lines of communication. An analyst of human affairs, Jomini had sought to avoid the brutality of combat. War, he felt, produced laws. Generations of West Point cadets had studied Jomini's belief that an army could win merely by concentrating force at the correct time and place. Force needed short lines. Eisenhower had memorized Jomini from books, but now, with Conner's help, the ideas came to life.

The most memorable of Conner's lessons for his young charge were those concerning the German army. The Germans, he said, would go to war again, prompting another war of coalitions in which the winner would be the side that fought together well. The United States should enter such a coalition only if the allied forces possessed a war council and had a commander. In such an alliance the Americans should not surrender tactical control of their own troops. Coordination must come from institutional arrangements that allowed the allied commander's orders to be respected only if they revealed a mastery of the art of warfare and the requirements of the moment.

Two principal pieces of wisdom came, sometimes in roundabout fashion, from Eisenhower's talks with Conner. The first was that if Eisenhower were to command large bodies of troops, he must have acquaintance with a work by the Prussian general, Karl von Clausewitz, entitled *On War*. Theorist and reformer, Clausewitz had achieved a high standing among modern military thinkers. Indeed, his book was a military bible.

Difficulties in overcoming the German enemy in 1914–1918 had prompted many U.S. officers to turn to Clausewitz. Years later Eisenhower recalled that he read Clausewitz three times: Clausewitz had axioms, and Conner "made me tell what each one meant." The best known was that war was "an act of force to compel our adversary to do our will." It involved bloodshed and, at least in theory, admitted no limit. War was justified only for a public purpose: *Deu Krieg ist ein Instrument de Politik* (war is an instrument of policy).

Conner's second insight was that Lieutenant Colonel George C. Marshall, a graduate of Virginia Military Institute who had assisted him in France, would be an important officer in the next world war. "We will have to fight beside allies," he said, "and George Marshall knows more about the techniques of arranging allied commands than any man I know. He is nothing short of a genius." He went on to say that "You and Marshall are a lot alike. I've noticed time and again that you attack problems in the same way."

The general's ambition for his protégé was contagious; Panama had proved to be a most advantageous assignment after all. Little by little the Eisenhowers' grief at the loss of their child diminished. The birth on August 3, 1922, of another baby boy, John Sheldon Doud, brought renewed happiness. Mamie, joined later by Ike, returned to Denver to have the baby, bringing John back to Gaillard with her two months later.

Eisenhower's assignments in the 1920s led him from Panama back to Camp Meade. He then received assignment to Fort Benning, Georgia, as the commander of a tank battalion. Meanwhile Conner, now deputy chief of staff in Washington, was taking action. Receiving a message that something unusual was about to happen and not to interfere, Ike found himself transferred to the adjutant general's department. After several months of recruiting duty in Denver, to his delight he received orders to the Command and General Staff College at Leavenworth.

Leavenworth brought a turn in Eisenhower's career, toward the responsibilities that would come during World War II. The army made new assignments for him every year or two, and in long retrospect they appear to have been made in kaleidoscopic fashion, one after the other. But Leavenworth was a move upward. Even though it had nothing immediately to do with rank, it put a stamp of approval on Eisenhower's ability to command.

The army's college for commanders, set up early in the century on the plains west of Kansas City, had become well known for the pressure it placed upon its students. A few had proved unequal to it. Major Eisenhower, after encouragement from his mentor, took its measure. He borrowed problem sets from his friend Patton, who already had attended Leavenworth. A fellow student, Leonard T. Gerow, became Ike's study partner. Converting the third floor of his quarters into a command post, with a table, maps, and shelves of books, he and Gerow locked themselves in the room for two-and-a-half hours at a time, five nights a week, stopping at 9:30 to ensure a full night's sleep. The two worked as a team: one read operation orders for each assignment and the other worked them out on the maps. The routine proved to be a formula for success. Ike graduated in 1926 as number 1 out of 245, with a grade average of 93.08 percent. Gerow was number 2.

After his performance at Leavenworth, Eisenhower was in demand. No fewer than three offers awaited him, including a place on the Leavenworth faculty. But none could compete with a summons to Washington from Pershing, who now headed the Battle Monuments Commission set up to study the battles of the American Expeditionary Force and maintain cemeteries in France. Eisenhower's assignment was to write a guidebook of the World War I battles for the man who had been in command, duty which took him, finally, to Europe. Eventually, he was stationed in Paris, from whence he could visit the battlefields. The Eisenhower family took an apartment on the Quai d'Auteuil overlooking the Seine at Pont Mirabeau.

His work in France made him expert on topography and transportation in the very place where Conner had said the next war would be fought.

The revised guidebook for the battlefields, completed in 1929, was remarkably well put together, a series of "short narratives establishing the relationship of each particular battle with American operations as a whole," accompanied by maps and five hundred photographs. Pershing wrote of Eisenhower's "superior ability in visualizing his work as a whole" and "executing its many details in an efficient and timely manner."

After his duty with Pershing, in 1927 Eisenhower became a student at Army War College in Washington, where he increased his grasp of military organization and national strength. In addition to attending lectures he had to write a paper and participate in group studies. He was chairman of a group that studied the American general staff, comparing it to those of Britain, France, and Japan. Another of his committees examined the war powers of the U.S. President and helped write a plan for wartime control of industry. He graduated in a year.

In retrospect, Eisenhower's most important project at the War College probably was his study of war's principles. Drawing on Clausewitz, he and his group discussed the need for an objective "the attainment of which will inflict or threaten to inflict more damage on the enemy than he would suffer through acceding to the wishes of his opponent." The object, something the Prussian general had described as a "center of gravity," must be possible, must cause the enemy to end resistance.

In the early 1930s came a stint of Washington duty. Ike and Mamie and John moved into the Wyoming Apartments on Connecticut Avenue, at Columbia Road near Rock Creek Park. His brother Milton and his wife were neighbors, for by this time Milton had become assistant to the secretary of agriculture. It was during these years that Milton introduced Ike and Mamie to the head of the Washington bureau of the new Columbia Broadcasting System (CBS), Harry C. Butcher, who would later become Eisenhower's public relations aide in Europe during World War II, and his wife Ruth. Butcher recalled the fun-loving, muscular Ike's parlor trick of standing stiffly erect and then falling forward as though crashing to the floor, at the last minute reaching forward to catch himself.

Ike's activities at the War Department included duty as a staff officer in the office of the assistant secretary of war, and then as an aide to the chief of staff, General Douglas MacArthur.

Suddenly, in the summer of 1932, Eisenhower found himself called into action. President Herbert Hoover, suspecting subversion by radicals, had ordered the army to evict forcibly the so-called Bonus Expeditionary Force, a protest gathering of World War I veterans, numbering some 20,000 men. Out of work and many of them destitute, they had converged on the capital city to collect immediately a bonus—$2,000 in endowment life insurance payable in 1945—that had been granted them by Congress. Hungry and desperate, these men felt that the government should hand over their bonuses now, when it could do them the most good. They had served their country dutifully, risking their lives in Europe, only to land on the skids due to the Great Depression back at home. Though the Hoover administration had refused their requests, the Bonus Army was determined to remain encamped in makeshift tents and shacks in Anacostia Flats, along the Potomac River. The U.S. Army moved in with tanks, burned the veterans' village, and forced them to disband. It was an unfortunate moment in the history of the U.S. Army and, for that matter, of the nation, for which, Eisenhower believed, the Hoover administration should have taken full responsibility. Instead, the army was the focus of public attention as the event was captured by press photographers. The black-and-white action shots revealed a bemedaled General MacArthur supervising the movement in dress uniform and high boots—normal peacetime attire in Washington was civilian clothes. Standing beside him, also in uniform, was Major Eisenhower, who considered the whole affair a miserable and unfortunate business. The decision to send the U.S. Army to disperse the veterans had come from the White House, not from the War Department. Eisenhower, sensitive to this use of the military against civilians, had advised that MacArthur not lead the eviction force personally. Obviously ignoring the recommendation, the general even gave an on-the-spot interview to reporters.

But most of Eisenhower's time during this period of his life was spent on activities little known to the American people. One of them was a plan for national economic mobilization. A widespread belief in the late 1920s was that American involvement in World War I (and in war in general) stemmed from the lobbying efforts of munitions manufacturers. Eisenhower worked as secretary of a congressional commission of six cabinet officers, four senators, and four representatives on "how to take the profits out of war." In 1918 he became friendly with Bernard Baruch, the head of the War Industries Board, the agency of the federal government that allocated the nation's manufacturing resources during war. Visiting plants that had manufactured World War I munitions, Ike had a good look at what he later would label "the military-industrial complex." Also, during this time he helped set up the Industrial War College to train officers to organize and manage wartime supply.

Meanwhile, Eisenhower's duties at the War Department, in addition to preparing the report of the War Policies Commission on industrial mobilization for war, included a considerable amount of writing for others. He drafted the annual reports of the chief of staff, MacArthur's report on dispersing the Bonus Army, and department papers and letters to congressmen concerning military subjects.

Planning for war was quite an education, but the frenetic pace took a toll on Eisenhower. And it was in the early 1930s that he began to encounter the physical troubles that would become severe later in his life. It was in his midcareer period when he discovered that work and tension do not mix. A physical examination in 1930 revealed hypertension, an abnormally fast heartbeat, and blood pressure as high as 145/70. The following year he began to have discomfort and much "tearing" in his eyes. He suffered a recurrence of a dysentery-like ailment that he had first experienced in 1919, which eventually (in 1956) would be diagnosed as ileitis, a chronic inflammation of the small intestine.

But his physical problems of the moment notwithstanding, Eisenhower was doing his best at a time when not much could have been expected from a military career. Opportunities had beckoned, first with Conner, then Pershing, and he had seized them. He was a graduate of Leavenworth and the War College. He had the benefit of an association with MacArthur. But the prospect was that he would end his career as a colonel in a staff office, perhaps meriting in the history of the United States a tiny footnote.

CHAPTER TWO

War

For a military man the 1930s was an awkward time. Eisenhower, one must say, had little understanding of the Great Depression. When the stock market turned down late in 1929 he did not sense what it portended. Nor did he fully understand the misery that engulfed city and countryside in the United States and indeed the western world. His response was in line with his training. He worried that "pacifistic propaganda will reduce army appropriations still further, including officer's salaries." Yet he favored the extraordinary powers taken by the President to restore the nation's confidence. "For two years," he wrote in his diary on February 28, 1933, "I have been called 'Dictator Ike' because I believe that virtual dictatorship must be exercised by our President." A few months later he wrote that "unity of action is essential to success in the current struggle. I believe that individual right must be subordinated to public good, and that the public good can be served only by unanimous adherence to an authoritative plan. We must conform to the President's program regardless of the consequences." As it turned out, his belief in the need for a dictator was unwarranted. President Franklin D. Roosevelt was no dictator, and he had no desire to be one. Unfortunately for the beleaguered people of several large European countries, notably Germany and Italy, government by true dictatorship proved to have egregious consequences, far worse than almost anyone could have judged. For Europe, and eventually for the United States, the depression led straight into World War II.

At the outset of the Roosevelt administration, Eisenhower supported the New Deal. After the election he noted in his diary that "While I have no definite leanings toward any political party I believe it is a good thing the Democrats won—and particularly that one party will have such overwhelming superiority in Congress. . . . I hope they are only 1/4 as successful as they said they would be!" As things progressed, however, the depression almost wrecked the army's budget, reducing appropriations from $271 million to $225 million for 1934. MacArthur prevented a cut of another $44 million, but the budget was still $110 million less than it had been in 1931 and required slashes in troop strength, already down to 125,000 men. Ike foresaw the country "going back to 1898. We will have left only a shell of a military establishment." By the end of that year he had become disillusioned and no longer supported Roosevelt. His conservative instinct—the importance of self-sufficiency, a basic part of life in rural Kansas—had reasserted itself. Eisenhower had determined that Roosevelt lacked a sufficient understanding of international relations and the extent of the dangers facing a United States that lacked the ability to defend itself. Meanwhile, he felt, the domestic reform programs were robbing Americans of personal responsibility.

During this time Eisenhower had the opportunity to learn more about national defense from his superiors. Major General George Van Horn Moseley enjoyed discussing the army's interest in legislation. Moseley, Eisenhower wrote, was "my most intimate friend among the senior officers of the army." After Moseley departed for assignment in Atlanta in 1934, Eisenhower wrote that he "missed the talks we used to have on such subjects as 'the state of the nation.'"

The person whom Eisenhower watched most closely, however, was MacArthur, an officer who violated the American military tradition that placed the army apart from politics. MacArthur enjoyed the company of reporters and discussing political topics. He spoke out against pacifists, socialists, and communists. "If General MacArthur ever recognized the existence of a line [between the military and political], he chose to ignore it," Eisenhower recalled. MacArthur's interest in politics included an ambition to hold a high office.

In March 1933 the general asked for Ike's services on a regular basis. A few weeks later the major wrote enthusiastically in his diary, "I was brought into General MacArthur's office not long ago with the title of 'Senior Aide.' My work will apparently be little different from that I have been performing for him for two years but he alone will be my boss—and I'll be more available for every kind of duty." Interestingly, considering later differences between the two, Ike was pleased to work with the man whom he considered "impulsive—able, even brilliant . . . essentially a romantic figure . . . a genius at giving concise and clear instructions." He was amazed by MacArthur's memory, "without parallel in my knowledge. Reading a draft of a speech or paper, he could repeat chunks of it." He shared MacArthur's veneration of the Constitution, concern for orderly government, belief in limited government for alleviating economic distress, and willingness, if ordered to do so by the President, to use military force to quell social disorder. The chief of staff admired Eisenhower's loyalty, knowledge of history, facility of expression, and interest in athletics, especially football.

MacArthur left Washington to become military adviser to the Philippines and asked Eisenhower to accompany him. Passage of the Tydings-McDuffie Act of 1934 gave the Philippines a commonwealth status to prepare for independence slated for 1946. There was much to learn about helping the Filipinos create a military force. And there were certain advantages. Eisenhower could pick his own assistant. Besides his salary he would receive $980 per month plus expenses from the Philippine government—a considerable increase in pay.

The Philippines, unfortunately, appealed to Mamie no more than had Panama. Her encounter with bats and vermin still fresh in her mind and aware of the good schooling that young John was receiving in Washington, she was not exactly eager to join her husband in the Islands. She and John remained in Washington for a year while John finished the eighth grade. Once they did arrive in the Philippines, John was sent to the Bishop Brent School in Baguio, 175 miles north of Manila. Meanwhile Ike had arranged living quarters for the couple in a suite in the Manila Hotel, wherein Mamie soon became claustrophobic: the ubiquitous mosquitoes forced them to keep the shutters closed all day and to sleep under heavy netting at night. She began to have stomach problems. In 1937 during a trip to visit John at school she became so ill that she almost died.

As he had hoped, while in the Islands Ike's primary concern was to establish a Philippine defense force. A few years before he had decried "the ability of Filipino masses to express intelligent opinion on the many questions involved until they shall have reached a substantially higher cultural plane." At the scene, he felt that his fears had been well founded. The Philippine legislature cut MacArthur's estimate of 50 million pesos ($25 million) for a thin-cordon defense of the islands to 16 million pesos—enough to support 930 officers and 7,000 enlisted men along with an equal number of one-year draftees. The United States was unwilling to supply more than World-War-I-issue Enfield rifles and a few aircraft. The Philippine defense force therefore had no hope of resisting an invasion. Eisenhower did what he could to remedy the situation, writing legislation that called for a war department with a general staff, training camps, headquarters, and an airfield. But almost all of his suggestions remained on paper.

The Philippine years did, however, bring Eisenhower some satisfaction. For one thing he became a lieutenant colonel in 1936. For another, MacArthur did not commence work each day until 11:00 A.M., retiring to quarters in midafternoon, leaving Eisenhower and his friends Majors James Ord and T. J. Davis on their own. After hours everyone had time for golf and bridge. When it became possible to set up an air force, Eisenhower accomplished a goal he had dreamed of for years: he learned to fly an airplane. After getting a private pilot's license Ike logged 350 flight hours on the open-cockpit bi-planes with which the Americans had furnished the Filipinos. In later years he sometimes would go into the cockpit of a plane and take over the copilot's controls.

It was also during this tour that Eisenhower came to know Major Lucius D. Clay of the Army Corps of Engineers, who had arrived to survey possible hydroelectric power sites. Ike persuaded Clay, whom he immediately liked, to take on the extra duty of acting as the chief engineer, overseeing camp construction and the training of Filipino engineers. Clay even began to take flying lessons. Years later, Clay would oversee the process by which Ike left military service to run for the presidency.

Eisenhower's most interesting acquaintance was Philippine President Manuel Quezon, who set up an office for him in the presidential palace. The Philippines were for Ike a laboratory for the study of politics, economics, public opinion, morale, technical knowledge, and leadership as practiced by a nonin-dustrial people. The conversations between Eisenhower and Quezon, at first confined to the nation's defense problems, became broader and deeper, coming to include taxes, educa-tion, honesty in government, and "the responsibilities and costs as well as the privileges of independence."

Eisenhower's decision to leave the Philippines came in 1939. By that time his respect for MacArthur had declined notably. The general's ego had required the domination of every con-versation the two men had. Furthermore, pressure on the War Department for more support in the Far East had produced friction between Eisenhower and MacArthur, which was only intensified by Eisenhower's willingness to speak up and his refusal, unlike MacArthur who became a Philippine field marshal, to accept rank in the Philippine army. They had a number of arguments, and MacArthur became suspicious that Eisenhower was trying to undercut him with Quezon and the Philippine legislature. Then matters came to a head. Without conferring with Quezon, MacArthur in January 1938 ordered the Philippine army into Manila for a parade, and then, when Quezon objected, denied having given the order, blaming Eisenhower. The officer from Abilene lost his temper. "General, all you're saying is that I'm a liar, and I am *not* a liar, so I'd like to go back to the United States right away." The relationship between the men who were destined to become two of the most famous generals of the twentieth century (Eisenhower in Europe, MacArthur in the Far East) thus soured. They would see each other from time to time during the epochal events of the war and cold war that lay ahead, but this did not alter their essential estrangement.

MacArthur's foibles were not Ike's only reason for returning. Another world war, as Conner had predicted, seemed to be well on the way. In Germany, Italy, and Japan the domestic response to the international economic depression and the resulting trade barriers was support for the military and for dictators who promised "simple" (violent) solutions to their respective nation's ills through military expansion abroad. The first such move was by Japan when in 1931 its army marched into the Chinese territory of Manchuria, which it quickly annexed, establishing a puppet government there and renaming the province Manchukuo. The United States responded with the Stimson Doctrine, refusing to recognize this expansion. The League of Nations launched an investigation but did nothing more to stop the aggression.

In the mid-1930s Italy and Germany had begun a series of aggressive moves of their own, Italy into Ethiopia and Germany, in two violations of the Versailles Treaty, achieved rearmament and the reoccupation of the Rhineland. In 1936 both countries aided the fascist revolt led by General Francisco Franco against the Republican government in Spain. By 1938,

Japan had invaded the rest of China, and Hitler's Nazi Germany had absorbed Austria. At the Munich Conference of September, Britain and France bowed to German military threats and, without consulting the erstwhile victim, agreed to give the western portion of Czechoslovakia, the Sudetenland, to Hitler. By the following spring, the German dictator already had broken his promise not to make any more territorial demands by marching his troops into Prague. The West European democracies protested and threatened war, so he signed a non-aggression pact (and a secret agreement to divide Poland and neighboring countries) with the Soviet dictator, Joseph Stalin. When Hitler invaded Poland in September 1939, World War II began.

Eisenhower, his temper flaring, decided that as an officer of the United States Army he would do whatever he could to stop a man (Hitler) whom he described as a "power-drunk egocentric . . . one of the criminally insane . . . the absolute ruler of eighty-nine million people." While he had tried everything he could think of to make it to the front lines in 1918, unlike Patton and perhaps MacArthur, he did not relish war. It was simply unavoidable given world conditions and the far-flung responsibilities of the United States. "The mad man that is governing Germany," Ike wrote, had driven the British and French "into a corner out of which they can work their way only by fighting. It's a sad day for Europe and for the whole civilized world—though for a long time it has seemed ridiculous to refer to the world as civilized." Eisenhower had indeed revealed his understanding of international relations. Germany, having easily defeated Poland, turned west the following spring, invading first Norway and Denmark, and then Belgium, Holland, and France.

Up to this point the Japanese militarists had been debating what they would do if the United States, in an effort to force their withdrawal from China, cut off the U.S. oil exports upon which their navy depended. Perhaps they should move north against Russia? Hitler's actions in Europe decided the matter, for now the Dutch, French, and British colonies in Southeast Asia, with their rich mineral resources, had become ripe for the picking. The Japanese signed the "Axis" treaty with Germany and Italy in September 1940 and proceeded with plans to establish what they called a "Greater East Asian Co-prosperity Sphere." Unfortunately for Japan, the latter would require American cooperation, something Franklin Roosevelt and his secretary of state were unwilling to give. Indeed, when Japan invaded southern Indochina in midsummer 1941, the United States cut off all trade with Japan and froze all of its U.S.-held assets. Unless something changed, conflict between the two Pacific powers was inevitable. Meanwhile, on June 22, 1941, Hitler, unable over the previous year to bring the British air force to its knees and fearing to invade the island nation without control of the air, turned to the east, launching the greatest land war in history: the "Barbarossa" invasion. Sending 3.2 million soldiers into Russia—obviously ignoring the so-called non-aggression pact—Hitler felt that the key to success would be to reach Moscow before winter took hold. This costly move, responsible by the war's end for the deaths 3.5 million German military men and over 20 million Soviets (military personnel and civilians), proved to be Hitler's greatest mistake.

Monitoring these events, the Roosevelt administration, though facing a strong isolationist sentiment in Congress, began to rearm, preparing the military services for war. In April 1939 the President reached down into the ranks and, with the advice of Pershing, selected General George C. Marshall over thirty-three senior officers to become army Chief of Staff. Marshall then set to work identifying other individuals best suited for wartime leadership.

The opening of World War II brought a rapid series of assignments to Eisenhower, one of the officers whom Marshall had noticed. Arriving by ship from the Philippines, he and Mamie had celebrated the New Year 1940 in San Francisco. Ike had orders to report to Fort Lewis in Washington state as a battalion commander, but was temporarily sidetracked to mobilize regular and national guard troops for maneuvers on the West Coast, which included an amphibious landing on a California beach. Then Ike was off to Fort Lewis and the 15th Regiment of the Third Infantry Division. He enjoyed his duty at the Third and in spare time wrote letters to fend off an attempt by Leonard "Gee" Gerow, his old study partner who was now a brigadier general and head of war plans in the War Department, to assign him to the department's General Staff. Again he felt the frustration he had experienced at having to miss action in World War I, and he recalled his discussions with Patton about how massed tank attacks would eliminate the stalemate caused in World War I by machine guns in defensive emplacements, thereby making combat purposeful again. He wanted command of an armored unit. In a letter to Patton, who was once again a colonel, he said he was "flattered by your suggestion that I come to your outfit. . . . I suppose it's too much to hope that I could have a regiment in your division, because I'm still almost three years away from my colonelcy. But *I think* I could do a damn good job of commanding a regiment." He had studied every intelligence report "coming out of this war, and to make sure that I study them well, I prepare lectures on them." But the effort to join Patton failed. In November 1940 he was chief of staff of the Third Division. Shortly thereafter he became a full colonel.

Events now began to move him upward. In June 1941 he became chief of staff of the Third Army (with headquarters at Fort Sam Houston in San Antonio) under General Walter Krueger, its 240,000 soldiers hailing from Florida to New Mexico. Ike and Mamie moved back to the place where they had met, this time to a large red-brick house with five bedrooms, a patio, and a lawn. Within two months the Third Army was "fighting" 180,000 men of the Second Army in the swamps of Louisiana, maneuvers designed to be the "closest peacetime approximation to actual fighting conditions that has ever been undertaken in this country." The exercise was both a physical and intellectual one, with critiques to highlight mistakes "that in war could mean death to a unit or an army." It was a test of the army's officer corps because staff officers who had served in World War I above regimental level had since passed out of the service.

By the time the Louisiana maneuvers ended, Eisenhower had so impressed General Krueger that he received promotion to brigadier general. Just months before, Ike had discounted the possibility of anyone his age reaching the rank of colonel. Now he had difficulty containing his emotion. "What do you mean, 'how does it feel to be a B.G.?'" he asked his friend T. J. Davis. "I'm working harder than ever; I used to be a deck hand, now I'm a stevedore. . . . Luckily, I've spent most of my life in large headquarters, so am not overpowered by the mass of details."

Two months later, on December 7, Eisenhower was taking a nap when his aide, disobeying orders that he not be disturbed, awakened him with news of the Japanese attack on Pearl Harbor. The telephone message ordering him back to Washington came from Colonel Walter Bedell Smith, secretary of the General Staff, on December 12: "The Chief says for you to hop a plane and get up here right away." Here again was another turning point, and this time a move to high command.

Eisenhower had first met General Marshall in 1927 outside Pershing's office in Washington. Through the years, perhaps to overcome his strong emotions, Marshall had adopted a quiet, candid, and to-the-point formality with everyone. He was five feet, eleven inches tall, athletic (he had played football at Virginia Military Academy) and had penetrating, deeply set blue eyes and short-cropped sandy hair that receded from his broad forehead. Like Eisenhower, Marshall had a tendency to overwork and chain-smoked cigarettes; he also admired General Fox Conner, was a student of military history, and was a man of considerable self-confidence.

Interestingly, it was Eisenhower's ability as a writer that impressed Marshall. At Pershing's request Ike had drafted topical summaries of World War I battles that were to be two chapters of the book, his own story of the war, that Pershing was preparing for publication. Eisenhower had been trying to see things through the eyes of the American Expeditionary Forces commander. With temerity but in a typically candid way he had suggested to Pershing that the reader could better understand the battles if the book were arranged in a topical format rather than in a chronological one. Pershing had asked Marshall what he thought of this suggestion. Stopping by Eisenhower's office, Marshall introduced himself and proceeded to bluntly say that he thought the summaries interesting but had advised the general "to stick with his original idea. I think to break up the format right at the climax of the war would be a mistake." The next time Marshall and Eisenhower met again had been in 1939 on the beach in northern California during the practice amphibious landing. Knowing that while in the Philippines Eisenhower had been living in a hotel where personal servants were always at hand, Marshall had asked: "Have you learned to tie your own shoes again since coming back, Eisenhower?"

No sooner did Eisenhower arrive in Washington than he had a gigantic strategic problem to solve. Marshall gave him just two hours to draft an Allied plan for dealing with Japan. His recommendation was to hold the Philippines as long as possible. More guns, ammunition, and aircraft, he said, would encourage the Filipinos' to continue to fight, buying the Allies some time. The United States must also develop a base in Australia, create supply lines, and, if possible, defend India. It was brave talk, logical in a theoretical way, and the best anyone could do. In subsequent weeks the Philippines fell to the Japanese, the worst defeat in American history, since the huge archipelago had become an American possession in 1898.

Marshall saw in Eisenhower many of his own qualities, especially an ability to analyze a wartime situation correctly and devise a simple and workable solution. "I can get many brilliant men to analyze and bring to me their problems; few will make their own decisions," he said. Accordingly, he made his new staff officer chief of the war plans division, then chief of a new operations division. The time had arrived for Eisenhower to begin practicing the lessons that Conner had taught him in Panama, to help his country fight what Clausewitz called that most difficult of undertakings, a war of coalitions. This one was particularly onerous, involving as it did the free French, Poles, and Great Britain and its combined commonwealth nations, including Canada and Australia. Roosevelt and Churchill in August 1941 signed the Atlantic Charter, a statement of war aims, although the United States was not officially at war until after Pearl Harbor. In early 1942 the United States and Great Britain established the Combined Chiefs of Staff to coordinate and carry out western Allied strategy. The senior American representative was Army Chief of Staff George C. Marshall. His British counterpart was Field Marshall Alanbrooke. The Soviet Union was not a member of the command arrangement, but both Churchill and Roosevelt sent envoys to the Kremlin in the month following the Barbarossa invasion and began shipping military supplies to Russia. As the war progressed, the communist Stalin, suspicious, even paranoid, continually demanded more help, and the Combined Chiefs tried to provide it, realizing their paramount interest in keeping Germany engaged in a two-front war. Indeed, the British (but not the Americans) signed a treaty with the Soviet Union in May 1942, and the three heads of state met three times during the war to coordinate their actions. These meetings were held respectively in Teheran in November 1943, Yalta in February 1945, and Potsdam in June of 1945.

Allied victory, Eisenhower quickly saw, thus involved binding in common purpose the disparate and often antagonistic branches of the U.S. military—naval, air, and ground—but also, and more important, the political cultures and wills of all of the nations of the Western Alliance. Instead of being the feuding conglomerate of strange bedfellows that Hitler hoped he would be fighting, under Eisenhower's direction, the west-

ern Allied army devised and executed a strategy that eventually brought victory. "Joint and combined staff work is terrible,"
he complained. "[It] takes an inconceivable amount of time.
Conner had been right about allies. He could well have included the navy." Eisenhower's diary for this difficult, even
frantic period reflected the continuing self-analysis of a seat-
of-the-pants psychology. "When high command invariably in-
volves a president, a prime minister, six chiefs of staff, and a
horde of lesser 'planners,'" he said, "there has got to be a lot
of patience—no one person can be a Napoleon or a Caesar."

In March 1942 Eisenhower was seeking ways to keep Russia
in the war and in the Alliance. In response to Ike's friendly
query, Conner, who long since had retired, wrote to his former
protégé that "the first thing to do is to determine the immediate task. As I see that the thing to do first of all is to relieve the
pressure on Russia."

All the while Eisenhower was dealing closely with Marshall. An item came to the Chief of Staff's attention about
promotion of an officer. In conversation Marshall forcefully
announced that only commanders in the field, not staff officers, would "get promotions in this war." Turning to
Eisenhower, he said, "Take your case, I know you were recommended by one general for division command and by
another for corps command. That's all very well . . . but you
are going to stay right here and fill your position, and that's
that!" The frustration Eisenhower had felt since 1918 about
his lack of real combat experience again surged within him,
and his temper flared. "General," he said, "I'm interested in
what you say, but I want you to know that I don't give a damn
about your promotion plans . . . I came into this office from
the field and I am going to do my duty. I expect to do so as
long as you want me here. If that locks me to a desk for the
rest of the war, so be it!" He got up, walked to the door, then
embarrassedly turned, looked at Marshall, and smiled. A tiny
smile formed on Marshall's face; a copy of his recommenda-

tion to the President that Eisenhower be promoted to major general reached Ike's desk three days later.

The ideas of the energetic head of the operations planning department had impressed Chief of Staff Marshall, and he began to think of appointing Eisenhower as commander of the European Theater of Operations. Ike and his staff had drafted a plan, codenamed Roundup, to open an early second front for the Germans through an invasion of France. His plan was approved in April by President Roosevelt and the British government, but the invasion of France would be postponed until June 6, 1944.

During a brief visit to England, Ike had a most cordial meeting with Prime Minister Winston Churchill, which further impressed Marshall. In early June 1942, Marshall asked Eisenhower to write an instruction for an American European Theater commander. When he presented it, the Chief of Staff replied, "I certainly do want to read it. You may be the man who executes it. If that's the case, when can you leave?" Eisenhower thereupon obtained an apartment in the Wardman Park Hotel in Washington for Mamie, said goodbyes, and on the morning of June 23, 1942, departed by air for his new command.

London must have seemed a strange place to Ike—foreign in a way, a sprawling city without tall buildings, sooty and foggy. It hardly felt like the setting for a military command post. Eisenhower's office, a few blocks from the quarters arranged for him at the Claridge Hotel, was at 20 Grosvenor Square, across the street from the embassy. Here he put together a staff, or, as he later described it, "a group that absorbs and analyzes the facts and statistics applying to all commands, fighting and non-fighting, and presents a consolidated picture to the commander on which he bases his decisions" and "then translates these decisions into detailed orders and later supervises execution." The group included a deputy, Major General Mark W. Clark, a West Point classmate of Ike's; a public relations aide, Lieutenant Commander (later Captain) Harry C. Butcher, his friend of years before; Colonel T. J. Davis, his friend from the Philippine days, as adjutant general; and Warrant Officer Marshall and Mary Alice Jaqua, stenographers. In September, Eisenhower's most important assistant, his chief of staff, Brigadier General Walter Bedell "Beetle" Smith, arrived from Washington where he had been secretary of the army General Staff and secretary of the Combined Chiefs of Staff. Smith, whom Eisenhower later called "a master of detail with clear comprehension of the main issues," had a long, pinched face with closely set eyes that seemed to display the discomfort its owner felt from his ulcer. Quick to yell at and threaten the staff, Smith nonetheless always gave instructions that were correct and pertinent to the mission at hand. The theater commander trusted him completely—it would be Smith, as Eisenhower's delegate, who would negotiate the Italian surrender and receive the unconditional one of Nazi Germany on May 8, 1945.

Ike's staff also included a young British woman, Kathleen "Kay" Summersby, who became Eisenhower's driver, receptionist, and friend. She was dark haired, slender, and pretty, and titillating rumors soon flew that she had an intimate relationship with the theater commander. After the war these rumors became the basis for gossip, a book, and a profitable made-for-television movie. No real evidence has been found to substantiate the rumors: indeed, a love affair with a member of his personal staff would have been so uncharacteristic of Ike as to be ludicrous. Keenly aware of the seriousness of his mission and the principles of leadership, including personal integrity, required to accomplish it, it is doubtful that Eisenhower would have in this way put his career in jeopardy. Finally, he loved Mamie very much.

At the outset it appeared as if London society might require all of Eisenhower's time, something that he could not allow. For a brief while the mixture of social obligations and military necessities created for Ike an air of unreality. In the middle of a crowded embassy reception Butcher called him out of a receiving line to report that two of the six planes of the first American air raid on German air bases in Holland had been shot down, and that one flyer, Captain Charles C. Klegelman, had heroically crashed his disabled plane on an enemy gun emplacement. As soon as the reception was over, Eisenhower went straight back to headquarters and ordered the Distinguished Service Cross for the dead airman. After that, he decided to attend no social functions. He put his staff on a seven-day week and moved his residence from the Claridge to a three-room apartment at the Dorchester, across from the anti-aircraft batteries in Hyde Park. At the end of the summer he found a little country place at Telegraph Cottage, a house in Kingston forty minutes from Grosvenor Square where he could concentrate better and, when necessary, let off steam by hitting golf balls or shooting targets with a pistol. His staff gave him a black Scottie that he named Telek, for Telegraph Cottage.

The summer of 1942 was a crucial time in faraway Russia, on the Eastern front; and as soon as Eisenhower had the opportunity he turned to that somber spectacle to ascertain what the Anglo-Americans could do to help the beleaguered Russians. The strategic problem was whether a loose alliance of ideological antagonists would be a source of strength or, as Clausewitz had warned, a weakness. Soviet Russia had been the object of much American suspicion since the Bolshevik Revolution of 1917. Upon hearing of Hitler's invasion of Russia in 1941, Senator Harry S Truman had said that the United States should supply enough aid to enable the two dictators to fight each other to a standstill. For his part, Churchill never doubted that Stalin's war aims included not only the defeat of Hitler but domination of Western Europe. Meanwhile Stalin did little to allay the fears of the western Allies that, as he had in August 1939, he might make a separate peace with Hitler.

Such were the questions of strategy that occupied Eisenhower's attention as the Allied commanders plotted their next move. The British, while ideologically aligned with the United States, drew upon an experience that differed from the Americans', causing the former to feel superior in both wisdom and hardship endured. After all it was they who had lost the flower of their youth on the battlefields of northern France between 1914 and 1918; it was they who had beaten back the *Luftwaffe* in the Battle of Britain and were now fighting Axis troops in the deserts of North Africa. They thus sought to humor the upstart Americans but to continue to fight as they thought best, using a peripheral rather than a direct approach to beat back the German army.

Both the teachings of Clausewitz and the uncertainty regarding the Soviets moved Eisenhower to oppose the British approach of striking on the periphery of Axis power, the invasion of North Africa, in place of a cross–English Channel invasion of occupied France. A direct thrust followed Clausewitz's dictum of aiming everything at the enemy's "center of gravity," his army. Eisenhower and Marshall, however, because of American military weakness, were unable to ignore the British strategic ideas in 1942.

Therefore the Combined Chiefs of Staff decided that the Allies' immediate task was not a cross-Channel attack but rather a North African invasion, Operation Torch, which later, if all went well, would continue across the Mediterranean and into the Italian Peninsula. The Combined Chiefs called for a landing in French North Africa and Eisenhower, although dismayed at the diversion of resources from the main objective, had no choice but to accede to their wishes. The British still had the preponderance of troops ready for battle. President Roosevelt knew he had to get them and at least some American troops into the war somewhere and approved the Combined Chiefs' designation of Eisenhower as the operation's supreme commander. The task was almost overwhelming; to succeed the invasion would have to be prepared secretly and executed with such strength that there would be little fighting. Accordingly, political considerations had to be dominant, as Eisenhower explained in his diary: it was "impossible to build up a force of sufficient strength to make tactical considerations the governing ones in undertaking this operation. . . . Success depends upon nonresistance on the part of the French army." He worried about "the extent of the unfavorable potentialities," including not only "chances of a very bloody repulse but a bringing into the ranks of our active enemies both France and Spain, which are now classed as neutrals. . . . We are simply sailing a dangerous political sea, and this particular sea is one in which military skill and ability can do little in charting a safe course."

The invasion of North Africa in November 1942 and the subsequent fighting, followed by the invasion of Sicily and Italy, constituted for the Allies perhaps the riskiest venture of the war. The Nazi war machine had already proven its strength many times over. In earlier fighting—which included the victory of the British Eighth Army under General Bernard Montgomery over General Erwin Rommel (the "Desert Fox") at El Alamein—the British, although outnumbering the enemy three to one, had lost three times as many men. Indeed, until that point in the war the Germans had seemed invincible. In 1939, using tanks in conjunction with dive bombers, General Heinz Guderian's version of the tactics explored by Eisenhower and Patton at Camp Meade in 1919, the Germans had penetrated north of Warsaw, turned south to attack the Polish army from the rear, and in three weeks taken half of Poland. By the end of the following spring they occupied the Netherlands, Belgium, and northern France. Paris had fallen in two weeks. Hitler had set up *Festung Europa* (fortress Europe)—artillery, tank traps, mines. In the autumn of 1940 it had appeared that Great Britain would be next to fall. The following summer the Germans had invaded the Soviet Union and penetrated to the gates of Moscow. All this because of audacity, superb equipment and tactics, and luck. In 1942 consequently, Eisenhower's task as supreme commander of Torch was enormous. There were few trained American forces to oppose German forces, the most awesome in modern history, supporting their Italian ally in North Africa. There were no weapons, besides artillery and aircraft, against superior German armor and tactics. German submarines patrolled the western Mediterranean, and the *Luftwaffe* controlled the air.

The landings for Operation Torch on November 8 nevertheless were a success. The beachheads, points at which the Allied amphibious landings occurred, were at: Casablanca, on the Atlantic coast of Morocco, where General Patton's Western Task Force, having sailed directly from Hampton Roads, Virginia, landed; Oran, 400 miles east of Casablanca on the Mediterranean; and Algiers, 200 miles east of Oran—all hundreds of miles west of the objective, the ports in Tunis. At Oran and Algiers the landing forces, totaling 35,000 each, were mainly British. Fortunately, the 100,000 Allied soldiers landed with only 1,800 casualties. "This is a fine command," Eisenhower wrote his son, "and, of course, it is every soldier's ambition to get command of something, even if it is only a platoon! I never once dreamed that my first big command would be an 'Allied' one and that I would have soldiers, sailors and airmen of two great countries under my direct control. I must say that it keeps a fellow stepping pretty rapidly to keep on top of the ball." Within two weeks Eisenhower had landed 150,000 troops and moved his headquarters from Gibraltar to Algiers. As supreme commander Eisenhower held tactical control with the help of his British deputies: air commander, Air Marshall Tedder; ground commander, Sir Harold Alexander; and naval commander, Admiral Sir Andrew Cunningham. The successful landing took considerable pressure off Montgomery's Eighth, which was moving toward Tunis from Egypt.

This is not to say that the North African campaign proceeded smoothly. To prevent further resistance by the French troops who had fired on the Allies as they landed, Eisenhower recognized the authority of Admiral Jean Darlan, who previously had collaborated with the Nazis in French North Africa. This caused a political storm. It appeared to many observers that Eisenhower had violated the Allied purpose. The war, af-

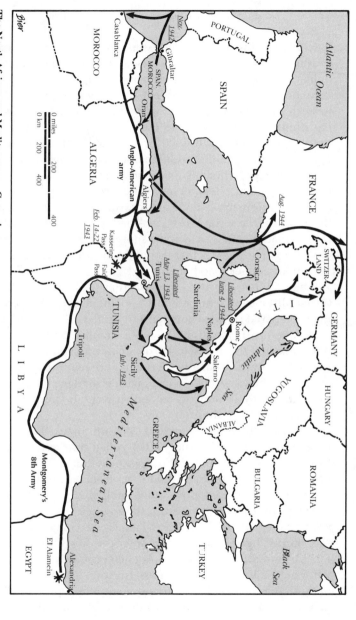

The North African and Mediterranean Campaigns

Bier

ter all, was against Fascist dictatorship. The American supreme commander seemed to have crossed over the line between military and political affairs and engaged in appeasement. Was this a precedent, they asked? What kind of behavior could the western Allies now expect of Stalin, especially if the Soviets' hardships became unbearable. Fortunately, Roosevelt upheld the decision. The Allied doctrine of "unconditional surrender," which declared the additional war aim of overthrowing the enemies' governments, announced at the Casablanca conference in January 1943, stemmed in part from this incident, an attempt to reassure the Russians, still complaining about the lack of a true second front, of Allied steadfastness. It was a tricky situation, one in which the supreme commander, demonstrating that war was merely politics by other means, had been both politician and diplomatist.

Then, in January 1943, bad weather took charge. Rain turned dirt airfields into swamps, and enemy aircraft operating from paved runways bombed and strafed Allied columns. It became nearly impossible to move supplies, and after the Allies reached the Tunisian border the campaign came to a virtual halt. By this point, the Germans were reinforcing Tunis by sea. Eisenhower, from his headquarters in Algiers, surveyed the situation by arduous automobile trips to the lines, a division here, a convoy there.

Gradually the offensive moved eastward toward Tunis until, by the middle of February 1943, Allied troops were on a line 120 miles inside Tunisia. Unexpectedly, Rommel's panzers, which Eisenhower believed would attack from the north, struck through the Faid Pass to the south and, after joining other German troops moving up from the southeast, a week later, went through the Kasserine Pass, almost reaching the Algerian border. In overrunning the American First Division and First Armored Division, they took 2,400 prisoners, wounding 2,620 men, and killing 190. At Kasserine over 200 Allied tanks were disabled and 4,000 thousand men were captured. The failure of the American commanders to establish defensive

positions at the pass was embarrassing. Eisenhower, after ordering men and equipment forward to retrieve the situation,
relieved the American commander of II Corps, Major General Lloyd R. Fredendall, and replaced him with Major Generals George S. Patton and Omar N. Bradley. He ordered British
Brigadier Kenneth Strong to replace his fellow countryman
Brigadier Eric E. Mockler-Ferryman as intelligence chief. The
British commander, General Harold R. L. G. Alexander, arrived at the front from Libya.

The pressure on the supreme commander was noticeable.
In letters he revealed that things were not what they should
have been. He was nearly exhausted. At one point the British
proposed that Eisenhower be removed from tactical command,
kicked upstairs as it were, while his British deputies, Tedder,
Alexander, and Cunningham, all senior to him in rank, ran
the war. Eisenhower would not hear of it. With support from
Marshall, he insisted upon unity of command and his prerogatives as commander, refusing the British proposal as well as
directives by the Combined Chiefs on organizational procedures. "The Americans," said Rommel later, "made up for their
lack of experience by their far better and more plentiful equipment and their tactically more flexible command." For
Eisenhower the lesson was that the Allied commanders must
uphold unity above all else. Having received his fourth star as
full general in the winter of 1943 (only Marshall and MacArthur
held such high rank at this time), by the spring the campaign
wound down to victory, with 275,000 prisoners, mostly Italian.

Meanwhile, in Italy Mussolini's government had capitulated
to the weak Badoglio regime, prompting Hitler to dispatch a
German army to occupy the peninsula, but the Allies were on
their way. After a pause to drive the enemy from Sicily, ensur-
ing control of the Mediterranean Sea, Allied forces were sent
to the Italian mainland. In September 1943 they landed at
Salerno Bay, south of Naples. The British considered the operation risky, because eighteen German divisions opposed six
of the Allies'. Eisenhower countered that Salerno was within

range of air support. When the Germans counterattacked, Ike asked for three more air force bomber groups and eighteen more landing ships and ordered Admiral Cunningham to send two battleships. Every plane, including heavy bombers, went into the air. The Americans and British then established a line across the Italian peninsula. A German lieutenant, awestruck at the strength of the Allies explained his capture this way: "I was on this hill as a battery commander with six 88-millimeter antitank guns, and the Americans kept sending tanks down this road. We kept knocking them out. Every time they sent a tank we knocked it out. Finally, we ran out of ammunition and the Americans didn't run out of tanks." Naples fell in October, although Rome remained in enemy hands until June 1944. The hard and costly campaign in Italy continued for the duration of the war.

With the Allies firmly in control of the Mediterranean, observers assumed that General Marshall would take command of the cross-Channel attack—Operation Overlord—and become the Pershing of World War II. Eisenhower, though immensely successful as the supreme commander of Operation Torch, would return to Washington as Chief of Staff. Ike wrote in his diary of his pleasure at hearing that Roosevelt and Churchill had expressed a desire for either him or Marshall to command Overlord. As much as Ike admired Marshall, he felt that he himself had put together a team that had shown it could do the job, and he hoped he would have the opportunity to command Overlord.

Eisenhower's career hung in the balance, and it is interesting to speculate what might have happened had he been relegated, one might say banished, to Washington. Would he have become the World War II successor of General Peyton C. March, Chief of Staff during the last months of World War I? March had been an exceedingly able Chief of Staff, and yet after World War I he was almost forgotten, overlooked in favor of Pershing.

As it turned out, the prize went to the man on the spot. After the victory in North Africa and during the invasion of Italy, Eisenhower's headquarters was in Tunis. Two years after Pearl Harbor, December 7, 1943, Roosevelt stopped there on the way back from the conference in Teheran, and in his off-hand manner he said to the general, "Well, Ike, you are going to command Overlord." The waiting had been difficult, and Eisenhower had talked at length with Colonel Elliott Roosevelt, son of the President, to discover if his father had said anything about the matter. The younger Roosevelt had nothing to report. Eisenhower resented the nonchalance of the President. Years later, after he himself had left the presidency, Ike told a friend that Franklin Roosevelt was "a cruel man." More to the point was the fact that Marshall by this time was indispensable to Roosevelt in the conducting of a global war, having come to dominate intellectually the deliberations of both the U.S. Joint Chiefs and the Combined Chiefs and having gained the trust of Congress. Marshall wanted the command of the cross-Channel invasion, but his sense of honor and duty, once he realized the President's position, prevented him from mentioning it. What Eisenhower did not know were the reasons for the selection. Roosevelt told his son James several months later that in North Africa Eisenhower had demonstrated that he was the "best politician among military men . . . a natural leader who can convince other men to follow him, and this is what we need in his position more than any other quality."

Now Eisenhower was impatient to oversee the buildup of what he knew would be the greatest invasion force ever assembled. He went home for conferences with Marshall and Roosevelt, arriving back in London in January 1944 to find himself in the midst of a contention over Allied strategy.

How to defeat Germany? The Russians were still struggling with the bulk of the German army, having thrown it on the defensive after the battle of Stalingrad in the winter of 1942.

Eisenhower favored plans that called for an assault in southern France combined with a landing at Normandy, but a short-
age of landing craft required a delay. Therefore the British
favored attacking Germany through Eastern Europe, through
the Balkans, but, bolstered by the increasing preponderance
of American troops and supplies, Eisenhower prevailed. Then
Sir Alan Brooke, British chief of staff, questioned Eisenhower's
strategy after Normandy—his plan to strike at the Germans
on a broad front using two spearheads, north and south.
Eisenhower explained that after the landing, the Allies would
pause long enough to amass troops and supplies. Then they
would break through the German lines of defense and proceed toward their objective, the Ruhr, the industrial heartland
of Germany located along the Rhine River, not far inside and
parallel to Germany's western border. British and American
troops under Montgomery would attack in the north with the
main strength through Belgium, while U.S. forces under Bradley would attack from France. It was to be a textbook example
of Clausewitz's offensive for the final overthrow of the enemy.
From their positions above and below the Ruhr, these drives,
according to plan, would encircle much of the German army.
A convergent attack was preferable, Clausewitz had written,
because, while it is risky without sufficient strength, if it "suc-
ceeds the enemy is not just beaten; he is virtually cut off." "Every ground commander," Eisenhower later wrote, "seeks the
battle of annihilation; so far as conditions permit, he tries to
duplicate in modern war the classic example of Cannae," where
Hannibal in 216 b.c. defeated a superior Roman army by
double envelopment. The British commanders, Brooke and
Montgomery, still of the opinion that their strategies were superior, proposed to send one spearhead north of the Ruhr, a
so-called "pencil thrust" under Montgomery, all the way to
Berlin. Eisenhower, usually able to cajole but when necessary
resigned to coercing the British, stayed with his plan. It was
not until Allied forces moved across the Rhine, that Brooke
admitted that Eisenhower had been correct.

Similar singlemindedness surrounded the London strate-
gists as they prepared for the invasion of Normandy. Clausewitz
had declared the defending force to be the stronger and that
an attack across water (he was speaking of rivers but the principle was the same) "always weakens and dislocates the offensive [force]." The intelligence staff sought to predict what the
defending German general—Rommel, with twelve infantry
and eleven panzer divisions—would do. Would he repulse landings at the beaches, or counterattack later? What's more, bad
weather could force a cancellation of the whole landing. Finally, they worried, if the Red Army did not, as promised, attack simultaneously on the eastern front, Hitler might decide
to repulse the Normandy invasion by drawing from his forces
in the east. Eisenhower's response to these dangerous possibilities was to count on: an element of surprise; Allied superiority on the beaches; control of the air, which included the
use of bombers; the support of French partisan fighters; and
the strategic landing of airborne troops to isolate and protect
the landing areas. What he could not allow was for the landing parties to be forced to dig in for a trench war, resulting in
another World-War-I-type stalemate. Success most of all depended on such surprise that no more than three enemy mobile divisions would be in Normandy on D-day, the code name
for the date of the invasion. This Eisenhower accomplished
by Operation Fortitude, which kept an entire German army
pinned at Calais in the north awaiting an invasion that never
occurred.

Early in the war the British, using a captured German en-
coding machine, had broken the German military code and
began listening to their transmissions. The operation was called
Ultra and enabled the Allies to both guard against attack and
achieve surprise. Ultra assisted the British air force to defeat
the *Luftwaffe* in the autumn of 1940, preventing a German
amphibious invasion of the British islands. In North Africa
Eisenhower learned the extent to which he could depend on
Ultra intelligence and how to incorporate it into tactical op-

erations. The Fortitude deception, with the assistance of Ultra, involved creating in the German mind a nonexistent army under General George Patton amassing in England to land in France at Calais, across from Dover, and entailed planted messages, cardboard tanks, a bogus invasion fleet, and false encampments.

By the end of May 1944, Eisenhower had amassed a sufficient force for a cross-Channel invasion—the largest invasion force in history—2.9 million men: twenty American divisions; seventeen British and Canadian; one French; and one Polish. Weapons included 5,000 bombers, an equal force of fighters, 5,300 ships, and 1,100 landing craft. His assistants were all British and included: Air Marshall Tedder, deputy supreme commander; Admiral Sir Bertram Ramsay, commander of naval forces; Air Marshal Sir Trafford Leigh-Mallory, chief of air operations; and Montgomery as assault commander. Ike was confident but knew that nothing could be certain. When H-hour arrived on D-day, June 6, he prepared a note for one last contingency. "My decision to attack at this time and place was based upon the best information available. The troops, the air and the navy did all that bravery and devotion to duty could do. If any blame or fault attaches to the attempt it is mine alone."

Good planning and follow through made the invasion a success. Before dawn on the morning of June 5, in the middle of driving wind and rain, the staff meteorologist forecasted a forty-eight-hour break in the storm. Eisenhower listened to conflicting advice—Leigh-Mallory predicted failure. Ike waited an agonizing 45 seconds, and then said: "Okay, we'll go."

The Allied force was opposed by 1.5 million Germans located in France and Belgium. The actual invasion included eight reinforced Allied divisions, 90,000 combat troops with 84,000 supply troops and 20,000 vehicles. The three airborne divisions and five amphibious divisions landed on a forty-mile front between Caen to the east and the base of the Normandy peninsula in the west.

A lone German division (in addition to the expected three) appeared unexpectedly to resist American forces, including Major General Gerow's V Corps at Omaha beach. But within hours the beachhead was secure. The Germans counterattacked in a piecemeal fashion. They had withdrawn most of their planes. Allied paratroopers that had landed inland had destroyed bridges, torn up railroad tracks, and cut telephone lines, causing fear and confusion behind enemy lines. By July 2, over 1 million Allied troops, 567,000 tons of supplies, and 172,000 vehicles were in the bridgeheads, miles into the countryside. The fighting on the beaches and in the hedgerows was vicious. In three weeks the Allies lost 8,975 men dead, 51,796 wounded. But German headquarters warned its commanders that Allied air superiority had smothered almost all their movement. Losses in men and equipment were extraordinary. Indeed, Rommel reported to Hitler that he had lost 97,000 men.

The breakout on July 25 showed how clearheaded and able Eisenhower and his lieutenants had been. Montgomery's attacks at Caen on the left flank, although never prosecuted as Eisenhower wanted, did attract German divisions, letting Bradley's Americans break out of their beachhead at St. Lo, pouring through a hole created by heavy bombers. Hitler's chief of staff, Colonel General Alfred Jodl, later commented that "the landing as a whole was well executed" but the breakthrough was "a piece of impertinence." Traveling by jeep, light observation plane, and staff car, Eisenhower had supervised the buildup, first from his headquarters at Portsmouth, then from Normandy.

If the breakout was masterful, what followed was a stroke of brilliance. Using Ultra, Bradley discovered a German counterattack, against the left flank of the Allied thrust south, in the making. Devising maneuvers in response to how the battle was evolving, Bradley held the village of Mortain to hinder the westward movement of the German panzers while looping his main attack against their southern flank. He sent one of his

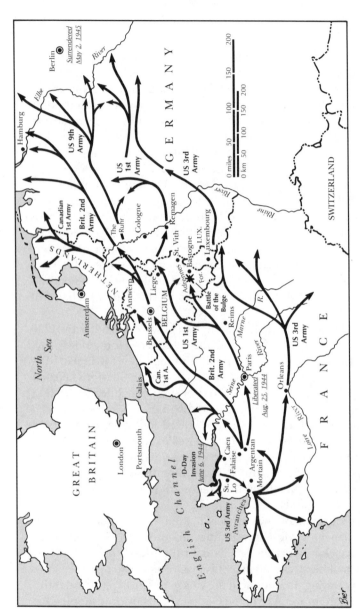

The Liberation of Western Europe

army commanders, Patton, to the south and then northeast toward Argentan and Falaise. Simultaneously, he needed Montgomery's troops to move south from Caen to the northern flank to cut off the retreating enemy at Falaise. Eisenhower was at Bradley's headquarters when the news came. The supreme commander nodded his approval and ordered Montgomery to strike south. After three days the Germans began to withdraw. Forty thousand German troops escaped before the Allies closed the door on 50,000 prisoners and 10,000 German dead.

Crucial to the Normandy victory, the Germans later agreed, was Allied air power. Heavy bombing raids, Operation Pointblank, on the German heartland piercing all the way to Berlin had, over the previous six months, virtually demolished the *Luftwaffe*. The bombing had also destroyed the Nazis' fighter production facilities, which, in turn, resulted in enormous losses among German pilots who found their Focke Wulf 190s and Messerschmitt 109 aircraft no match for the sleek new Allied P-51 Mustang fighters escorting the bombers to their targets. Then, in the weeks before D-day, having established air supremacy, Eisenhower took operational command of the Eighth Air Force bombers to implement his Transportation Plan: the objective to cut the railroads to Normandy and, without giving away the plan, to isolate the battlefield from resupply. While this was not as effective as desired, in the days before the invasion the interdiction raids completed the task by destroying bridges. In the weeks that followed, Eisenhower saw to it that his troops had all the close support they needed. Bradley's armored columns broke through, as mentioned, at St. Lo through a gap in German fortifications created by a B-17 bomber run—similar to the tactic used at Salerno. And when Patton's tanks ran into a pillbox or the Germans counterattacked, as at Mortain, air corps pilots assigned as ground observers in lead tanks used their radios to call in dive bombing and strafing P-51s and P-47 Thunderbolts, a devastating and swiftly moving form of artillery. It was a replay, this time on the side of democracy, of Guderian's *blitzkrieg*. It was combined, mechanized warfare at its most ferocious and deadly.

After the fall of Paris the Allies had to pause or risk overextending their supply lines. By this time the Germans had lost 200,000 troops—equally divided between prisoners and dead. Eisenhower was commanding 55 combat divisions, 2.5 million men, half of them American. Headquarters was now at Versailles. He supplied the troops from across the Normandy beaches and, beginning in August, from Marseilles on the Mediterranean until he could support them also from Antwerp. But in September the supply lines had stretched to their limit, and the enemy had dug in on the Siegfried line on the German border. The war of movement had temporarily ended.

Something had to give, but leaving the Ardennes Forest, south of Belgium between France and Luxembourg, lightly defended was a risk. Intelligence reported the withdrawal of German tank units from other parts of the line. As Eisenhower wrote in his diary the following week, "it was not deemed highly probable that the enemy would, in winter, try to use that region in which to stage a counteroffensive on a large scale. Nevertheless, this is exactly what he did." On December 16, shrouded by radio silence and fog, the Germans launched a surprise offensive with twenty-five divisions, later named the Battle of the Bulge. Eisenhower had miscalculated.

"Danger, exertion, uncertainty, and chance," said Clausewitz, make up "the climate of war." Accordingly, he called for character in a military commander—"the ability to keep one's head in times of exceptional stress and violent emotion." Eisenhower knew this well from his days with Conner. "The history of war," Ike later wrote, "is replete with instances where a sudden panic, an unexpected change of weather, or some other unforeseen circumstance has defeated the best-laid plans and brought reverse rather than victory. . . . No matter how confident they may be of their ultimate ability to foil the enemy and even to turn the situation into a favorable one, there always exists the danger, when the enemy has the initiative, of something going wrong. No responsible individual in war is ever free of mental strain; in battle such as the one initiated by the German attack in the Ardennes, this reaches a peak. But in a well-trained combat force, everyone has been schooled to accept it. Hysteria, born of excessive fear, is encountered only in exceptional cases." English-speaking Germans, dressed in American uniforms, disrupted the Allied lines. To make matters worse, there was a rumor afloat at this time that these infiltrators would attempt to assassinate the supreme commander. Eisenhower, demonstrating his equilibrium, responded characteristically. "Hell's fire, I'm going out for walk. If anyone wants to shoot me, he can go right ahead."

After several days of anxiety and action by Eisenhower, the danger receded. Realizing the threat to supply dumps at Liege, and the advantage the enemy might gain from attacking, as he did, the juncture of Montgomery's 21st Army Group and Bradley's 12th Army group, Eisenhower used the Ardennes attack as an opportunity to regain the initiative and return mobility to the war. He moved the 101st Airborne Division and part of the Tenth Armored to hold Bastogne. Their mission, and that of the Seventh Armored at St. Vith farther north, was to delay the enemy. He then ordered the 82nd Airborne to threaten the German flank on the northern edge of the German penetration, or bulge in the line. He needed infantrymen and looked everywhere, including the services of supply and prison stockades. He signed an order enabling black Americans to serve alongside whites in what was still a segregated army. He alerted commanders to fight to the finish. Placing all troops north of the Ardennes under Montgomery's command, including the American First and Ninth armies, he then ordered an attack south. At the same time Patton's Third Army was to move north toward Bastogne—another pincer like the counteroffensive at Mortain. Finally, he sent a delegation under Tedder to Moscow to do what it could to obtain a Soviet offensive, which the Red Army launched in early January 1945. Clouds and fog meanwhile had lifted, and on December 23 American and British fighter-bombers destroyed enemy tanks, C-47 transports airlifted supplies and ammunition to the Allied troops on the line. The Germans lost 120,000 men (dead and wounded), 600 tanks and assault guns, and 1,600 planes. Allied losses were 77,000, including 8,000 dead and 48,000 wounded.

The failure of the German offensive in the Ardennes was the beginning of the end of World War II in Europe. For the Allies, the operation since Overlord had proceeded generally according to plan. There had been setbacks—the Ardennes surprise, Montgomery's failure to capture the water approaches to Antwerp until late autumn, and, in September, a failed attempt to broach the lower Rhine by airborne assault, Operation Market Garden. But, while building strength continuously to avoid what Clausewitz termed a fatal "culminating point" of an offensive where lines are so extended that the advantage goes to the enemy, the Allies pursued and ground down the Germans in artillery barrages. Then, in a stroke of good fortune for the Allies, the Germans failed to blow up the railroad bridge across the Rhine at Remagen, south of the Ruhr, and an American platoon cut the demolition cables the fleeing enemy had laid, raced across, and set up positions. "Hot dog!" shouted Bradley when he heard the news. Bradley reached Eisenhower by phone, and the two ignored British protests that a crossing was not a good idea. "To hell with the planners," was the response. "Sure, go on, Brad, and I'll give you everything we got to hold that bridgehead." The Germans never recovered. Field Marshal Albert von Kesselring, their commander in the west, later explained that he knew the Allies regarded the Rhine as a "great barrier and would pause to regroup. That would give us a chance to pause and regroup. The magnetic way in which the Remagen bridgehead drew these divisions prevented their being reinforced."

In movements that another enemy general later described as "strikingly daring" and "faultlessly executed," Allied forces moved into Germany. German divisions surrendered or melted away. Eisenhower ordered an advance not to Berlin, as desired by Montgomery, but toward Red Army positions at the Elbe River. From there his troops spread north, incidentally pre-empting a Russian occupation of Denmark, then south to wipe out pockets of resistance and a possible Nazi redoubt in Bavaria. Faced with insurmountable circumstances—the loss of their petroleum supplies due to Allied bombing; the Allied movement of 91 combat divisions, 970,000 vehicles, 18 million tons of supplies, and 28,000 combat aircraft into their country from the west; the occupation of Berlin by the Red Army; the suicide of Hitler in his Berlin bunker; and the spontaneous surrendering of many of their troops—the German high command signed an unconditional surrender at Allied headquarters in Rheims on May 7, 1945.

Years later German General Bodo Zimmerman wrote that the most important Allied edge in the European assault was, what Eisenhower had required from North Africa onward, the "full powers of command over an armed force consisting of all three services," while each of the German arms "fought its own battle."

In the Allied campaigns across France and Germany, Eisenhower was in tactical command. Montgomery, supremely egotistical and difficult as a subordinate, at several points nominated himself to be the Allied ground commander, however, his inability to break out as he promised at Caen during the assault on Normandy, his failure to close the Falaise pocket, the ill-fated Market Garden operation, and his reluctance to accept orders for the approach to Germany were perhaps sufficient in themselves for some sort of action by the supreme commander. But when, after the German winter offensive, Montgomery delayed a counterattack and then demanded to be made commander, Eisenhower drafted a message relieving him. It was not until then, upon being told of the situation, that Montgomery apologized. It is difficult in retrospect to imagine that anyone besides Ike could have accomplished the tasks of Allied command.

The Eisenhower-Montgomery debate, despite historical reconsideration to the contrary, entailed more than just a disagreement over strategy or Eisenhower's frustration with a dilatory subordinate. The supreme commander had an acute awareness of both the limitations of supply and the importance of overall morale—the unity of the Allied coalition. As historian Martin Blumenson has shown, Montgomery's insistence on a single thrust into northern Germany would have required more fuel and ammunition than was available and would have given the Germans an opportunity to concentrate their defenses at one point. Eisenhower's double thrust on a broad front, on the other hand, conserved Allied resources, kept the Germans spread out and guessing, and preserved the concept that the Allies were working as a team.

In the postmortems on the victory in Europe in 1945, critics accused Eisenhower of failing to take Berlin. They overlooked the fact that he would have had to take it upon himself to change strategy and along with it the objectives of the war. His orders from Roosevelt and the Combined Chiefs were to defeat Germany by working with the Soviet Union to destroy the German army. The Soviets had coordinated attacks on the eastern front and, at wartime conferences, had agreed on the Elbe as a line of demarcation. The United States needed Soviet intervention in the war against Japan, and the President wanted their participation in the United Nations, which he saw as the guarantor of peace in the postwar world. From Normandy until V-E day, Eisenhower's forces, which numbered during this time 5,412,219 troops, had suffered 586,628 American casualties, among them 135,576 were dead. The British, Canadians, French, and other Allies lost 179,666, including about 60,000 dead. The Soviet Union, for its part, had lost 20 million dead. Now Berlin was in the Soviet sector of postwar Germany, and the Russians were closest to it with the largest force. Liberating the city would require fourteen days of fighting before 120,000 German defenders surrendered. Before doing so they lost 60,000 dead, the Red Army even more.

And so the war was won. Roosevelt's successor, President Truman, traveled to Europe in July 1945 and arrived at Brussels en route to the Potsdam Conference to discuss the postwar division of Europe with Churchill and Stalin. When Eisenhower arrived to meet him, the new President's gratitude was boundless. The general had received his fifth star— a promotion to general of the army, a permanent rank—just before the Battle of the Bulge. Now there was another offer. "If there is anything you want in the days ahead," Truman said, "including the presidency of the United States," he would help Eisenhower get it. After Potsdam, Eisenhower accepted an invitation from Stalin to visit the Soviet Union. The trip was cordial, reinforcing the general's belief that if cooperation with Soviet forces had been closer, victory would have been earlier, the peace on a "firmer foundation."

Victory had its extraordinary moments for Dwight D. Eisenhower. In London he received a sword from the Lord Mayor and gave a speech at the Guildhall about the need for partnership among nations in a world where wars would no longer be necessary. Upon his return home he addressed a joint session of Congress, receiving the longest ovation in the legislature's history. Then it was on to New York City for a tickertape parade in his honor. And then, at last, came a visit to Abilene where his hometown sponsored a parade, after which he gave a speech in the city park that was named for him.

But the victory had not come cheaply, and for Eisenhower the personal costs had been high. In 1941 the face of the brigadier general had displayed the appearance of youth, free of lines, his eye a sparkling blue. The war had been his unrelenting preoccupation for three and one-half years. Leading troops in his view meant leaving his headquarters often, visiting the lines, always moving from place to place. "The feeling that pervades the forward areas," he later wrote, "is loneliness. There is little to be seen; friend and foe, as well as the engines of war, seem to disappear from sight when troops are deployed for a fight. Loss of control and cohesion are easy, because each man feels himself so much alone, and each is prey to the human fear and terror that to move or show himself may result in instant death." At Faid Pass in 1943 he had been at the front very early on the morning of the German breakthrough. Admonishing a colonel for not putting out mine fields and preparing positions, he departed at 3:30 A.M. The Germans came in thirty minutes later. In 1945 the face of Dwight D. Eisenhower held deep lines, his tired eyes were gray.

CHAPTER THREE

The Road to the White House

With the collapse of Nazi Germany in April 1945 there came the serious question of how long Allied cooperation would continue. Even during the war the Allied strategic coordination had been tempered by distrust, including worries about Russia reaching a possible separate peace with the Nazis because of Western delay in establishing a second front, suspicion over the 1940 massacre in the Katyn Forest of 15,000 Polish officers who were prisoners of the Red Army, and unhappiness with the Soviets' delay in the liberation of Warsaw, which resulted in the city's demolition by Nazi SS storm-troopers.

In the months that followed the German surrender, Eisenhower, as military governor of the American zone of Germany, was now burdened with the responsibility, more diplomatic than military, for which precedent was either nonexistent or unclear. The demilitarization and de-Nazification of Germany had indeed been the Allies' wartime goal, but who would define and implement that objective now? The provisions of the Yalta agreement (the February 1945 meeting in the Soviet Crimea on the Black Sea in which Roosevelt, Churchill, and Stalin decided upon postwar arrangements for the defeated Germany) were for an Allied control commission to make these decisions, but this would have required a continuing agreement between Soviet and Western members of that commission (that never materialized).

For Eisenhower, his hatred of the Nazis and awareness of the need for continued cooperation with the Soviets went hand in hand. At the same time he realized that a Germany stripped of its own industries would end up becoming a burden to the U.S. economy. As military governor he concluded that he had no real choice but to do his best to implement the original goals of the coalition. The ultimate purpose of the victory, after all, had been a Germany at peace with other nations. And he would do all he could to foster good feelings in the Soviet leader. The only hope for avoiding a recurrence of the death and destruction he had seen all about him, he felt, was to encourage a postwar international coalition. The goal would be long-term, mutual self-interest.

Meanwhile, however, Eisenhower had to figure out how the victors would deal with a multitude of prisoners of war (POWs), liberated concentration camp inmates, and refugees who all needed proper food, sanitation, and shelter. Carrying out the agreement at Yalta, Eisenhower repatriated two million Soviet citizens—POWs, slave laborers, and political refugees (whom Stalin promptly sent into his prison work-camp system). Much further suffering was nevertheless in store for the German people, as untold numbers perished from hunger or cold. Furthermore, the Western allies brought charges of war crimes against three million Germans, bringing two million former Nazis to trial and punishing one million of them.

Then, once again, came new duty for Eisenhower. This time he was appointed as army chief of staff. If someone had said to him in 1939 that in six years he would be the senior officer of the United States Army, he would have scoffed. At that time he had been only recently promoted to colonel and had not even entertained the thought of reaching brigadier general. Now, in 1945, he was, of all things, possessor of the five-star insignia and a new rank invented in 1944, general of the army. As it happened, he returned home from Germany in November to brief Congress on events in Germany, became ill with bronchial pneumonia, and had to enter a hospital. By the time he recovered, two weeks later, President Truman had appointed him to his new post. The chief executive needed Marshall as special envoy to China, where civil war had broken out, and he needed Omar Bradley as director of the Veterans Administration. Upon hearing of his new appointment, Eisenhower protested that he wanted to retire, but he accepted after receiving a promise that the tour would be brief. Alas, it lasted from November 20, 1945, to February 7, 1948, and by the latter date, the United States had passed from a time of relative serenity to one of great anxiety about its position in the world.

As chief of staff Eisenhower moved from one frustration to another. Against his better judgment, it was he who had to preside over the most massive and precipitous demobilization of the armed forces in American history. The one redeeming hope he held was that the President and Congress would support the army's proposal for the establishment of a system of universal military training—modeled after Switzerland's citizen soldier training—the mandatory training of all eighteen-year-old American men to provide them with a grounding in citizenship and give the armed forces a sufficient strength to deter aggression and support its interests. The best thinkers in the army had supported the concept of universal training since World War I. To Eisenhower's alarm, Congress refused to enact the plan, despite his urging and that of Marshall. By 1948 the American part of the military machine that had brought Germany and Japan to their knees was in ruins. The National Security Act of the previous year had established a Department of Defense, within which existed a separate Air Force, National Security Council, and Central Intelligence Agency, but it left the previously existing services autonomous, their chiefs of staff and secretaries all reporting to a relatively weak secretary of defense, a civilian in the President's cabinet. When Eisenhower told the President and congressional com-

mittees that the nation could not maintain overseas occupation forces and guarantee its own defense without a $15 bil-
lion defense budget, they responded with an $11 billion bud-
get. The United States possessed the atomic bomb, they said.
Ike was quick to respond that this "horrendous weapon" was
unusable in circumstances short of a surprise attack similar to
that at Pearl Harbor. While he opposed giving nuclear-weapons capability to the United Nations without a reliable system
of inspection to ensure that all parties abided by an agreement not to develop their own nuclear weapons, he believed
that the A-bomb did not truly strengthen the United States'
military or diplomatic position. Having drastically reduced
both conventional and reserve capability, he felt that the
United States lacked an alternative means of inhibiting aggression. It was for a man of Eisenhower's understanding and
dedication an awful time.

All this perhaps would have made little difference were it
not for the fact that Stalin and his comrades in the Communist party of the Soviet Union had no intention of relaxing
their hold on their nation or of giving up territories taken
during the war. By mid-1945 they, accordingly, were intransi-
gent in the international postwar councils, and in the areas in
which wartime agreements had given them joint control, they
were busily carting every piece of stranded military equipment
back to Soviet territory.

The origin of the cold war has been the subject of many
books, and it is impossible to place precise responsibility for
the events that unfolded. By this time the United States had
already had major difficulties with this particular Russian government. Distrust of the Bolsheviks, their methods of taking
and holding power, and their apocalyptic Marxist ideology had
resulted in the United States' refusal, from 1917 to 1933, to
extend diplomatic recognition to the Soviet Union. The administration of President Franklin D. Roosevelt finally did so
grudgingly because new national interests were at stake in
Europe and especially the Far East after Japan had begun an
offensive expansion. During World War II America and Russia's

common enemy, Germany, had forced a level of cooperation, which was considerably less than the level of cooperation that the Americans enjoyed with the British. Notably, early in the war the Soviets discovered from their spies that the Americans and the British were working jointly to develop an atomic bomb but were keeping it a secret from them. By 1946, Soviet efforts to continue the flow of Lend Lease aid (the program by which the United States sent wartime supplies to both Britain and the Soviet Union) to their country and to secure a postwar reconstruction loan from the United States failed. The Truman administration, faced with urgent economic demands, newly confident because of its possession of the atomic bomb, and suspicious of Stalin's renewed anticapitalist propaganda campaign, had decided to use the possibility of economic aid as leverage to obtain Soviet accession to Western war aims of national self-determination in Eastern Europe.

By the spring of the following year, Truman received notice from the financially strapped British of their need to withdraw their long-standing military presence in the Eastern Mediterranean. Realizing that neither Congress nor the American people saw the magnitude of the problem, the President announced a new U.S. foreign policy, one committed to holding back the expansion of communism. Soon becoming known as Containment, or the Truman Doctrine, this was in fact the American declaration of cold war. But even Containment, the accompanying $400 million of aid to Greece and Turkey, and the announcement in June 1947 of the Marshall Plan, $12 billion to rebuild Western Europe, made little difference to the squabbling U.S. armed services and their supporters in Congress. The creation of a Defense Department that included a separate air force, army, navy, and marine corps, and the establishment of the Joint Chiefs of Staff brought no agreement on an overall strategy or any willingness by Congress to appropriate more money to keep the nation's defense on the ready.

Eisenhower found the situation increasingly dangerous. In May 1946 he had confided to his diary that the public largely failed to understand "that our form of government is under deadly, persistent, and constant attack. To lead others to democracy we must help actively." American strength, he said "is a combination of complete devotion to democracy . . . and practice of free enterprise." Accordingly, he advocated that the nation maintain "industrial and economic strength; moral probity in all dealings; and necessary military strength." The following November he noted that a number of "well-meaning friends have suggested a political career for me" and had not listened when he said, "no." He remarked "I've been under intensive strain since 1938 . . . I'm suspicious of anyone who believes he could take over the presidency successfully in these days and times." However, the problems of postwar America, especially its security and diplomacy, called out for leadership by one of Eisenhower's expertise.

Since he was not consulted as to the formation of policy, Eisenhower could only respond to it. He supported Containment but disliked the crisis atmosphere whipped up by those who had enacted it. He considered the problem with the Soviets a political and economic rather than military one. And he disagreed with people who felt that a U.S.-Soviet war was imminent, inevitable, desirable, or that Russia's aim was military conquest (he demanded evidence that Stalin wanted war or was mobilizing). At the same time, he advocated U.S. preparedness, industrial strength, and conventional military capability and supported the Marshall Plan.

Perhaps what fueled the frustration he was feeling at this time was that he remained popular, his status as hero undiminished. There were constant requests to make appearances, and, indeed, that he make political pronouncements. The Red Cross, the USO, veterans organizations, and church groups all sought him for the lectern. He refused many of these invitations because, as he put it, "fair presentation of the whole subject requires consideration of subjects outside the strictly military." He feared creating an impression that "the U.S. Army wants to achieve some position other than that of servant of civil power." Still, he felt a sense of guilt in declining many of the offers. And, as always, many of his duties involved the political arena. For example, he had to prepare the contingency plans in the event that the President had to order the army to take over the coal mines where miners were striking. And, of course, diminishing appropriations required that he decide just where to cut the army's budget. "I'm on the side of the congressional purpose of saving money," he insisted in February 1947, "but if I'm pushed more, I'll simply have to ask them 'how' to do it." So, while he rationed out his appearances carefully, during his tour as army chief of staff he gave numerous speeches and in the process established contacts with prominent and wealthy businessmen, some of whom became his friends. Meanwhile he relearned what he had come to know during his earlier tour in Washington, D.C., that the army—because of its unending efforts to obtain consideration of its programs in Washington and the New York media, but also because of its leaders' personal egos, hatreds, political and partisan prejudices—was inevitably immersed in politics.

The general rejoiced when, in February 1948, his "tour" had ended and he could leave the Pentagon. He had dreamt of going off to a small, rural college to write and teach and talk to students. As it happened, small colleges, probably intimidated by his stature, failed to seek him. Thomas J. Watson of the International Business Machines Corporation (IBM) in New York thereupon courted him to become president of Columbia University. The position, Watson said, would afford him a good measure of tranquility and the chance to reflect upon while keeping abreast of public affairs. Also appealing would be the fact that as Columbia's president he would be free as never before to criticize U.S. policy. He agreed and promised to set up his new residence in Morningside Heights in New York City by June.

Before he could venture into civilian life, however, he had one more short-term but, as it turned out, important commitment. Two of his businessman acquaintances, Douglas Black, president of Doubleday publishing company (and a trustee of

Columbia University), and William Robinson, executive vice president of the New York *Herald Tribune*, had persuaded him to write his wartime memoirs as a means of "setting the record straight." Taking a leave of absence from military duty, a so-called terminal leave, he read the memoirs of U. S. Grant, two direct and plain-spoken volumes (incidentally by a successful army commander who entered civilian politics) to gain a sense of his task. Then, using his wartime correspondence and office records to prod his memory, he organized the material chronologically into chapters and dictated them to a stenographer. After revising for clarity he gave the chapters to staff researchers, who verified every statement. He worked at a furious pace, putting in sixteen-hour days to finish in the allotted time. *Crusade in Europe* (still in print) became one of the best-selling works of nonfiction in the present century (well over a million copies sold). Rather than a percentage of sales, his royalties were a flat prepayment of $635,000. After completing this task he officially retired from the office of army chief of staff—as a five-star general he was on active duty for life, something that he could change only by resigning his commission—and moved to New York.

As it turned out, the presidency of Columbia little resembled Eisenhower's ideal of retirement and involved a variety of unexpected activities. He enjoyed discussing history, economics, and science, and he told his old friend Everett Hazlett that he was certain that his academic work would be absorbing if only he could give attention to it. Unfortunately this was impossible. Administrative duties of every sort took his time. He greeted dignitaries, made speeches, negotiated with employees, appeared at ceremonies, and managed university real estate. Instead of exchanging ideas with faculty and students, he found himself grappling with a university budget whose deficit threatened faculty salaries and academic standards. He did find opportunities for physical exercise, camaraderie, and emotional recovery. Indeed, for Eisenhower excursions away from his daily responsibility were by now essential. He enjoyed playing golf and joined the Augusta National in Georgia. An avid bridge player, he continued to play, and even found time to do some fishing, hunting, and skeet shooting.

At Columbia also he began what was for him a novel activity, oil painting. The artist Thomas E. Stephens had arrived at Morningside Drive one day to do Mamie's portrait. Seeing the oils, Ike picked up a brush and began his own portrait of Mamie. He found the experience fascinating, and before long he had converted a room in the house into a studio. He explained that his productions were not paintings but "daubs, born of my love of color and . . . pleasure in experimenting."

Finally, the time at Columbia left him free enough to do something he loved, to "chew the fat," as Kevin McCann recalled, and he began to form associations with individuals who later constituted the group he named "the gang." William Robinson and Cliff Roberts, a New York investment banker, helped him invest the money he had earned from his book. At the Century Club, a prominent men's social club, he met such people as Governor Dewey's 1948 presidential campaign chairman, Herbert Brownell. Another new friend from this period was the president of Brown University, Henry M. Wriston, who once remarked that people thought the general was idle because he played golf but that he was actually, "one of the most industrious men I ever knew." With all of these new friends Eisenhower hardly relaxed as much as he should have. He talked with them during evenings at their clubs or in their houses, thereby enlarging his ideas of what might be good for the country, say, rather than just Columbia University.

During this time Eisenhower's commitment to capitalism and democracy—so he explained in a letter to a friend—had become "almost fanatical," the rhetoric of a man interested in politics. Among his worries was what he saw as a challenge from within, a tendency to compromise American values through bureaucracy, subsidies, and handouts, all of which, he felt, could produce "loss of personal initiative and responsibility, lowered production, a stagnated economy, commandeering of property and, finally, dictatorship." At Columbia he instituted a program of annual conferences, so that, as he later wrote, the university might marshall its "moral and intellectual strength . . . as a power for good throughout the country and the Western World." This was a purpose different from that which most faculty had in mind for the university, and he thus received their barbs for diverting its resources via the conferences to everyday problems of society, perhaps politicizing the campus. He either did not hear the criticism or would not listen to it. Citizenship, he believed, required understanding the dangers that went with freedom, including "opposing ideologies." Therefore he established a program called the American Assembly, an annual event to bring together individuals from many occupations to discuss questions facing the nation. In sessions on foreign policy Ike stressed the need to help Americans draw the line between "tragic unpreparedness" and "unconscionable cost." In domestic affairs he urged the Assembly to discuss solutions to labor-management troubles, alternatives to socialized medicine, and the need to reduce federal aid to education. For its meetings Eisenhower obtained the use of Arden House, the hilltop estate of Averell Harriman in upstate New York (easily reached from New York City, up the Hudson on the rail line to West Point or to Poughkeepsie and then across the river by car to the hill), to which he summoned groups of leaders in business, labor, politics, finance, and higher education to cooperate for the common good. Indeed, the American Assembly became virtually synonymous with the idea of cooperation in postwar America, of bringing what in times past had been disparate groups together with Columbia faculty. The Assembly, by the end of Eisenhower's tenure, became an important source of good will and, indirectly, of funds for Columbia. It was one of his principle successes as the university's president.

But in retrospect, Eisenhower's educational accomplishments at Columbia were considerable. He started a program for conservation of human resources under the economist Eli

Ginzberg, an Institute of War and Peace Studies, and a new engineering center. Because of his pressure the university's endowment increased, and with it faculty salaries. Within two years he had eliminated the university's heretofore chronic budget deficit.

Meanwhile the rapidly occurring world events began to tug Ike back into national service. The president of Columbia began to bring people together to talk about possible solutions to international problems at the Council on Foreign Relations (a private, elite New York organization dedicated to the study of American foreign relations and publisher of the quarterly *Foreign Affairs*). The passage of the Marshall Plan in 1948 and the Soviet reaction to it was a pressing issue. Meanwhile, Bedell Smith, most recently the U.S. ambassador in Moscow, had written that Russia had declared war on European recovery and would try to prevent German resources from contributing to a new Europe. The European recovery administrator, Paul G. Hoffman, had asked the Council to recommend a policy for Europe now that it looked like the division of Germany would be permanent. The Council asked Eisenhower to become chairman of a study group. He did and the group ultimately recommended the political unification of Western Europe through implementation of the North Atlantic Treaty. It recommended German rearmament and steps by the Europeans to assure that Europe was prepared to resist aggression. Eisenhower said Bernard Baruch, now in retirement, was the individual who might get the countries of Europe who were known more for warring upon each other than for cooperating to do their part. Economic concessions, he believed, could emerge from political accords. Eisenhower urged Secretary of Defense James Forrestal to push for economic union in return for any U.S. participation in a postwar treaty organization.

Study group member Tracy S. Voorhees, former undersecretary of the army, in 1949 advocated conversion of the Marshall Plan's economic assistance to purely military aid. This was in response to the first successful detonation by the Soviets of a nuclear device, talk by both superpowers of a hydrogen bomb, and the communist conquest of mainland China. William Dieboldt, Jr., Council on Foreign Relations staff economist, countered that the Soviet Union was not inclined to attack Western Europe militarily. Therefore, military expenditure in Germany, he said, would detract from its hopes for a economic recovery. As a foremost expert on Europe and military affairs, Eisenhower found himself squarely in the middle of these discussions.

It was becoming clear that world events were drawing him away from Columbia. Because of his position—public Law 333 of 1946 had established his permanent rank as general of the army and provided assistants to help with his "continuing responsibility" for study, correspondence, and public appearance—the President was free to call upon him. What was remarkable was not that Eisenhower did not remain at Columbia but that he remained as long as he did.

The first call to return to Washington came from Secretary of Defense Forrestal in December 1948. The Soviet blockade of the West's access to Berlin and an accompanying war scare had begun the previous spring, and yet no one in the Pentagon even seemed able to bring about a reasonable level of cooperation among the three squabbling military services. "The current situation," Forrestal said, speaking of international affairs, was grave, because "our diplomatic opponents have finally demonstrated their intention of avoiding any path that might lead to even partial settlement of our differences." The Joint Chiefs of Staff nonetheless spent their time poaching on each other's territory, acting as if their respective services were enemies, so Eisenhower began going to Washington once or twice a week to preside over their meetings. In February 1949 he agreed to act as the chairman of the Joint Chiefs of Staff for a brief period. (No permanent chairmanship yet existed by legislation.) He was not optimistic, confiding to his diary that the President and Forrestal "apparently assume that I have some miraculous power to make some of these warring elements lie down in peace together."

A large part of the interservice bickering stemmed from rivalry over the foreseen role that each service would play in U.S. strategy now that the nuclear era had dawned. U.S. contingency plans for a war with the Soviet Union actually projected bombing only in the "initial phases," when some 15 to 30 atomic bombs of the Nagasaki type (plutonium implosion) would be delivered on industrial targets. This would be followed by movement of allied troops and bombing of military bases. But in the Pentagon there was little if any understanding of these realities. Neither the new department of the air force nor the navy believed ground forces could have a role in future conflict. The future (and congressional appropriations), they believed, belonged to the service that could deliver the nuclear bomb. Consequently, they disagreed about their missions—the air force considered bombing its responsibility, believed it needed a new bomber, and suspected the navy wanted to encroach; the navy argued that only with the support of fighters launched from large aircraft carriers could bombers reach targets and that it needed a new type of "supercarrier" to accomplish the mission.

What to do? "The basic evil," Eisenhower soon was saying, "was the freedom with which each service attacks any decision of the joint chiefs of staff or secretary of defense that it does not like." None of them revealed any awareness that national security required an ability to "speak serenely and confidently, keeping open [U.S.] access to needed raw materials," keeping the allies in a "position of strength without bankrupting ourselves," and ground forces. Convinced that a U.S.-Soviet war would not occur if at all for another ten to twenty years—it would take that long, it seemed to him, before the Soviet Union was able to stockpile the 100 to 200 atomic bombs that they would need—Eisenhower asked the military chiefs for "an agreed-upon strategic concept" as the basis for a budget.

Argument finally bordered on insubordination, with each

of the three sides considering itself the guardian of national security, and nearly drove Eisenhower to distraction. In the spring of 1949 he was so weary of interservice rivalry that he decided both sides, air force and navy, were probably wrong, although he sided with the air force and its belief that it should have primary strategic responsibility in the atomic age.

Health problems, aggravated by the pace of his schedule, began to plague Eisenhower. One evening after a rigorous day with the Joint Chiefs he collapsed in his Washington hotel room, an attack that he called a "severe digestive upset." It was in fact a heart attack. Earlier he had shown signs of exhaustion, and he had what psychologists now call a type A personality. Further aggravating factors to his condition were his habit of cigarette smoking (four packs a day), high blood pressure when agitated, and painful arthritis and bursitis in the left shoulder. Eisenhower and his doctor, in an effort to protect Ike's political viability, decided to conceal the seriousness of his medical problem. For several days after the "attack" he was not able to get up from his bed. As soon as he could travel, on advice from his doctors at Walter Reed Army Hospital, he accepted an invitation from the White House and went to President Truman's vacation retreat at Key West, where he was forced to abandon solid food for a while and quit smoking. "My doctors tell me," he wrote Joseph E. Davies, "I have made a splendid comeback from my recent illness and will remain in fine shape if I do not again become neglectful of exercise and proper care for myself. Hereafter I think I shall come to Washington only about once a week." When he was well enough to travel again, he made trips to Georgia to play golf at the Augusta National but returned to Washington only rarely.

From his vantage point in New York City he could see that the reorganization of the defense department had done some good. By August 1949, the Joint Chiefs of Staff had a permanent chairman, and a new undersecretary of defense was authorized to deal with matters of strategy and procurement of equipment for all the armed services. A vote of the Joint Chiefs against building a supercarrier temporarily ended debate on that matter, and an investigation began on proposed development of the huge, 4,000-mile-range, B-36 bomber.

But none of this, in Eisenhower's view, could ensure the nation's security. By the end of the 1940s the army was unable "to mobilize effective land power to support air and sea power in any emergency requiring a major mobilization." It had purchased no new equipment since 1945. An occupation army for Europe and the Far East of 670,000 officers and men was needed, plus a two-and-one-third division emergency force in the United States. The army was 100,000 men short. Universal military training was still a possibility, but even if Congress passed such a measure, an unlikely prospect, there were insufficient troops to conduct training. "No economy and efficiency," Eisenhower said, "can be produced in military preparations except on planned and steady basis." Refusal to heed the lessons of the previous war (World War I), he said, was caused by a public failure to "believe we ever will get into a real jam."

The United States seemed to have no solution to the new postwar difficulties it was experiencing. Having refused to accept a nuclear disarmament proposal by the United States in the United Nations, which would have allowed U.S. possession of nuclear weapons until after the Soviets had abandoned their nuclear-weapons development program, Stalin chose to retain his focus on what had been his war aims against Hitler. In the face of international pressure, he did back down from his efforts to secure territorial possessions in Africa and northern Iran and to gain a naval base from Turkey at the Dardenelles, the entrance to the Soviet-dominated Black Sea, but he would not allow political freedom in the areas occupied by the Red Army in East Germany, eastern Austria, and Eastern Europe, including the Baltic states (he had annexed them) and the Balkans. By 1948 he had incorporated all of the occupied region of Eastern Europe into his political and economic sphere, installing governments as he went. The Soviet position was understandable and to a degree justifiable, considering the immense Russian contribution to the victory over Nazi Germany and Russia's historic security interests. The impediment to postwar detente was distrust, Stalin's refusal to accept the legitimacy of democratic governments (the Western war aim), and the view of Western leaders who beheld in Stalin a form of the same totalitarianism against which they had just waged war. With such a juxtaposition of circumstances, values, and attitudes, cold war, if not inevitable was enormously difficult to avoid.

Stalin soon seemed to confirm the West's suspicions, and the cold war had begun to warm up. In 1948, he had responded to the Marshall Plan and actions to unify the western zones of Germany with a communist takeover of Czechoslovakia and the military blockade of access routes to Berlin. For a time many observers feared war, and then, in the spring of 1949, the United States signed with West European nations its first peacetime military alliance, the North Atlantic Treaty Organization (NATO). The same year, although an allied airlift broke the Berlin blockade, the Soviet Union detonated its first atomic device, and the communist Mao Tse-tung's troops overran China, forcing the nationalist government of Chiang Kai-shek (which was strongly backed by the United States) to retreat to the island of Formosa (Taiwan). To make matters worse the Republican opposition in Congress, departing from its earlier bipartisan cooperation in foreign policy, declared that these events were further evidence of treason by the Democrats, who they said had begun appeasing Stalin at the Yalta conference in 1945 and continued doing so with the policy of Containment. Disloyal Democratic State Department officials, according to their broadsides, had allowed the Soviets to obtain American atomic secrets and had allowed China to fall to communism. The Truman administration's attempt to counter Soviet moves in the spring of 1950 was the writing, by a joint policy planning group, of National Security Council Paper Number 68 (NSC-68), which proposed, in addition to the development and construction of a hydrogen bomb, the rapid building of "the powerful, economic, and military strength of the free world," U.S. and allied capability to respond to any communist threat. The problem was how to get the plan, which would require tripling the defense budget, through a parsimonious, if not outright isolationist, Congress.

The Soviet explosion of a nuclear device in late August 1949 had brought a sober appraisal from Eisenhower, one which contained a key to understanding his next twelve years. The existence of the Soviet atomic weapon would require an array of U.S. measures, including a "stand-by mobilization plan," civil defense, and a network of dependable allies. A strong Western Europe was essential. Finally, he said, the United States should insist on a verifiable international control of atomic energy before relinquishing "our overwhelming advantage in the development of atomic weapons."

Then came the Korean War. North Korean troops, with Soviet encouragement and assistance in planning, on June 25, 1950, attacked across the 38th parallel, the 1945 line of demarcation separating the Soviet-backed "liberators" in the north from the American-backed south. Eisenhower hurried to Washington to see friends at the Pentagon. "They seemed indecisive," he noted in his diary. Assuming, in retrospect correctly, that Stalin had given North Korea's Kim Il Sung a green light to attack the South, Ike believed there was danger of Soviet miscalculation about what the West would tolerate. "I believe we'll have a dozen Koreas soon if we don't take a firm stand," he said. He then reminded his army friends, who might have forgotten their Clausewitz, that "an appeal to force could not be partial" and that "in a fight we (our side) can never be too strong." He left a memo for General Bradley urging him to "study every angle to be prepared for whatever may happen, even if it finally came to the use of an A-bomb." Intervention to save South Korea was not something the United States could do alone. The United Nations, he said in a letter, must take a stand. The following week he lunched with the President and his former chief, General Marshall, whom Truman had recalled from retirement yet again, this time as secretary of defense. Although unsure that the President understood, Eisenhower told Truman of the need for "speed and strength." In the following weeks, a group of university presidents called a conference on national objectives—national security, a strong U.S. economy, a plan for the rapid mobilization of the armed forces—at the Waldorf-Astoria Hotel in New York City. Guests included former President Hoover and thirty-three individuals prominent in banking, journalism, and manufacturing. Eisenhower told them he believed that the program of universal military training and a strategy to accompany it could prevent further communist aggression. The United States, he said, now needed to have 3 million men and women in the armed forces.

It is difficult to exaggerate the importance of the war in Korea to the United States' involvement abroad after World War II and ultimately to Eisenhower's destiny. The war's major events included: the North Korean invasion; the United Nation's support of the American initiative to repel the aggression; the appointment of General MacArthur as commander of UN forces on the Korean peninsula and the commitment of American forces to assist South Korea; the South Korean army's retreat to the perimeter of Pusan on the peninsula's southeastern tip; the remobilization of the American economy and armed forces; a UN offensive to liberate North Korea and unify it with the South after MacArthur's surprise amphibious landing at Inchon, near Seoul; and the stunning UN defeat and retreat back across the thirty-eighth parallel after entry into the war of the Chinese People's Liberation Army in November 1950. President Truman then fired MacArthur from his command in the Far East in April 1951, after the general, returning to his political ways, repeatedly and in public criticized the American strategy of fighting a limited war and seeking a negotiated peace on the basis of the pre-invasion status quo. The final misfortune for Truman was his inability to achieve a negotiated armistice despite UN successes on the battlefield after May 1951, and thus the development of a stalemate there not unlike that in France during most of World War I. In the spring of the following year, Truman, his public opinion polls plummeting, decided not to run for reelection in 1952.

Meanwhile Truman had announced implementation of NSC-68, and Congress, responding to the Korean emergency, funded all of the document's provisions. During the Korean War and soon thereafter the United States, accordingly, sent military supplies and troops to Europe and signed mutual security treaties with Japan, the Republic of Korea, Taiwan, Australia, and New Zealand. Indochina was deemed vital to American security, and the United States increased its support to the French there. As for the overall American troop build-up, by 1953, after increasing the annual defense budget to over $60 million ($40 million for the Korean War alone) the United States had 23 army and marine divisions totalling 1.7 million personnel (in 1950 there had been 12 divisions composed of 665,000 personnel), 974,000 air force personnel (up from 411,000 in 1950), and 808,000 naval personnel (up from 382,000 in 1950). All totalled the U.S. armed services now had a personnel of 3.5 million people. By the time of the Korean War armistice, which was finally signed by the new Eisenhower administration in July 1953, 2 million Americans had served in Korea, including the 54,000 who died there.

Eisenhower was therefore not surprised when in December 1950 another request came from Truman, this time to help organize NATO into a military organization. Here, at last, was a job in which Eisenhower could fill his long-held prescriptions for his country's ills. A European military alliance, he had written Hazlett, was "about the last remaining chance for the survival of Western civilization." The Atlantic Pact, implemented in 1949, was a way in which "free countries may band together to protect themselves." His approach to world peace was to husband strength, in the event of war to "achieve victory expeditiously, surely and economically," and at the same time to keep American individual liberties unimpaired. The problem, he had determined in the months preceding his appointment, was drift in Washington. "Goddamit," he asked, his temper and blood pressure rising, "is there no desire to know where we are going?"

Taking a leave of absence from Columbia, Eisenhower, as NATO commander, toured Europe in January 1951. He visited capitals and talked with heads of state. In Paris he asked René Pleven to "reaffirm the glory of France" and received the effervescent reply that there was "new confidence already."

Upon returning home for a visit before going to Paris to establish his NATO headquarters, Eisenhower hoped to persuade conservative members of Congress to apportion the appropriate funds to provide American arms and troops for NATO. The European and world balance of power was delicate, he contended. If one took Western Europe and areas of the world under its control, with their potential for military exploitation, and allowed them to fall under Soviet control, "our safety would be gravely imperiled." He urged a new version of Lend-Lease; the United States, he said, should provide the guns and Europeans should provide the men.

At a cabinet meeting to discuss the establishment of a good and strong NATO, Eisenhower laid out his position. He said that he understood totalitarian regimes. The reason that 350 million Europeans needed to fear 190 million "backward people" was Western disunity. Though the Russians had imposed "unity at the point of a bayonet," it was still unity. European leaders, "could tell Russia to go to hell," provided they got together, raised enough men, and produced enough equipment. Communist parties in Western Europe were no menace. The danger was a widespread European neutralism fostered by communists. The Western alliance also needed to include German troops. He knew first hand what kind of fighters the Germans were. They had been reformed, and they believed in democracy. Now they needed to believe in themselves, and the United States could give them the chance to do this. The West Europeans were capable of raising fifty to sixty divisions within a few years, but ten or twelve divisions from the United States were needed right now. Since the United States then had only two divisions in Europe, an attack by the Soviets would render them lost. With ten or twelve U.S. divisions stationed and ready in Europe and with European forces up to strength, matters would be far different.

As NATO commander Eisenhower was doing what he did best, developing strategy. His next step during his visit to Washington was to explain to Congress and the cabinet how he would use additional troops in Western Europe. Europe was a bottle, he said, with the base being Russia and the neck Western Europe, "stretching down to the end of the bottle, Spain. On either side of this neck are bodies of water that we control, with land on the far side of the water which is good for air bases." His strategy would be to apply air and sea power on both sides while relying on solid land forces in the center, although he also would provide arms to Turkey and Yugoslavia. His goal was to effect a vise-like trap in the shape of Hannibal's at Cannae. Then if the Russians sought to move ahead in the center (Western Europe), he would "hit them awfully hard from both flanks." After a brief retreat the center would hold and the Soviets would have to pull back.

Though his was a good plan, he worried about domestic political support for American positions abroad. What he discovered in Washington was not comforting. Congress was currently debating about whether the President possessed the unilateral power to deploy troops. Ike decided to see what he could do by himself, and arranged a meeting with Senator Robert A. Taft of Ohio.

Called "Mr. Republican" by most Washington columnists, Senator Taft was GOP senate minority leader and, having been a senator since 1938, the obvious choice for his party's presidential nomination in 1952. Perhaps the opposite of charismatic, Taft was a poor orator and disliked Washington parties.

With his rimless glass and receding hairline, he looked more like a banker than a politician. He was, however, incredibly intelligent—graduating first in his class at Yale before going on to Harvard Law—and he had come to dominate his party intellectually. Taft was an isolationist, believing that the United States should accept its limits in the postwar world. The major lesson of World War II, in his view, had not been the danger of appeasing aggression—as the British and French had at Munich—but rather that European politics were nationalistic or socialistic, alien, and entangling. He was thus skeptical of the Truman Doctrine, and his power in the Senate had been a factor in Truman's decision not to seek a formal declaration of war against North Korea. Later, when things went badly and Truman fired MacArthur as Far East commander, Taft spoke of impeachment.

The problem for Eisenhower was that though he obviously disagreed strongly with Taft's positions, he needed this man's support if he were to accomplish anything in Europe. He thus decided to draw his trump card, to obtain compromise or begin a campaign to reduce the senator's influence. Calling in two staff officers, Eisenhower wrote a statement removing himself from consideration as a candidate for president in 1952— there had already been much speculation about a possible Eisenhower candidacy—if Taft would support NATO. When the two met, in retrospect a fateful rendezvous, the senator refused to commit and the general tore up his statement. Eisenhower had taken his first real step, as it turned out, toward the presidency.

His quick tour of Europe in January 1951 had been essentially diplomatic. He wrote President Truman of his delight that the administration had decided to contribute six divisions to NATO. He thought it important that "no one had ventured this figure as a solution." Troop strength, he said, "could vary within fairly wide limits,'" but his aim was within four to eight years to "reduce the American ground forces." Putting strategic necessity ahead of political orthodoxy he expressed a desire to have the dictator General Francisco Franco of Spain contribute twenty divisions to NATO and, interestingly, even arranged clandestinely (through intermediaries) with the communist Tito of Yugoslavia to commit troops in event of Soviet aggression.

By the spring of 1952, the NATO commander had accomplished much, including, most important, the preparation for West German participation in the alliance. Averell Harriman, chairman of the Temporary Council Committee, reported that Eisenhower's plans would create "substantial combat-worthy forces by next year, increasing thereafter, towards Standing Group targets." At the Lisbon Conference in April 1952, Harriman's committee projected 50 divisions—half combat-ready—and 4,000 operational aircraft, entailing American appropriations of $8 billion. It was a satisfying result. President Truman told Harriman that Eisenhower "seems to be on top of the situation and he also seems to understand the international situation better than another 5-star general I can name," (alluding, no doubt, to MacArthur).

It was thus in 1951–52 that an Eisenhower run for the presidency became feasible. No sooner had he arrived in Paris than demands began to pour in from the United States that he become a candidate. He resisted. His situation as an officer on a mission essential to the western world, his belief (probably correct) that chances for nomination and election hinged on an appearance of reluctance, and personal preference all dictated that he not make any such announcement.

But the decision was not easy. The nation's most prominent Republican, two-time presidential candidate, Governor Thomas E. Dewey, had been urging Eisenhower to run. The New York governor's purpose, he had said in the months following his defeat by Truman in 1948, was no less than to save constitutional democracy. Eisenhower's close friend from the Philippine days, Lucius Clay, now Governor Dewey's director of civil defense, agreed and said the same. Eisenhower began to believe that he "didn't have much choice."

As early as 1943, journalists had talked about an Eisenhower candidacy, and the idea had, in an abstract way, struck Eisenhower as appealing. He and his brother Milton had even discussed it. Sitting around in the evening after a day of fishing, they had talked the idea through. Ike said most policy makers were ignorant about foreign policy and military strategy. What bothered him about running, however, was his lack of experience in party politics and the possibility that he might not be very good at it. The public, he feared, would expect more from him than he could deliver. He also dreaded campaigning. No one likes to start something in which defeat is likely, and this was especially true for a man who had devoted his life to the art of winning. He disdained the self-seeking aspect of politics and could not help thinking of the pleasures of retirement. Golf, fishing, and painting appealed to him, and he especially liked the idea of continuing teaching—conveying to young Americans the history and principles of their country. Certainly, for an individual with some serious health problems, a peaceful retirement would seem to be the most desirable choice. But for Dwight David Eisenhower, duty and ambition would not allow it.

In the summer of 1948 he talked with individuals representing the liberal faction of the Republican party about the possibility, if Dewey lost in November, of becoming the GOP candidate in 1952. When Dewey did lose, a group led by New York attorney Edwin Clark; journalist and Willkie activist Russell Davenport; and president of Minute Maid Corporation and finance chairman of the Ford Foundation James Brownlee swung into action—with Eisenhower's consent—to start a draft-Eisenhower movement. First they conducted a survey of the individual states to determine the possibility of their candidate's success. Then, in July 1949, Governor Dewey came to see the general at Morningside Heights. Eisenhower, said the governor, was a "public possession" and the only man who could "save this country from going to hades in the handbasket of paternalism, socialism, and dictatorship." The following month, President Truman sent George Allen, a mutual friend, to offer Ike the Democratic nomination for senator from New York, which Ike promptly refused. Meanwhile, Eisenhower gave speeches. The one at the American Bar Association, in retrospect was one of the most important of his career, for it established his Republican credentials. He called Americans to a "middle way," and—broaching a foremost issue of the day—a "far tighter voluntary cooperative unit than we now have," between labor and management.

Eisenhower sought and received advice, both from his friend Robinson and via Robinson from Clarence B. Kelland, former executive director of the Republican National Committee. As Eisenhower made speeches he tended to lambast the New Deal and had a tendency to make off-the-cuff remarks. In one speech he made a comment that the way of life that he supported did not put security ahead of all other virtues, that if all one wanted was security one could find that in prison—something he sincerely believed the New Deal to resemble, with its high taxes, controls on business, and programs for social reform. This, of course, sounded like a repudiation of Social Security, which was impolitic considering the widespread public acceptance of the program. When Kelland pointed this out to Eisenhower, it quickly became clear to him that every remark he made was on record, something to which his command experience had accustomed him, and he decided that his best path would indeed be a middle one between radicalism on the left and the conservative Republican right.

Back in Paris, Eisenhower supported General Lucius Clay's Crusade for Freedom broadcasts, touting democratic freedom via Radio Free Europe to Eastern Europe, and promoted the effort of the American Assembly to produce studies of how a democracy can retain its freedom by defending itself. The domestic imperative driving Eisenhower's international concern was the preservation of the American people's way of

life. The federal budget for 1951 was $85 billion, with $65 billion for defense, up from $13.5 billion in 1950. There would
be a deficit of $14 billion. The Russians might commit "the
great blunder of venturing upon global war," but Ike doubted
it. The men advising the President, he knew, had "no better
access to secret or otherwise valuable information than I
have. . . . Everything done to develop a defense against exter-
nal threat, except under conditions readily recognizable as
emergency, must be weighted and gauged in the light of probable long-term, internal, effect." Otherwise a strong commitment to defense might actually damage U.S. democratic freedom through censorship, price controls, and a government
controlling the allocation of materials.

Among the many individuals interested in an Eisenhower
candidacy (and, beginning in 1948, working for it) the most
dynamic was Clay. Indeed, this retired four-star general and
Eisenhower confidant was becoming a key mover in the events
of American political history. Eisenhower trusted this tall army
officer with whom he had served in the Philippines as perhaps no one else save his brother, Milton. A descendant of an
old Southern family, Clay was a political general in the best
sense of the term. Devoid of political ambition for himself, he
knew personally House Speaker Sam Rayburn and the influ-
ential Democratic Senator Richard Russell of Georgia. Clay
had been assistant to former Senator Byrnes when the latter
served in the White House as coordinator of war mobilization, and had become Eisenhower's deputy in the occupation
of Germany, shielding his boss from controversy by urging him
to relinquish occupation duties as soon as possible. By 1951
he was chairman of the board of Continental Can Corporation. The Democrats, Clay believed, had been in office too
long. They had gained "a certain feeling of ownership."

Pressure mounted as Senator Henry Cabot Lodge, Jr., together with Clark, Hoffman, Brownell, and Baruch came to
Paris to reinforce what Clay was saying. Dewey, they said,
thought the conservative Taft could not win but was confident

Eisenhower could. Eisenhower already knew what Dewey thought, but Clay's method was nonetheless to court the candidate, meet with senators (including James Duff, Lodge, Harry Darby, and Frank Carlson) and a fund raiser, Harold Talbott, and move between them and Eisenhower. Clay returned to New York and told Dewey that as of yet he had no idea whether Eisenhower would run. There had to be a "real possibility" of winning the party's nomination, he told the New York governor, before the general would consider running. He then sent Eisenhower a letter reporting the success of the latter's Labor Day radio speech after which fifteen and a half million Americans had contributed $1.3 million to Radio Free Europe. Clearly, Eisenhower was an enormously popular and influential American. As for the Truman-MacArthur controversy, Clay advised Eisenhower to remain aloof. Taft forces were siding with MacArthur and wanted to portray Eisenhower as a supporter of Truman, he reported.

Besides raising money, Clay's mission now was to keep Eisenhower, currently busy with his NATO duties in Paris, posted and be a "persuader." Clay appealed to the general's sense of mission, the danger that nothing accomplished in Europe would have permanency unless he became President. Brownell arrived in Paris and warned Clay of the danger of isolationism. Brownell told Eisenhower that he had only to reiterate "his view on the proper role of the United States on the world scene." Lodge also arrived and reported that domestic issues would play a minor part in an Eisenhower campaign.

In October 1951, Eisenhower wrote in his diary that "persons may, in spite of my silence, succeed in producing a grassroots draft" and that when all these individuals assert "that I have a duty, it is not easy to just say NO." At Edwin Clark's urging (and in response to a newly developing Taft momentum), Eisenhower secretly authorized Senator James Duff to establish an organization to coordinate the Eisenhower-for-President forces. The following month, Ike traveled to Washington to brief Truman on NATO. (Truman again attempted to persuade Ike to run in 1952 on the Democratic ticket.) While the NATO commander's airplane was parked on the tarmac at La Guardia Airport, he met his brother Milton, Clay, and others and agreed that Lodge, the son of the famous senator who had organized the congressional opposition to the League of Nations in 1919, should manage his campaign. John Hay Whitney, the New York financier, and Talbott would become financial co-chairmen. The advisers would be Senator Duff, Dewey, Brownell, Barak Mattingly, and Representative Hugh Scott. The machinery was moving into place. Lodge opened the national Eisenhower-for-President headquarters in Topeka, Kansas, an office at the Shoreham Hotel in Washington, another office at the Commodore Hotel in New York, and contacts with pro-Eisenhower groups in twenty-one states. Clay then met with designated convention delegates to dispel any doubt that they may have harbored concerning Eisenhower's intentions.

Gradually, as Eisenhower knew they would, matters became awkward, for if he was to accept responsibility for these campaign activities, he would be violating army regulations, jeopardizing his mission by letting himself be distracted, and risk appearing as political as MacArthur. He wrote Lodge that he would participate in no preconvention activity. Meanwhile, he received a letter from Truman asking for a private indication of his intentions. Truman added that he himself might run again to "keep the isolationists out of the White House." Eisenhower's reply was purposely ambiguous. He said, deceptively, that he was remaining quiet "in all this struggle for personal position in a political party." He did not say that he would repudiate efforts made in his behalf or report what he was doing behind the scenes.

Then, in mid-February 1952, he made his move. His name was on the ballot in the New Hampshire primary, and Brownell was arguing that Taft would receive the nomination if Eisenhower did not return to the United States before the convention. A gloomy letter arrived from Bedell Smith. The "Eisenhower-Taft situation," he said, "is a fifty-fifty bet." If Eisenhower were campaigning, Smith went on, there would be no question of the result, nor would there be if the decision rested on expression of the popular will. Meanwhile, Smith reported, at the Defense Department, Bradley was frustrated about the failure of the Joint Chiefs to reach a firm decision on a viable plan for universal military training. Only Anna Rosenberg, assistant secretary of defense for personnel, Smith explained, had any hope for it, while, "Most of them, including, to my surprise, Gen. Marshall, seem to have given up and to be ready to abandon the sinking ship."

Then in a carefully orchestrated display, 30,000 people gathered for an Eisenhower-for-President rally at Madison Square Garden. Jacqueline Cochran, the well-known aviatrix, filmed the event and flew to Paris to show it to Ike and Mamie. It "brought home to me for the first time," Eisenhower told Hazlett, "something of the depth of the longing in America today for change—a change that would bring, they hope, some confidence that the disturbing problems of our country will be sensibly attacked and progress made toward solving them." The following week he won the New Hampshire primary, receiving half of the vote to Taft's 38 percent and Stassen's 7 percent. A week later, in the Minnesota primary, he received 109,000 write-ins on a ballot in which Stassen, the native-son candidate, received only 129,000. Ike realized that it was time to announce his intentions. Though recently afflicted with a bad cold and a case of conjunctivitis, for which he had been briefly hospitalized, he met Clay and agreed to resign his army commission so that he could enter the partisan fray.

The new candidate, as one might expect from a protégé of Fox Conner, now turned his entire attention to the campaign. The only way to achieve a goal, he averred (and of course was demonstrating yet again) whether military or political, was to have a strategy. The approach would not necessarily be a frontal assault. "Sometimes you may have to engage in a flanking

movement . . . [or] a feint, to draw your adversary out of position. Sometimes you may have to retreat a little bit. But all the
time, your eye is on that objective." He would do his best to
appear to be the sought-after rather than the seeker in order
to avoid debate and division in the party, but privately he told
friends that he planned to come out swinging.

His formal resignation occurred after the treaty for the
European Defense Community was signed on May 27, at which
time he could tell his staff he had accomplished his mission.
Then he wrote Truman, finally to come clean. He told the
President he had miscalculated in thinking that he could "avoid
the impingement upon my time and attention of political
movements then in progress." He asked for a termination of
his assignment as NATO commander so that "any political
activity centering about me cannot possibly affect the military
service."

By this time the campaign was rolling. Hoffman, George
Whitney, the president of J. P. Morgan, Sidney Weinberg, and
Clay had little trouble raising money. CBS assigned David
Schoenbrun to follow Eisenhower on the campaign trail, and
Emmett John Hughes and C. D. Jackson from Time-Life agreed
to write speeches for Ike.

In the months between January 1951 and June 1952,
Eisenhower thus had moved boldly. He believed that U.S. isolationism had contributed to the rise of Hitler and World War
II. Now a new variety of the disease had led to communist
aggression, the stalemate in Korea, and the real possibility of
a global nuclear war. The New Deal, if taken any farther, would
ruin the American way of life, diminishing initiative—expanding the federal bureaucracy, increasing taxes, borrowing
money, handing down regulations, emphasizing security rather
than opportunity. Deficit spending, he asserted, was habit form-
ing, "each dose increases the need for the next one."

In the years after World War II, domestic and international
affairs intertwined as never before, and the question that needed
the nation's attention was what the world's leading democracy

should do in an era of international tension and unprecedentedly powerful weapons. Had the atomic bomb made war impossible? Eisenhower had written that in wartime democratic governments organize to defeat the enemy. In peacetime such governments exist for the economic and social betterment of the populace, purposes at odds with "consistently heavy defense expenditures." The nation, he determined, had to prepare for a time of neither war nor peace. "We are building defenses against the possibility of an emergency which will never be of our making," he noted. Nothing, he said, neither a cold war nor local conventional wars, must weaken "our resolution promptly to attain respectable strength." National strength, he said in a discussion, was the product, not the sum, of three elements—spiritual and moral strength of a people, economic and financial capacity, and a military establishment. If a country were deficient in any one, the result would be deficient, since "if you multiply something by zero, the result is zero."

Eisenhower decided such real strength was not possible for the United States in the current circumstances. Most Americans failed to understand the problem. By 1951–1952 the war in Korea, like Pearl Harbor a decade earlier, had revealed the bankruptcy of isolationism, this time the neo-isolationism of the congressional conservatives. Yet, if the Korean conflict had persuaded Congress of the need to send troops and weapons to NATO, it also, by focusing public attention on the Far East, could detract from internal West European stability and growth. General MacArthur, concerned primarily with Korea and advocating an Asia-first U.S. foreign policy, had approached Congress for support, appealing principally to a vocal Republican minority but attracting much sympathy across the country. Now the public was really confused.

The great contest for the presidency formally began in Kansas, a location in Abilene—named Eisenhower Park—where rain turned the ceremony of the candidate's announcement speech into near chaos. Television cameras showed a sparse crowd running for cover from the downpour. The next day, fortunately, Eisenhower appeared at a press conference in the local movie theater, the Plaza, looking dapper in a gray suit and drawing reporters in with his grasp of issues ranging from the rising national birthrate and the problems of farmers to the state of the U.S. economy and military. When asked a question to which he did not know an answer, he flashed his famous smile and said in his best West Point cadence that he honestly did not know but would find out. The man who had become a symbol of Allied victory in World War II seemed to have a bag full of tricks. When reporters asked whether they should address him as "general," he responded, "just call me Ike, or Mister." He had no formula for ending the Korean War, he said, but would work for a "decent armistice." He was in favor of civil rights but felt that the matter should be handled by the individual states. He opposed a Fair Employment Practices Commission, legislative control of the economy, and socialized medicine (though he did support the right of Americans to "decent medical care"). Convinced that domestic turmoil was tearing up the nation's morale, but realizing that he must work to restore unity to the GOP, he refused to say whether he would support the reelection of Senator McCarthy. Unfortunately, by this time the senator was dominating newspaper headlines with his unfounded and outrageous charges, which, sadly, many people believed, that the federal government was riddled with communists (bringing a new term, "McCarthyism," into parlance). While careful not to endorse the fanatical senator, for his part Eisenhower did say that he opposed "any kind of Communistic, subversive or pinkish influence" in government.

By the time of the Republican convention in Chicago, Eisenhower had met delegates from all over the country and distinguished his program from that of Taft by explaining that the senator's isolationism towards Europe was inconsistent with his interventionism towards Asia. Japan, Ike said, was the nation's only true strategic concern in the Far East and that it "must not be jeopardized by ill-advised ventures in Korea and Formosa." Criticizing politicians who insisted on riding the communist issue, he said there was no more reason to fear the Russians "than there is to fear polywogs swimming down a muddy creek." Americans needed mainly to "pull together."

The nomination turned on whether the Eisenhower forces could obtain a change of the rules to enable pro-Eisenhower delegates to have voting seats. "Fair Play," was the term used by the Eisenhower forces to rally the convention for a resolution to allow the convention itself, rather than the Republican National Committee—composed of Taft supporters—to accept or refuse credentials. This was crucial because efforts by Eisenhower supporters in Texas and Georgia had resulted in local-party delegate nominating conventions which, to the dismay of the state Republican bosses, elected Eisenhower rather than Taft supporters. These Eisenhower delegates were the key to any Eisenhower nomination, but many of these people, without credentials from their state GOP organizations, upon their arrival in Chicago would be denied admission to the floor unless the rules were changed. Lodge worked behind the scenes with Senator Richard M. Nixon of California (letting him know that Eisenhower was considering him for the vice presidential slot), Governor Harold Stassen of Minnesota (a longtime supporter of Eisenhower's candidacy), Governor John Fine of Pennsylvania, and Arthur Summerfield, who controlled the Michigan delegation, to obtain the Fair Play resolution by a vote of 658 to 548.

With the real battle (over Fair Play) out of the way, Eisenhower was nominated at the end of the first ballot. Eisenhower went to Taft's hotel room to say he wanted to be friends, and Taft, in what became one of the most famous newspaper images in the history of Republican politics, went out into the hall for a photograph with the candidate. It was, of course, only the beginning of Eisenhower's battle with the Old Guard. In the days that followed, Dwight D. Eisenhower resigned his commission as an officer in the United States

Army and officially accepted the Republican party's nomination for president.

The choice of a running mate was a political calculation. The Eisenhower team needed someone from the West to balance Ike's eastern image; someone with conservative and anticommunist credentials to bring along the Old Guard and right-wing Republicans who were disappointed at Taft's defeat; and an individual of youth to balance Eisenhower's age. The choice was Richard Nixon. In 1948 Congressman Nixon of California, as a member of the House Un-American Activities Committee, brought charges against former State Department official Alger Hiss for espionage. This widely publicized case brought Nixon to the nation's attention and helped set the stage for McCarthy's campaign of Red baiting. Finally, Nixon was only thirty-nine years old at the time, appealed to the right wing of the GOP, and, perhaps most important, had held the California delegation to the Fair Play resolution. It was, of course, another fateful Eisenhower decision.

The campaign of 1952 brought out the least desirable characteristics of American politics. The Republican platform accused the Democrats of shielding traitors. It damned Truman's policy of Containment and sought the "liberation" of Eastern Europe from the Soviets. Eisenhower reassured the Old Guard that he deplored the secrecy of the negotiations at Yalta (though not the resulting agreement) and the loss of China (though criticizing a policy of isolation). According to one writer, "American political life in 1952 had hit rock bottom, owing to McCarthyism and the G.O.P.'s lust for office."

Eisenhower's Democratic opponent was Governor Adlai E. Stevenson of Illinois, the grandson of a vice president of the United States, and a person of integrity. A graduate of Choate preparatory school, Princeton, and Northwestern Law School, he had worked in Washington during the New Deal. He had won the Illinois governorship in 1948 by the largest margin in the state's history, 572,000 votes. He had come out against an anticommunist bill in the state legislature because he considered it a violation of constitutional liberties. On domestic legislation he was even more conservative than some Republicans, opposing much of Truman's Fair Deal, including public housing, repeal of the Taft-Hartley Act, which slightly weakened the New Deal's Wagner Labor Relations Act that had legalized union activity, and federal aid for medical care and agriculture. Stevenson also believed that the protection of civil rights was the responsibility of the states, and he worried about the national debt, advocated cutting bureaucracy, and agreed with the charges that Truman had tolerated corruption in his administration. Despite all this, Truman liked him and asked him to run as the Democratic candidate against Eisenhower.

The most trying and, in retrospect, most unfortunate moments of the campaign came when Eisenhower sought to appease the Republican right wing in Indiana and Wisconsin. Although his agenda had been formulated, he still had to build a coalition of Republican politicians to support his campaign. This meant (as indicated above) that he needed the Old Guard. They agreed with Eisenhower's desire to shrink the federal government but not his willingness to retain New Deal programs such as Social Security or his approach to national security. Was Ike not, they asked, a party to treason? After all, he was a friend and associate of General Marshall, who McCarthy and Senator William E. Jenner of Indiana considered to have committed treason. The political arena, Ike quickly discovered, was all he had feared it would be. Still, the Republican candidate believed that he needed to nullify the Republican right, and he also believed that there was some truth in the Old Guard's concern about communist sympathizers and possible subversion. Neglect, indifference, and arrogance, he said, had given anticommunist extremists an excuse to indulge in their excesses. While Eisenhower defended General Marshall from McCarthy's wild accusations, he refrained from doing so while speaking in the Wisconsin senator's home state. Reporters noticed the omission, and it quickly became national head-lines. The regrettable episode, a momentary bowing to the advice of his professional staff, infuriated Truman, and he would never forget it.

Somewhat less awkward was the revelation that Nixon had a secret campaign fund. At this point Eisenhower hardly knew his running mate, the man who had helped rally the Califor-nia delegation. As mentioned, he had selected Nixon on the advice of party managers. It then came out that Nixon secretly had received excess campaign money and gifts from several wealthy Californians. Rather than repudiate him, Eisenhower, moved to reduce the damage and, hopefully, to resolve the issue. Remaining aloof, to Nixon's dismay, he sent word to his running mate to hold a press conference at which he must tell the truth. Nixon resented this treatment, privately losing his temper, but going ahead with what became the famous "Check-ers speech," in which he denied any impropriety and referred to his wife, Pat's, common cloth coat and the family dog, "Checkers."

Nixon's problems dismissed, the Eisenhower special—the last of the genuine whistle-stop campaigns—literally remained on track. Ike's train included a platform car and carried the slogan "Look Ahead, Neighbor" emblazoned across the front of its streamlined locomotive. In addition to Ike and Mamie, the train carried advisers, staff, and members of the press. Eisenhower insisted on having every stop scheduled because, in his words, "advance preparation saves wear and tear on the nerves."

The erstwhile general proved a superb candidate. His en-thusiasm, confidence, determination, knowledge, and intelli-gence all were evident, but perhaps his most appealing attribute of all was his common touch. Jackson and Hughes wrote the speeches at the Commodore Hotel from material supplied by Brownell and Stassen, but the candidate went over every word himself, penciling out words, sentences, paragraphs, inserting arrows to scribbled additions, omitting any word or phrase that could label him an "intellectual" like his opponent. There was a rapport between himself and audiences. The advertising firm of Batten, Barton, Durstine and Olson purchased spot television commercials in such popular programs as *I Love Lucy* that were designed to convey Ike's frankness and integrity. "He looked somewhat like the American eagle ought to look," Republican advisor Bryce Harlow recalled. "And he had this astoundingly mobile face, which can look craggy one minute, and the next minute that warm, friendly grin of Ike of Kansas. The smile would melt audiences." Ike's grin, Clay said, evoked a feeling of "we're glad you're here." He might make a mistake, people felt, but he "won't make a mistake in his heart." Several million veterans of the European war, of course, came out to see their former supreme commander, "Ike." Mamie was well received too, and her presence helped the campaign's momentum. At one point the Eisenhowers awakened at 5:30 A.M. to see a crowd gathered outside their train at Salisbury, North Carolina. Putting on their bathrobes, they went to the rear of the train to wave to the crowd.

In November, after five defeats in presidential elections, the Republicans had finally regained the White House. Eisenhower received 34 million votes to Stevenson's 27 million—or 55.1 percent to 44.4 percent, 442 electoral votes to 89. Ike led the ticket everywhere, receiving 100,000 more votes in Wisconsin than the popular McCarthy. West Virginia and eight states of the Deep South went Democratic; all the rest voted for Eisenhower, including Florida, Tennessee, Texas and Virginia—the first time any of which had gone Republican since 1928. Eisenhower also brought in a Republican Congress, although with a bare majority of 8 in the House (221–214), and one (48–47) in the Senate. The congressional results were not quite what the candidate had wished, but the American people, especially those veterans who were making the suburbs of

American cities boom, had demonstrated that they agreed with the campaign buttons that testified, "I like Ike."

The reason why Eisenhower won, aside from his attractive personality, was fairly clear once the dust had settled. Affluence—the number of U.S. households with televisions had increased from 5 million to 15.3 million between 1951 and 1952 and would more than double by 1956—had combined with a generalized fear in America about world communism and the threat of atomic war to replace the earlier politics of Depression and war. There had not been a great deal of difference between the two candidates on the issues. It is probable that the general's war record, his statement that if elected he would "go to Korea," and his willingness to take his campaign to the South, where he advocated states' rights on tidelands oil and refused to endorse the New Deal's Fair Employment Practices Commission (barring racial discrimination in hiring) had been the decisive factors.

And so Eisenhower, at sixty-two years of age, had out campaigned an opponent ten years his junior. He traveled more (51,376 miles through 45 states) spoke more (giving speeches in 232 localities), held more press conferences, and never appeared tired. It was an amazing performance, especially when one considers that he had not run for political office and, for that matter, had not until the previous year declared a party affiliation, or even voted. It was one of those fortunate turns of fate in which the American people, perhaps instinctively, sensed a leader uniquely qualified to deal with problems unprecedented in magnitude. Few of them knew, of course, that Eisenhower's personality, military schooling, career in the highest echelons of military policy since the 1930s, and experience as a wartime commander prepared him for the position perhaps better than any President in the twentieth century. Some aspects of politics and campaigning came awkwardly at first, but, as in every other activity he had undertaken since his departure from the Panama Canal Zone and

Fox Conner's tutelage, he knew what he wanted to do, learned quickly, and, ultimately, excelled. The question remained whether an ability to win campaigns, both as a military commander and as a candidate for the presidency, would translate into success as the nation's second cold-war commander-in-chief.

CHAPTER FOUR

Dilemmas of Power

When Eisenhower entered the White House in 1953 he had much to think about. A new mood had overtaken the nation concerning its place in the world, one that if not pessimistic was at least realistic, as Americans seemed to be more concerned with consolidating gains than with trying on new adventures. The desire to enjoy the material wealth of a triumphant American system prevailed. Communism, however, seemed militant and on the march, and obviously the people had doubted that either President Truman or the Democratic nominee, Governor Stevenson, knew how to deal with it. The election of 1952 had gone far toward restoring the nation's confidence, bringing into the presidency a man from the past, the general who had led the nation to victory in Europe and had become a symbol of that triumph, a man of heroic proportions who somehow also embodied the virtues of his fellow countrymen. In mid-January 1961, as Eisenhower was leaving office, and afterward, it was possible to claim nonetheless that Ike had not lived up to his promise or even that his presidency had failed. The cold war remained, and the world was still exceedingly dangerous. One historian recently has asserted critically that President Eisenhower did not develop and follow a clear and consistent plan for national security policy. Much of his time was spent, said the historian, attempting to rein in the Pentagon and its allies while at the same time determining the best way to handle changing Soviet leadership and policies. There is truth in this assertion, but there is, of course, no way of knowing what would have happened had Eisenhower done things differently. Despite his almost mythical status as the victor in Europe, Eisenhower never had as much influence as people thought. Even as a military commander he fell short of receiving all the men and supplies he had desired and was not satisfied with the degree of personal control that he had over the resources at his disposal. His method both as supreme commander and commander-in-chief was to move toward a goal—the objective—armed with the best available information about his allies and antagonists. In the process, he established the United States firmly as the leader of the free world and institutionalized an internationalist U.S. foreign policy which, despite its shortcomings, pitfalls, and the seemingly enormous odds against it, increased the domain of liberty, avoided world war, and specifically worked toward the day that a successor in the White House would witness the peaceful demise of communist systems.

The question in the spring of 1953 was how long the new President could sustain the postinauguration "honeymoon" period. The world situation was becoming increasingly volatile. Press Secretary James C. Hagerty would recall that President Eisenhower spent most of his time dealing with foreign affairs, not because he enjoyed it but rather because he had no choice. The Soviet Union would not negotiate about Germany and Eastern Europe and was preparing to detonate its first thermonuclear device. In Korea, with armistice talks deadlocked at Panmunjom, Soviet airmen were attacking American bombers in Russian MIG-15 jet fighters with North Korean markings while waves of Chinese soldiers assaulted the South Korean army and their supporting American ground positions. Western Europe, still rebuilding from World War II, had neither an adequate defense force nor economic unity.

Iran had taken over British oil fields in the name of national-ism, while in Indochina, Ho Chi Minh's Communist Viet Minh were at war with French troops determined to hold on to their errant colony. In China, Mao Tse-tung seemed to be on the verge of sending a force from mainland China to invade Tai-wan and crush Chiang Kai-shek's remaining army. Balanced against these facts and possibilities was the news in March 1953 of Stalin's death, anti-Soviet riots in East Germany, and the growing realization by both superpowers that the forces of the other could at any time launch a devastating nuclear attack.

Indeed, what distinguished the cold-war era from all previ-ous periods in world history was the existence of nuclear weap-ons in the possession of two opposing camps. Eisenhower was the first President to face from the very beginning of his term in office the possibility of nuclear war. Moving through a se-ries of problems of unprecedented danger and difficulty he handled himself with calmness and skill.

Since his days with Conner in Panama, Eisenhower had considered principles that applied to a problem and then de-veloped a plan. Clausewitz had taught that "war and its forms result from ideas, emotions, and conditions." To discover the resources a nation should mobilize, the Prussian had written, "we must first examine our own political aim and that of the enemy. We must gauge the strength and situation of the op-posing state" and "do the same in regard to our own." Applied to the United States in 1953, a time of limited war in Korea and seemingly indefinite cold war, Clausewitz's ideas meant that mobilization, while appearing to develop strength, could be a source of weakness. As Eisenhower saw it, the puzzle was something like this: the Soviet Union desired and expected the spread of its form of government. This danger was long-term and, while immediate U.S. efforts to counter its spread might succeed, they just as easily could trigger a global war, or short of that, ruin democratic institutions by necessitating the establishment of a garrison state at home. In sum, no clear distinction existed in Eisenhower's mind between domestic and foreign policy, both being part of national strategy. This was a precept upon which the President and Secretary of State John Foster Dulles agreed. The question was how to proceed from there.

The President set about organizing the White House and the executive branch to his specifications. Drawing upon findings of previous studies of White House organization as well as his experience of command, he required the best possible people near him to obtain, sort, and review information, make recommendations, and then see that his decisions were implemented. To coordinate the flow of paper he asked his former Pentagon and NATO staff assistant, Brigadier General Paul T. Carroll, to establish a White House staff secretary's office. When Carroll died in October 1954, another trusted assistant, his former military aid in Paris, West Point graduate and Princeton Ph.D. in international relations, Colonel Andrew J. Goodpaster, became staff secretary. Goodpaster was well educated, had all the necessary security clearances, and soon became Eisenhower's alter ego—advising the President in both domestic and foreign affairs—his White House equivalent of "Beetle" Smith.

Although the National Security Council (NSC), an interdepartmental advisory body of cabinet-level officials to formulate, recommend, and implement foreign and defense policies, was already up and running, Eisenhower felt that it could be running better and picked a Boston banker, a graduate of Harvard Law school and a retired army general, Robert Cutler, to head a study group on ways to improve the NSC. Eisenhower then asked Cutler to become his special assistant for national security affairs. The latter would implement the committee's recommendations, expanding the operations of the NSC, broadening its membership, and making it a sort of war cabinet on the British model.

At first the former supreme commander doubted that nuclear weapons truly had changed the exceedingly violent course of international relations in the twentieth century. History was a record of the advance and use of technology in war. Indeed, unless both sides understood the awesome destructive power of uranium fission and now the horrendous hydrogen fusion weapons, not just the United States but mankind was in jeopardy. This new situation thus did little to reduce the danger facing the nation. Clausewitz said war tended toward absolute destruction, a possibility that now seemed to be approaching. The leaders of the Soviet Union, having broken the American monopoly on nuclear weapons were willing, Eisenhower believed, to advance communism by force, and if they did, he would respond in kind. The events of the following years, however, taught the President another lesson. The cold-war era was vastly more complex than earlier ones. The means of waging war can influence purposes, this he knew. "We are rapidly getting to the point," he said, "that no war can be won." The Scylla of war, he decided, was as devastating to a nation as the Charybdis of being overrun. Politics were no longer "merely man against man or nation against nation. It is man against war."

Eisenhower's introduction to the thermonuclear (hydrogen fusion) age came the week after his election in November 1952, when the secretary of the Atomic Energy Commission (AEC), Roy B. Snapp, briefed him at the Augusta National golf course. American scientists had detonated a hydrogen device (a true hydrogen bomb was not yet available) code-named MIKE, on the island of Elugelab near Enewetok in the Pacific. The blast had the equivalent force of more than ten million tons of TNT (the TNT equivalent of the bomb dropped on Hiroshima was twenty thousand tons) and had vaporized the island, leaving an underwater crater 1,500 yards wide. Eisenhower believed that the United States's official response should be low key; anything else could appear boastful, even provocative. But he also felt that the government should explain the threat (that these new weapons literally held for the world) to the American people.

To get a better comprehension of the international circumstances in the face of the new military possibilities and formulate a course, late in the spring of 1953 the President ordered a study, codenamed Solarium, that called together three groups of national security specialists, including, interestingly, George F. Kennan, the intellectual father of Truman's Containment policy, former director of the State Department's Policy Planning Staff, and U.S. ambassador to the Soviet Union. Now retired from government service, Kennan resided at the Institute for Advanced Study in Princeton. The charge of the study groups was to investigate the implications for American strategy of Stalin's death, the possible breakdown of armistice negotiations in Korea, and the possession by the Soviet Union of large numbers of nuclear weapons. Beginning their deliberations in early June, the groups reported their conclusions on July 16 at a closed meeting of the NSC. The results of these studies became the Eisenhower-Dulles national security policy.

The Solarium reports were startling. A large-scale surprise nuclear attack by the Soviet Union in 1955, the groups agreed, would result in between 6 and 12 million U.S. casualties, paralyze two thirds of the nation's industrial production capacity, destroy one-third of all American bombers (which were at the time the only delivery vehicle capable for retaliation), and produce "morale and political problems of a magnitude which it is impossible to estimate, or even comprehend." Goodpaster considered one of his boss's most important qualities to be "precision of statement, and an ability to deal with the nuances of questions." In response to these findings, Eisenhower declared that winning a global war under circumstances in which both sides had such awesome power to destroy would be as bad as losing one, a Pyrrhic victory.

A planning document, the so-called Proposed New Basic Concept, embodied the recommendations of Solarium, and it is difficult to exaggerate its importance. An elaboration and modification of Containment as spelled out in NSC-68, the new document assumed that the Soviet threat was a long-term one but that the United States could take initiatives against it. Stalin's death had not removed the Soviet menace, but the West, with its nuclear weapons—and conventional NATO forces which included a rearmed West Germany—could deter a Soviet attack. The United States and its allies nevertheless would need both conventional military forces "adequate to deter or initially to counter aggression" and "massive atomic capability." As the time approached (by the end of the decade) when nuclear weapons were plentiful, one also might expect a slackening of revolutionary zeal in the Soviet Union with an accompanying popular pressure for more readily available consumer goods. The assumption here was that with time the Soviet government would become less militant and threatening.

Meanwhile, at home the United States would have to maintain confidence, a balanced budget, a larger economy free from inflation, and—referring to the anticommunist crusade of Senator Joseph R. McCarthy, Republican of Wisconsin—the protection of the citizens from unwarranted fear or intimidation. Abroad, the United States needed to "concentrate on creating strong, independent, and self-sufficient groupings of nations friendly to the United States." Americans would have to confine U.S. foreign assistance to support for the development of "these regional groupings" in Western Europe and the Far East "centered on Germany and Japan" and also send "selective and limited military aid and technical assistance" to other free nations. As regions became economically and politically independent, American soldiers could withdraw.

Unwilling to allow the opponents to decide the place and methods of a possible encounter, the Eisenhower administration intended to create an active national defense that employed a variety of methods. To reduce Soviet influence in Eastern Europe it would need to "exploit vulnerabilities" of the Soviet bloc by "covert and overt means" while trying to "persuade the Kremlin that their fundamental concepts were fallacious." There should be public announcement of what the United States considered to be Soviet bloc advances, and as necessary to counter them, "selected aggressive actions of a limited scope, involving moderately increased risks of general war." In the Far East, U.S. strategy would entail a noncom-munist protective barrier and a regional trading area border-ing the Asian continent from Japan and Korea in the north-east to Vietnam in the southwest. Nonmilitary action here meant political and economic support for French and South Vietnamese forces fighting the Viet Minh in Indochina, and protecting South Korea "while seeking [its] political unifica-tion."

However, the most important area, the administration felt, was Western Europe. As Eisenhower pointed out to Prime Minister Churchill in early 1953, neither the United States nor Great Britain could afford to see Western Europe "pass under communist domination, either through military action or through subversion and internal decay." Such protection had to be achieved, however, without an arms race that would bur-den the poor and hungry of the world. The President's hope was to get the Soviet Union interested in other approaches to international relations and through negotiations to join with it for a mutual reduction of tensions and joint humanitarian efforts.

Liberty was impossible without security, but the opposite also was true—security was impossible without liberty. Docu-ments emerging from the Solarium conference spoke of ways to bolster U.S. strength, with options ranging from a cautious and long-term firmness to pressing communist power until it capitulated. Agreeing generally with the former approach, but containing elements of the other, the risk of general or even peripheral war, they concluded, was not high. The United States would have to keep sufficient conventional military forces at home and abroad for many years, to prevent seizure of friendly countries via "local communist minorities." A sub-sidiary goal was to reduce the area currently under Soviet control in Central and Eastern Europe. The United States, according to the Solarium report, could assume "the strategic offensive." The United States should also try to induce China to be wary of domination by Moscow. In case of local aggression, the United States might announce that it would "feel free to use atomic weapons" and if general war broke out would make it clear that its "immediate retaliatory action" would "not be inhibited by government processes." The dual nature (both foreign and domestic) of the threat to liberty, tempered as it was with a threat (in the event of general war) to humankind's survival, obviously was unlike that faced by people of any earlier era.

The rise of Stalin's successor, Georgi Malenkov, fortunately held out new possibilities for the future of the Soviet Union. The new Communist party secretary talked of solving disputes between nations by peaceful means, "on basis of mutual understanding." Eisenhower recognized the opportunity for better relations and made a speech that observers later called the best of his presidency. At a meeting of the American Association of Newspaper Editors in Washington he said a "chance for peace" existed. If the Soviet leaders would sign bilateral agreements on verifiable arms limitation and international control of atomic energy, the United States would turn over a portion of the money it saved from reduced weapons production to a fund for world aid and reconstruction. The "monuments to this new kind of war," would be "roads and schools, hospitals and homes, food and health." The best the cold war could offer was a "life of perpetual fear and tension" in which "every gun that is made, every warship launched, every rocket fired, signifies in a final sense, a theft from those who hunger and are not fed, those who are cold and are not clothed." It was not "a way of life at all, in any true sense" but rather— alluding to another famous speech (by William Jennings Bryan, 1896)—"humanity hanging from a cross of iron."

The response was spectacular. The newspaper editors in attendance gave it glowing reviews. The Soviet newspaper

Pravda published it in its entirety. It was after this that the Soviet Union began negotiations for a treaty on Austrian neutrality (which it later signed), approved armistices in Korea and Indochina, and began negotiations on arms limitation— all items Eisenhower had mentioned in the speech. But peace in the sense of security with liberty, including verifiable disarmament, remained to be seen, and the United States in Eisenhower's view had no choice but to be strong militarily.

Since 1946 the United States and the Soviet Union had been at an impasse on nuclear arms limitation. The Americans insisted upon a "foolproof system of inspection and control" before any actual reduction in nuclear arms could take place, while the Russians advocated the immediate outlawing of nuclear weapons, without safeguards. The advent of the H-bomb brought an attempt by both sides to break the impasse. But in the months that followed, the CIA estimated that Soviet troop strength would remain constant until 1959 and, while avoiding actions that would "clearly involve substantial risk of general war," the Soviets, according to intelligence estimates, would pursue world revolution by propaganda, economic aid, espionage, infiltration, subversion, sabotage, bribery, assassination, and guerilla war.

Meanwhile, Eisenhower launched a campaign to educate Americans. Seeking another use for the new energy source, he called for "atoms for peace." The public had heard allegations that J. Robert Oppenheimer, the scientific director of the atomic bomb project who now opposed building thermonuclear weapons, was a security risk. At about the same time the Soviets detonated a fusion device (which newspapers erroneously—it was so large it rested on a platform—had identified as an "H-bomb"). In a speech at the UN general assembly on December 8, 1953, Eisenhower nevertheless called for the formation of a UN agency to collect the world's nuclear weapons materials and convert them to electric power. It was well received by both delegates and, except for the Soviets, world opinion.

But the thermonuclear age seemed impervious to human intervention. Soviet leaders refused Eisenhower's UN initiatives. On March 1, 1954, the AEC began another series of tests in the Pacific. The first one, codenamed BRAVO, was designed to test "dry" thermonuclear bombs that could be carried in B-36 and B-47 bombers. Detonated on a reef on the perimeter of Bikini atoll, BRAVO surpassed all expectations, exploding with a force equivalent to 15 million tons of TNT and releasing a great deal of radioactive fallout—a terrible new reality. The fallout contaminated villagers on distant islands and a Japanese fishing boat, the *Fukuryu Maru* (*Lucky Dragon*), that was eighty-two miles away, well outside the "restricted" area. The United States had created a weapon that in the words of one historian "defied human description." Within the weeks that followed one of the Japanese fishermen who had been aboard the *Lucky Dragon* died. Lewis Strauss, chairman of the AEC, said the nation's new hydrogen bomb was big enough to "take out" New York City, a phrase that made headlines. The chairman did not say (because it remained classified) that if dropped on New York City, depending on wind direction, fallout (500 roentgens) from such a bomb also would have killed half the population of Washington, D.C., and most of the people in between the two cities.

Eisenhower's strategy for the new era drew upon his experiences as the first Supreme Allied (NATO) Commander in Europe. As mentioned, his contingency plan, in the event of a Soviet invasion of Western Europe, had been to hold the attackers with ground forces long enough for allied air and naval power from the north and south, on the Baltic and Mediterranean flanks, to wipe out reserves, supplies, and communications behind the advancing Red Army. Now, with thermonuclear weapons and even better conventional capacity inherited from the Korean War, he altered his defense plans. Eisenhower's so-called "New Look" approach was to ward off a Soviet attack on the United States and Western Europe while at the same time seeking to diminish power in the Soviet Union and its influence throughout the world, creating, in the words of the report, a "climate of victory." The U.S. mainland was now within reach of (Soviet) weapons that could "knock it out within the first thirty days of combat." The issue of nuclear disarmament was "largely academic," since it could not be accomplished "without the most rigid and complete system of inspection" something he felt "perfectly certain the Soviets would never allow." Therefore, his strategy was to build a self-sufficient Western Europe, including West Germany. Furthermore, he looked forward to a reunified Germany under Western control. Relying more on technology than had his previous plan, now nuclear forces stationed in Europe would deter a Soviet attack and, if necessary, come in from the north and the south. With the nuclear arsenals in place, the long-term aim was to withdraw U.S. troops from Europe, but it was assumed that the United States would maintain its military presence in Europe for the foreseeable future.

Eisenhower's new policy went into effect on December 22, 1954. It reduced U.S. military divisions overseas to seven—two in Korea and five in Europe, with three aircraft-carrier task forces in the Far East. Since nuclear weapons would now be part of any European war, Eisenhower sought a capacity to deter or at least blunt a possible Soviet offensive attack: a far cry from Eisenhower's prewar and immediate postwar plea for deterrence through universal military training. Now an alert of actual Soviet attack in Western Europe would bring a strike by strategic air forces combined with the use of tactical nuclear weapons in forward positions. Rejecting preventive war, Eisenhower and NATO planners nonetheless adopted a strategy that challenged the readiness of allied air forces and intelligence agencies and the wisdom of the commander-in-chief. General war (and untold worldwide devastation) hinged on the reliability of the warning system. The cold-war commander-in-chief accepted the situation, along with plans for removing himself and the American government to safety in the event of a nuclear attack. Codenamed Outpost Mission, by 1955 a special air force detachment was formed to move the President, the cabinet secretaries, Supreme Court justices, and members of Congress to underground bunkers outside Washington, D.C. Upon alert of such an attack, helicopters would take Eisenhower to one of four command posts—either in the air, at sea, at Raven Rock, a 235,000-square-foot bunker near Gettysburg, or a similar bunker at Mount Weather near Berryville, Virginia. Congress had its own relocation site in West Virginia.

But how would the government determine if an alert was authentic, if an attack were truly imminent? Eisenhower authorized the Science Advisory Committee of the Office of Defense Mobilization to study the question. A subgroup of the committee, the Technical Capabilities Panel (TCP), reported in early 1955 that both superpowers remained vulnerable to surprise attacks because sufficient numbers of weapons would not exist for mutual assured destruction (MAD), and thus obvious deterrence, until 1960. In the meantime, this vulnerability, said the TCP, required the nation to develop both an intercontinental ballistic missile (ICBM) program and better knowledge of Soviet capabilities. It recommended aerial photographic surveillance of the USSR to detect any mobilization of troops or weapons and identify possible targets for NATO strategic forces. American reconnaissance planes began clandestine flights over Soviet territory in 1956 and continued to do so for the next four years. Codenamed U-2s, (the "U" was for "utility," a purposely ambiguous term) they were high-flying, long-winged, glider-like planes appropriately painted a ghostly dull black with no markings. The flights, administered by the CIA (only a handful of officials knew about them) were conducted at an altitude of 70,000 feet, beyond the range of interceptor aircraft and anti-aircraft guns and missiles. The U-2s proved quite useful: the photographs that they supplied were effective for gauging Soviet missile capability and military readiness; they took air samples to measure levels of radioactive fallout in the atmosphere; and they tested Soviet air-defense radar.

What the U-2s discovered helped hold down the costs of the American defense posture. After a $2.2 billion cut in general military spending, the President was able in 1958 to prune $8.35 billion from such items as bombers and tanker aircraft, antiballistic missiles (ABMs), Polaris submarines, a radio-telescope, antisubmarine weaponry, solid missile propellant, air-to-surface missiles, a sought-after increase in the long-range penetrating power of the B-52 bombers, and launching bases and fuel for the Titan ICBMs.

By 1955, Eisenhower discerned progress. The two main approaches of the strategy outlined at the Solarium conference—building strength while not abandoning purposeful negotiations—seemed to be working. Sufficient progress had occurred in negotiations with the Soviets that Eisenhower could say they "seem prepared to accept business-like procedures." The Soviet Union, as mentioned, had acceded to an agreement to withdraw from Austria, creating a neutral nation, and to discuss a mutual verification of nuclear testing. A united and rearmed West Germany among the Western nations under the NATO council was achieved soon thereafter.

In the summer of 1955, Eisenhower met with world leaders, including those of the Soviet Union, the first such meeting since the end of World War II, at a summit conference in Geneva. Though the summit failed to end the antagonism between East and West, it was successful in some ways. Premier Nikolai Bulganin and Party Secretary Nikita Khrushchev (the latter had risen to dominance in the politburo, a fact that was not at first recognized by the Americans) on one side and Eisenhower and Secretary of State Dulles on the other talked matters over—the beginning of a "spirit of Geneva" that would carry forward in correspondence and, four years later, in a visit by Khrushchev to the United States, the first ever by a Soviet general secretary. Desiring to continue the progress demonstrated by the armistices in Korea and Indochina and the Austrian state treaty, Eisenhower put forward an initiative to reduce the danger of surprise attack, the so-called "open-skies" proposal. Each side, he proposed, would exchange blueprints of military installations and then allow the other to fly over its territory to verify that there had been no secret military buildups. Although Khrushchev (not eager to expose his nation's true state of military preparedness) condemned the idea as espionage and thus killed any hopes of its adoption at Geneva, Bulganin expressed interest in the plan; and it was perhaps Eisenhower's offer (the recent opening of Soviet archives might provide a better answer) that prompted the Soviets to ask the United States, in a joint agreement with Great Britain, not to use nuclear weapons, to cease nuclear test explosions within two years, and to ban nuclear weapons in both West and East Germany. In early 1957, Eisenhower took his initiative to the United Nations, where support for the cessation of nuclear-bomb testing had increased because of scientific reports about the dangerous effects of radioactive fallout. "Open skies" received unanimous support in the UN General Assembly. About this time, some journalists began to use the term "detente" to describe the new superpower relationship.

Still, trouble had not stopped in Eastern Europe, where in 1955 the Soviet Union formed its counterpart to NATO, the Warsaw Pact. Still, for a while in late October 1956 it appeared that GOP platform promises to push back the iron curtain might be deliverable. Three years earlier, news of Stalin's death had brought rejoicing and riots in East Germany and elsewhere. Among operations launched by the CIA at the time was an effort to stir discontent in the Eastern bloc countries through Radio Free Europe broadcasts and the distribution of propaganda leaflets written in the native languages of East European countries, which were dropped from helium-filled balloons. In 1956 these broadcasts contained a taped segment of Chairman Khrushchev's denunciation of Stalin's crimes— including murder—against party members. East Europeans were thrilled. In Poland the result was the rise to leadership of

Wladyslav Gomulka, who insisted that there were roads to socialism other than that prescribed by the Soviets. In Hungary the dissidents were even more exuberant, in October 1956 placing in power a man, Imre Nagy, who sought the Hungarian withdrawal from the Warsaw Pact.

Khrushchev decided that things had gone too far, that vital Soviet interests were in jeopardy. While NATO was distracted by the Suez crisis (explained below), in early November, Soviet troops moved into Budapest, as street fighters threw rocks and firebombs at the invading tanks. The unrest was ill-fated, the uprising futile. When it was over, two hundred thousand Hungarians had to flee to the West, and thousands were killed. Eisenhower, seeing U.S. complicity in a tragedy, curbed the emphasis on encouraging dissidence in U.S. propaganda broadcasts, replacing it with an emphasis on trade and economic assistance.

The commander-in-chief, meanwhile, reorganized the Pentagon. Faced with budget cuts, the navy worried that the White House had decided to rely almost exclusively on the atomic bomb and was afraid that the air force would become that weapon's sole carrier. The air force, although more confident, at the same time felt that it must fend off the navy. The rivalry of the armed services caused them also to "back-scratch," a member of Eisenhower's reorganization task force recalled. "The air force wanted a new air wing, and the navy wanted a new airplane carrier. The army didn't want anything at the moment, but thought it would soon and so all three services recommended both the extra air wing and the carrier." It was in an effort to end the interservice scrambling, with the accompanying crash programs that only heightened the levels of tension, that Eisenhower acted. The nation's defense, he saw, would be complicated, expensive, ongoing, and stressful. The administration, he said forcefully, would have to "bear the burden of making responsible decisions."

The President asked a group headed by Nelson Rockefeller to draft legislation that he made part of his 1958 state-of-the-union address. The resulting reorganization established unified commands, assigned missions related to objectives, and set up a direct line of communication between the President and the secretary of defense to operational commands in places such as Europe, Japan, and Korea. It also strengthened planning and operations staffs and established a director for planning and coordination. The secretary of defense was now free to act as a legislative liaison and oversee public affairs, personnel, and the department's spending.

But in the final analysis, Eisenhower's reorganization was not as effective as he had hoped it would be. The internecine warfare and political pressure fueled by self-interest continued. In a manner similar to his courting of conservatives and liberals, Eisenhower appealed to Pentagon officials, weapons lobbyists, peace advocates, and Congress. Each had an agenda that it pursued easily, justifying its actions by claiming that in cold war, as in war, the nation's security was at stake and that everything pertaining to it therefore had to be hidden from enemy (and public) scrutiny. Few persons at the time knew, for example, that the United States had miniaturized thermonuclear warheads, reducing them from twenty-one tons to less than a ton; it had stationed its intermediate-range missiles (IRBMs) in Britain, France, and Germany; that U.S. ICBMs were under construction; and that the Titan II and the submarine-launched Polaris missiles, unlike their liquid-fueled Soviet counterparts, utilized solid fuel (which was lighter and easier to handle than liquid fuel) and were capable of lightening-fast launches. Fewer still knew about the U-2 program. While conventional wisdom held that the Americans were ahead in the arms race, the actual details (and American superiority) were relatively unknown.

Such were the circumstances in which the long-anticipated if somewhat difficult-to-gauge era of nuclear plenty arrived, two years earlier than expected, in 1958. The President ordered the AEC to study targeting systems proposed by the Joint Chiefs of Staff, and American war planners analyzed 20,000 Soviet targets. Meanwhile, production of nuclear explosive was exceeding expectations, or needs. By the end of 1960, the AEC report stated, the United States would have a surplus of 30,000 to 40,000 kilograms of U-235, the explosive substance used in both atomic and (as a first-stage propellent in) hydrogen weapons; Eisenhower and AEC chairman John McCone even discussed, in jest, the possibility of selling the excess U-235 to stem the outflow of the nation's gold, or putting some of it in Fort Knox as support for the currency. McCone projected that the United States would have $22 billion worth of U-235 in eight years. The effect of unleashing the "5,000 or 7,000 weapons" that soon would be in the stockpile (by the 1980s the numbers would reach nearly 25,000) Eisenhower said, was clear. "There just might be nothing left of the northern hemisphere." He wondered what was to be done with "this tremendous number of enormous weapons." Now that long-range B-52 bombers were armed with Rascal missiles, which could be launched when the airplanes were still hundreds of miles from their targets, the number of nuclear weapons the nation actually needed was already lower than current stockpiles.

Eisenhower's cold-war strategy began to have difficulty during the previous year. Whether the American people would be able to endure a lengthy posture of confrontation had long been his concern, second only in importance to whether his strategy would have the desired effect on the nation's opponents. His worry was that the Soviets would simply respond by attempting to find security in weapons or that, heaven forbid, they would want to vent their frustrations by launching a preemptive strike. Meanwhile the U.S. economy had entered a recession. By mid-1957, unemployment reached 7 percent, with corporate profits down by 25 percent, a serious problem. Then, suddenly, a series of other unforeseen events occurred. In October the Soviet Union launched the 184-pound *Sputnik I*, the first man-made, earth-orbiting satellite. The following month it launched the 1,120-pound *Sputnik II*, which carried a dog. Then Khrushchev began to brag about the development of a Soviet ICBM. "Suddenly here was this new delivery system, a missile, that might come in on us so fast, 30 minutes from Russia, that we wouldn't have knowledge of," recalled Secretary of Defense Neil McElroy, "and theoretically we could have everything destroyed on the ground." A special committee headed by H. Rowan Gaither of the Ford Foundation reported (and soon leaked to the press) its view, which was later determined to be erroneous, that the Soviets would achieve nuclear/technological superiority by 1960, something that would require the United States, if it hoped to catch up, to launch a $10 billion crash missile-building program plus fallout shelters costing $5 billion. Finally, in December, an American Vanguard rocket, under development to carry satellites into orbit, blew up on the launchpad.

As he had done after the German winter offensive in 1944, Eisenhower moved on several fronts simultaneously. To increase the quality of the advice he was receiving and persuade the public that his policies were sound, he asked James Killian, the president of the Massachusetts Institute of Technology, to take charge of a new group, the President's Science Advisory Committee, to monitor advice from the AEC and the Joint Chiefs. Then, mainly to calm fears, he asked for a supplemental appropriation of $1.2 billion, to provide more protection for the Strategic Air Command through increased alert and dispersal of the aircraft to various bases across the country and accelerated ICBM programs. Meanwhile, nuclear testing continued. The Castle series of tests of 1954 had included six detonations (one of which was BRAVO), the Redwing series of 1956 had included ten. The Hardtack series in 1958 was the most elaborate ever conducted, and it included the testing of antimissile warheads. By the autumn of 1958 the United States had conducted 125 tests of nuclear devices since 1945, this in contrast to 44 by the Soviet Union and 21 by Great Britain over the same period.

None of this seemed to have any calming affect on the American public. Appearances (perhaps it was the nationally televised spectacle of the Vanguard rocket exploding or the unrelenting criticism of U.S. policies by hostile columnists such as Joseph Alsop) were for them reality. Americans came to see a "missile gap," with the Soviet Union pulling out ahead. Try as he could, Eisenhower was unable to erase this impression from the public consciousness, and it lasted all the way to the election of 1960.

Yet another problem that Eisenhower faced at this time, as will be detailed in the next chapter, was his health. It is probable that after suffering a slight stroke, the President's physical appearance and demeanor, including slurred speech, influenced popular attitudes and politics.

Khrushchev, meanwhile, exploited his advantage. In March 1958, he announced a moratorium on nuclear testing, which was designed to be embarrassing to the United States. It was "simply intolerable," Eisenhower said, "to remain in a position wherein the United States, seeking peace, and giving loyal partnership to our allies, is unable to achieve an advantageous impact on world opinion." Secretary of State Dulles wondered what the United States should do, considering its unwillingness to give up nuclear weapons and the "impossible conditions we have in fact put on disarmament." Eisenhower had concluded that the primary threat to the nation was not the Soviet Union but, rather, the arms race itself. The United States would reduce its holdings of nuclear weapons, he replied, "if we could be sure that all had done so." "My theme is that *we* must find ways of reducing the *need* for armaments." Security, Dulles said, does not require us to develop *every* military potential, but to have "sufficient [power] to deter attack." Eisenhower agreed. The task of "reaching some reliable agreements" with the Soviets, making possible "with confidence to reduce armaments transcends all other objectives we can have" he said. "Security through arms is only a means (and some times a poor one) to an end. Peace, in a very real sense, is an end in itself."

Again the President decided to approach the Soviets. He suggested that the two nations "at once put our technicians to work to study together and advise as to what specific control measures are necessary." When the groups met they proposed negotiations on surprise attack. By July, they suggested aircraft flights with representatives of both countries aboard to sample atmospheric radioactive debris and proposed an end to tests. Eisenhower ruled that a test ban was a first step toward nuclear disarmament. Both Dulles and the new AEC chairman, John McCone, also favored a test ban. "Some risk," said the latter, was necessary to eliminate the health hazard of radioactive fallout and, "at the same time . . . to slow down the arms race." Eisenhower ordered a test moratorium to begin on October 31, 1958, upon the completion of the Hardtack series. The American people had placed national security (and superiority in weapons) ahead of the danger posed by fallout, but by now the reports of atmospheric contamination were in the newspapers. For example, it was reported that samples of milk contained radioactive strontium 90. The United States accepted the Soviet principle of unsupervised test suspension, and the Soviets at last agreed that details of verification must precede a test-ban treaty.

The two sides seemed ready to compromise. "What we are aiming at," Eisenhower said, refocusing on the threat of surprise attack, is to determine that Soviet bases "within such and such a line have not been brought to a state suggesting imminent attack." Meanwhile development of new devices to detect and monitor underground nuclear testing allowed Eisenhower to move toward his goal of verification. In the spring of 1959 he proposed a bilateral atmospheric test ban of nuclear devices. "Could we not, Mr. Chairman," he asked Khrushchev, "put the agreement into effect in phases beginning with a prohibition of nuclear weapons tests in the atmosphere?"

Then a new move by Khrushchev made compromise impossible. His East German client, Walter Ulbricht, was finding it increasingly difficult to tolerate a prosperous and vital West Berlin located deep within his faltering communist nation. In

addition Khrushchev desired to stymie an ambitious, independent, and nuclear-armed Federal Republic of (West) Germany
(and a similarly armed People's Republic of China to his
South). Unwilling to wait any longer, the Soviet leader gave
the United States six months to negotiate a treaty to end the
postwar occupation of Berlin. Compliance would mean the
U.S. recognition of the German Democratic Republic and the
legitimacy of a divided Germany, and, possibly, that the United
States would lose the treaty basis for the presence of Western
troops and separately controlled zones in Berlin. Refusal, said
Khrushchev, would result in a separate treaty between East
Germany and the Soviet Union that would close Western access to Berlin. A defining point in the dispute came in early
March 1959, when Eisenhower called a special task force of
the NSC and explained that he intended to hold his ground.
Refusing recommendations that he send a combat team on
one of the ground corridors to assert U.S. rights of unob-
structed passage, he told his staff that there would be "no
ground battle around Berlin with the [East] Germans and the
Russians—that is out." The President intended to "face up to
the big decision," if the Soviets take Berlin by force. In the
meantime he would "do everything feasible to negotiate" a
peaceable settlement. Ann Whitman, the President's personal
secretary, wrote in her diary on March 5 that there was "more
serious talk of possible war. The President at one point said
'you might as well go out and shoot everyone you see and
then shoot yourself.' . . . But this mood does not last, and routine matters go on pretty much as usual." Four months later
Ike confided that "We will not abandon our rights and responsibilities," but he left a way out of the impasse by saying, "unless there is a way made for us to do so."

Eisenhower's approach, a firm and patient resolve, followed
the Solarium guidelines and was successful, at least for a time.
Khrushchev softened his position, and in succeeding months,
with Eisenhower's acquiescence, arranged to visit the United
States. "Why should our two countries fight each other?" said

the deputy Soviet premier, Frol Kozlov, in making the arrangements. "The Berlin problem should be resolved by the Germans themselves."

The chairman's visit to the United States, the first by a Soviet head of state, was a fascinating, if not altogether happy event. U.S. reporters asked disrespectful questions of the rotund party leader. Drunks heckled him in New York. Tomato-throwers in Los Angeles caused cancellation of a planned trip to Disneyland. American officials nevertheless watched the flamboyant Khrushchev—a man of sturdy peasant stock—and concluded, prematurely it turned out, that he wanted to end the hostility between the two powers. At Camp David, the presidential retreat in the Maryland mountains, Eisenhower said he would negotiate the Berlin crisis but only after the Soviets retracted their ultimatum. The two men discussed the present difficulties in China over Quemoy-Matsu (discussed below), Khrushchev pointing to the parallels with Berlin—another militarily untenable, but to the communists, threatening, outpost on their soil that belonged to nations with potential nuclear capability. Khrushchev seemed mollified and allowed his Berlin deadline to pass.

In retrospect, other than the reduction of tensions over Germany, the much-talked-about "spirit of Camp David" came to little. Lodge soon reported that the Soviet delegation at the United Nations was making insulting and "scurrilous" remarks about the United States. "We could never agree with the Russians on [nuclear testing] inspection," McCone said. "And until you had some means of verification and inspection, no agreement with the Russians, in my opinion, was any good. I think everybody pretty well agreed on that." Still, hope existed that the superpowers' difficulties could be resolved in a summit meeting in Paris, after which Eisenhower would accept a Soviet invitation and become the first U.S. President to visit the Soviet Union.

Against the objections of the Pentagon, the CIA, his science advisers, the AEC, and members of the cabinet, the Presi-

dent thereupon decided to accept a nuclear-test-ban agreement without pre-existing provisions for verification. In his
search for an end to the madness, Eisenhower had gone a
distance toward the Soviets. By 1960, the United States no
longer was emphasizing a Germany unified by free elections,
no longer seeking speedy rearmament of that nation, nor was
it hoping to withdraw its troops from the region any time soon.
(Ike's successor in the White House would send in more.) Both
in Europe and in Northeast Asia (Korea, Japan, and the
Formosa Straits), U.S. forces remained on the scene, the stabi-
lizing core of defense arrangements, controlling nuclear weapons.

American foreign policy during the Eisenhower years followed
the priorities established by the Solarium conference and, although not without missteps in the various areas of the globe,
matched ends with means. The circumstances in the Far East
were troublesome. Armistice negotiations in Korea had begun in 1951 but were at a standstill. After stepping up bombings in North Korea, Eisenhower sent word to the People's
Republic of China of his readiness to use nuclear weapons to
resolve the Korean conflict. Such measures, he told the NSC
in May 1953, considering the enormous cost of transporting
the necessary conventional weapons and ammunition from
the United States to the Korean combat zones, would be a less
expensive way to finally wipe out at least some of the enemy
dugouts that honeycombed the rocky Korean hills. Whatever
the reason (Stalin's death, a stepped-up U.S. bombing in the
north, U.S. pressure on South Korean president Syngman
Rhee, weariness with the war, or Eisenhower's resolve and stark
message to the enemy—or a combination of these), the Red
Chinese and North Koreans signed an armistice (but no peace
treaty) with Rhee's South Korean republic in July.

In Southeast Asia, Eisenhower refused to help the French
in May 1954 when their forces were completely surrounded
by Ho Chi Minh's troops at a mountainous place in north Viet-

nam named Dien Bien Phu. Perhaps it was Eisenhower's way of staying out of Vietnam. Did he want to intervene but only with British support, a promise by the French to withdraw from the area, and consent of Congress? He told Dulles that these were all important conditions for American involvement. Certainly he worried that a communist takeover in Vietnam would be the beginning of all of Southeast Asia's slide into the Red camp, upsetting the balance of power. Solarium criteria told him that force, especially the unilateral kind, was not the answer to the problem in Indochina. The people of Vietnam, a land rich in much-coveted raw materials, had been oppressed during the twentieth century by Japanese and then French occupiers. Therefore, to contemplate U.S. intervention, Ike wrote to a friend, "was to lay ourselves open to the charge of imperialism and colonialism or—at the very least—of objectionable paternalism."

It was at this juncture that Secretary of State Dulles proposed a Southeast Asian Treaty Organization (SEATO), to be composed of the United States, Great Britain, France, Australia, New Zealand, the Philippines, Thailand, and Pakistan. The new alliance would help ensure that South Vietnam would remain independent, reflecting American hopes that the nation would be the southern anchor of the hoped-for barrier against communism (along China's border). Created by the Geneva accords, a conference in Switzerland of the parties to the Vietnam conflict and Great Britain following the fall of Dien Bien Phu, South Vietnam would be the region of the Indochinese peninsula south of the seventeenth line of latitude. Elections to unify the Northern and Southern regions were to be held in 1956. In the meantime, a U.S.-sponsored South Vietnamese president, Ngo Dien Diem, received 700 U.S. military advisers and more than $1 billion in U.S. aid, $800 million of it military. These U.S. actions brought stability to South Vietnam for a while, allowing the United States to attend to other parts of the world. Indeed, by 1960—the Vietnamese elections never having occurred because the United

States feared the vote would have registered a majority for the communist North Vietnamese leader Ho Chi Minh—South Vietnam, although a problem, was less of a concern to U.S. policy makers than neighboring Laos, where the communist Pathet Lao seemed about to take control. Still, Eisenhower's decision to prop up the South Vietnamese was in retrospect a fateful commitment.

A third and in some ways a more troubling location was along the Chinese coast midway between Indochina and Japan, the Formosa Strait. The island of Formosa, now known as Taiwan, had been under protection of the United States since its liberation from the Japanese in 1945. After his defeat by the communist forces of Mao Tse-tung, Chiang Kai-shek and his Nationalist forces had sought refuge there. With the opening of the Korean War, Chiang had signed a mutual defense treaty with the United States. American military presence in Taiwan was designed to put pressure on Red China, hopefully causing dissention between Mao and his Soviet ally. But Eisenhower also hoped that the treaty would stabilize relations between the two Chinese regimes. This was perhaps an impossible expectation. Just as Mao had vowed to take Taiwan, Chiang had pledged to re-establish his authority on the mainland and was conducting raids along the Chinese coast. In January 1955, Mao's army fired artillery barrages at islands occupied by some Nationalist troops in the Quemoy and Matsu groups, just off the mainland, and sent troops to occupy one of the Tachen islands to the north.

What to do? Eisenhower valued the 400,000 Nationalist troops on Taiwan. They were, he said, a "constant threat and deterrent to Communist Chinese aggression anywhere in the Pacific." The Quemoys, Matsus, and Tachens were less important. Complicating matters was the fact that the Red Chinese were holding forty-one Americans whom they had captured when they took over the mainland in 1949. The crisis in the Formosa Strait provided the United States an opportunity to take a stand. The United States, Secretary Dulles said, needed

to put its "power into the scales." Eisenhower agreed, believing Moscow, with only one-third the industrial base of the
United States, could not afford to support Peking in such a
confrontation. He sought support from Britain and asked
Congress for authority—the so-called Formosa Resolution—
to use force as necessary to protect Taiwan. He then announced
U.S. readiness to defend the Quemoys and Matsus by whatever means necessary, including nuclear weapons. "We just
can't," he told Senator Leverett Saltonstall of Massachusetts,
"permit the Nationalists to sit in Formosa and wait until they
are attacked, and we just can't try to fight another war with
handcuffs on as we did in Korea. If we see the Chinese Communists building up their forces for an invasion of Formosa,
we are going to have to go in and break it up." Privately he
urged Chiang to withdraw from the Tachens and insisted that
he stop his raids on the mainland. It was a subtle approach.
Declassified documents reveal that Eisenhower had agreed to
defend the Quemoys and Matsus, which he pointed out were
virtually within "wading distance of the mainland," but only
from attacks that actually also threatened Taiwan. He sought
to convince Chiang that the offshore islands were "outposts"
not "citadels" and that "no force on earth could hold them for
a long time." "We could slow them up with atomic weapons,"
he told Press Secretary Hagerty, "but I do not think that it
would be wise unless we are forced to do it, to atomize the
mainland opposite them. . . . they could just wait for a while
and start the attack over again." Meanwhile, the President made
conciliatory overtures to Mao through the British, Australians,
and Canadians attending the Bandung Conference on non-
aligned nations. The tension lessened; the combination of
forcefulness and conciliation seemed to have worked.

A second Formosa Strait crisis occurred three years later, in
1958, when the mainland Chinese resumed shelling Quemoy
and Matsu. In consultation with the Joint Chiefs of Staff, Dulles
prepared an estimate of the Communists' intentions. If the
United States did not intervene, Mao might launch an assault,

damaging the morale of the Nationalists to such an extent that they would lose control of Taiwan. The key to the puzzle, Dulles said, was American resolve. The risk of "extensive use of nuclear weapons, and even general war," he told the President, "would have to be accepted."

There seemed no way to persuade Chiang to pull his troops back from the offshore islands. Adding to the difficulties was the unpopularity of the American position at home. Many Americans opposed risking war over the islands. Eisenhower again sent statements of support for Taiwan and the offshore islands to Moscow and London, said nothing that would provoke the Red Chinese, and pressed Chiang to reduce his forces, even offering assistance in removing them. By the end of October 1958, the world beheld the bizarre spectacle of shelling by mainland Chinese forces only on odd days, allowing supply ships escorted by American destroyers to get through on even days. The United States soon stopped its escort service, and the crisis ended when the Communists stopped their shelling altogether.

No less threatening to world peace were events in the Middle East, geographically on the cold-war divide between East and West. Because of the region's location on the world's largest petroleum deposit, it was a vital resource to American allies in both Western Europe and the Far East. Arab antagonism toward the newly established state of Israel also made the region a cockpit of world tensions. In the end, Eisenhower was less successful in preventing the expansion of Soviet influence there, but he did accomplish his larger goal of keeping the oil flowing and maintaining good relations with the moderate Arab states, while at the same time retaining close relations with Israel, a democracy strongly supported by the American Jewish community and militarily the most powerful nation in the region.

In the middle of October 1956, U-2 flights discovered that the Israelis had achieved a state of military readiness to do battle against Jordan and Egypt. The background to the conflict was complex but included, briefly, the fact that Egyptian President Gamal Abdul Nasser had aspired to lead Arab states in an anti-Israeli and anticolonial union that he called the United Arab Republic. He had received arms from Czechoslovakia and had extended diplomatic recognition to the People's Republic of China. Responding to these events and to the U.S. Congress's reluctance to subsidize Egyptian cotton on world markets, Dulles halted negotiation on proposed American aid to build a dam at Aswan (which would have provided Nile River irrigation for the fields, thereby increasing their cotton yield), and Nasser in response nationalized the vitally important (to world shipping) Suez Canal, heretofore under British control. Eisenhower had told Israel that raids against the Egyptians could precipitate foreign intervention. "There would be no brake or deterrent possible," he said, "against any Soviet move into the area to help the Arab countries." Ignoring him, the Israelis, in coordination with the British and French, who sent troops to restore British management of the Suez Canal, launched a surprise invasion of the Egyptian Sinai Peninsula. Soviet Premier Bulganin bristled and warned the West that Soviet missiles were aimed at London and Paris. Eisenhower wondered how an Anglo-French occupation could hold the canal against Arab nationalism. The invasion, he feared, would be "interpreted by the world as power politics and would raise a storm of resentment that, within the Arab states, would result in a long and dreary guerilla warfare." "If one has to fight," he told a friend, "then that is that. But I don't see the point in getting into a fight to which there can be no satisfactory end, and in which the whole world believes you are playing the part of the bully and you do not even have the firm backing of your entire people." He sent a warning to the Soviets but urged withdrawal of foreign troops from Egyptian territory. He then took the matter to the UN Security Council.

The British and French troops withdrew from the Sinai, and the United States retained the friendship of the Arab states, including Iran and Saudi Arabia. In the United Nations, Lodge reported, Afro-Asian nations were "enthusiastic" in praise of "an honorable [U.S.] act performed in a big and clean-cut way." Unfortunately, earlier policy had weakened the American position with Egypt. The Soviets, upon receiving an invitation from Nasser, built the Aswan dam and in return received a naval base at Alexandria.

The Eisenhower Doctrine of 1957 was the administration's response to the Suez crisis. Like the Truman Doctrine ten years earlier, it guaranteed U.S. aid to Middle Eastern nations that resisted communist aggression.

The only time during his presidency that Eisenhower sent troops to a foreign country came in 1958 in response to a domestic crisis in Lebanon, which Eisenhower believed had international implications. President Camille Chamoun of Lebanon felt threatened by the unrest that recently brought a coup in Iraq. In the preceding months Chamoun, the Maronite Christian leader, had run into his own difficulty with Muslims who participated in his government but opposed his ambitions for a second term in office. He also suspected that Nasser, who had elicited Syrian membership in his United Arab Republic, was behind the unrest in the entire area. At the same time, the governments of Jordan, Kuwait, Iran, and Saudi Arabia seemed threatened as well. The Soviet Union and its allies, Egypt and Syria, it seemed, were threatening to keep an oil-dependent western world at bay by controlling the oil of the Persian Gulf. Director of Central Intelligence Allen W. Dulles, the brother of the secretary of state, told congressional leaders that Iraq's king had asked for U.S. help and predicted that Saudi Arabia would look favorably on the undertaking. In Jordan, King Hussein uncovered a pro-Egyptian plot to overthrow his government. Meanwhile, Israel was preparing to occupy the west bank of the Jordan River, and the British were ready to send troops to assist Hussein.

Eisenhower, desiring that Nasser not conclude that the United States was hesitant about its support, moved skillfully by linking his purposes to NATO support. His approach was to get there quickly, and, in the words of Goodpaster, "with such a preponderance of force that there was no invitation [whether by Lebanese rebels, Nasser's agents, or the Soviet Union] to resist." He put U.S. strategic air forces on alert and moved naval task groups to the area. General Nathan Twining, then chairman of the Joint Chiefs of Staff, recalled that Dulles worried about a Soviet response. American strength, the general had replied, was sufficient; the Russians were "not that stupid. Besides, they could see S.A.C. [Strategic Air Command bombers] flying all over the world, and all these carriers and everything we've got heading towards the Suez." Four battalions of U.S. Marines and one Army battle group (6,700 troops) landed in Lebanon, and by the end of the month 15,000 troops had control of the airport and dock areas. The President then sent his friend, Deputy Undersecretary of State Robert Murphy, to get at the source of the instability. This was as far as Eisenhower would go. "If these people," he told Dulles in private, "are not capable of doing their business with us protecting their capital and their rear, then there is little more that we can do about it." If the United States, he said, started "pushing around too much we would shortly have the whole Arab world against us." Murphy told Chamoun that the United States would not support a second term and negotiated an agreement between him and the opposition that eased tensions, bringing about an outcome satisfactory to all parties included.

The President exchanged letters with Khrushchev, expressing a willingness to take the matter to the United Nations. The United States, he said, unlike the democracies of the 1930s, was behaving responsibility to restore order. As Twining had surmised, the Soviets spoke belligerently but behaved cautiously. Within three months the situation quieted.

Unlike the oil-rich Middle East, Latin America, in the southern half of the Western hemisphere, was removed to a certain degree from the cold war. There the threat was less Soviet domination than internal disorder—impoverished, powerless people controlled by wealthy landowners and American corporations that dealt in coffee, bananas, and minerals. Twenty years earlier in the Philippines, Eisenhower had encountered people for whom the modern American concepts of freedom and opportunity had little meaning. The average Filipino, he recalled, thought *independencia* meant "good." The nature of the problem in Latin America made quick solutions impossible and long-term answers seem expensive. Americans, including the President and his secretary of state, preoccupied with the threat of a surprise Soviet missile attack and communist expansion in Asia, nevertheless worried about possible Soviet efforts to exploit the anti-U.S. sentiment in their own "backyard." This, rather than the real belief that the United States could or should do much in Latin America besides encourage a healthy trade, made Latin America a U.S. foreign-policy concern.

When, in 1954, elections in Guatemala brought to power a regime that nationalized the holdings of the United Fruit Company, Eisenhower ordered the CIA to quietly replace President Jacobo Arbenz Guzman with a pro-U.S. government. The agency's clandestine intervention succeeded. The Arbenz government fell. Unfortunately, the episode did little for the image of the United States as a friend of democracy, for, with the new government in place, Guatemala remained an oppressive dictatorship.

In Cuba, decades of paternalism, exploitation, and neglect had produced a revolutionary movement. The leading revolutionary, Fidel Castro, overthrew the dictator Fulgencio Batista on January 1, 1959, and in the succeeding months, after proclaiming himself to be a follower of Marxist-Leninism, Castro took his island nation into the Soviet camp. He nationalized all of Cuba's privately held land and other assets and used terror to suppress his opponents. The United States, appalled by Castro's actions, pressed the Organization of American States (OAS) to impose sanctions on Cuba. The administration sponsored legislation cutting the Cuban sugar import quota and then broke formal relations and began to seek ways to replace the new Cuban leader. "If you're going to make any move against Castro," Eisenhower told CIA director Allen Dulles, "don't just fool around with sugar refineries. Let's get a program which will really do something about Castro." A secret operations group—reporting only to the President— ordered sabotage, propaganda, and preparations in Guatemala for an invasion of the island by forces composed of anti-Castro Cuban exiles. The CIA training of the rebels began, but their training facilities in Guatemala were equipped to handle only 500 men, not nearly enough to face Castro's 32,000 regular troops and 200,000-man militia.

Meanwhile, U.S.-Cuban relations worsened, and Castro moved even closer to the Soviets. But the OAS refused to label him either a communist or a threat to other Latin American nations, and not even the CIA would admit that Cuba was under communist domination. Anti-U.S. sentiment, it was clear, would increase in Latin America and elsewhere should the United States resort to force against Castro.

By December 1960, Eisenhower, his presidency virtually over, had not found a way to pull the Cuban situation together. There was no emigré political leader who the United States could support, an insufficient counter-Castro force, no good plan for an attack, and uncertainty over just which countries would support such a U.S.-backed countercoup. The President should have canceled the build-up of the anti-Castro force that the CIA was trying to train. Instead, he passed the whole problem on to his successor.

The President moved in a more promising direction when he addressed the economic backwardness of Latin America. His purpose was, in the final analysis, a psychological one—to win friends among the Latin American people. The enemy was not merely the Soviets or communism, it was 1.9 billion Latin American people living in poverty and disease. There-

fore Eisenhower felt that a Latin American common market
might stabilize prices and production, easing economic hardship. In collaboration with his brother Milton and his chief
advisor on foreign economic policy, Clarence B. Randall, he
sought U.S.-Latin American economic cooperation and mutual assistance. By this time, U.S. investment in Latin America
had reached $1.7 billion, while awareness among Latin Ameri-
cans of their comparative misery was growing. The problem,
the President felt, was a lack of sympathy by Congress and the
American people. In 1957, during a visit by Vice President
Nixon, anti-U.S. demonstrations and rioting broke out in Ven-
ezuela. The administration, jarred by the unrest, sponsored
the Inter-American bank. With contributions from member
nations, the bank could lend to any Latin American nation
that met its conditions. This, it turned out, was the basis for
the Alliance for Progress, ratified in the Act of Bogota in 1960.

On the other side of the globe, U.S.-Soviet relations had
soured in the late spring of 1960. Both sides were at fault, though
Eisenhower had been the instigator. The American U-2 reconnaissance flights, while enormously helpful in reducing the
fear of surprise attack and moderating the arms race, had been
both risky and provocative undertakings. Perhaps seventeen in
all, these flights were blatant incursions into Soviet airspace. In
addition, U.S. Navy and Air Force flights, so-called ferrets, constantly flew over, photographed, and tested Soviet border defenses. Researchers recently have revealed that between 1950
and 1970, tens of thousands of such flights occurred, often
incurring protests by the Soviets, which the United States remained silent about or simply denied ever hearing. Over 250
U.S. airmen were shot down, with perhaps as many as 24 killed
and 138 missing.

On May 2, 1960, the CIA U-2 pilot, Francis Gary Powers—
despite agency insistence that no pilot ever would be taken
prisoner—found himself floating to earth by parachute after
a surface-to-air missile destroyed his plane near the Soviet city

of Sverdlovsk, today's Ekaterinburg, where local police arrested him. Washington put out a false story about a weather flight that the President, following a contingency plan, confirmed. Khrushchev then sprung his trap, producing Powers and photographs in a press conference.

Eisenhower was dismayed. Never comfortable with the flights, he had halted them temporarily when he felt their risks outweighed the possible gains, first in June 1956, then again in March 1958, and yet again in 1959 during the Berlin crisis. He had seen the possibility of a propaganda defeat and a loss of momentum toward mutual arms reduction if the Soviets ever brought down a U-2. One "tremendous asset in a summit meeting, as regards effect in the free world," he had remarked, "is [my] reputation for honesty. If one of these aircraft were lost," he had said prophetically, it could "dissipate my reputation for a different mode of behavior from that of Khrushchev in international affairs." Putting himself in the other man's position, he told advisers that he would consider a similar violation of American airspace by a Soviet plane to be an act of war. And though he saw evidence that the Soviets wanted a summit and progress on arms control, he nevertheless had agreed, fatefully, to "one or two flights" in late April or early May 1960, just before the planned summit meeting in Paris.

Having arrived at Paris, the Russian leader loudly demanded an apology, saying he would not sit down with the President until he thus humbled himself, but Eisenhower would not give one. The flights were, he said, necessary to spot preparations for a possible ground offensive and counter the risk of a surprise missile attack. What's more, they were but the counterpart by the free world of on-going and often clumsy Soviet espionage. The conference thus never occurred. Khrushchev, he decided, no longer truly wanted a summit anyway.

The failure of the 1960 summit, occurring as it did amidst Soviet bluster and acrimony, reflected poorly upon Khrushchev. For him, apparently, the U-2 affair was an opportunity to appease his Soviet critics who were concerned about nuclear weapons in West Germany and China and reductions in the Soviet defense budget. He may also have acted to placate the leaders of East Germany and the People's Republic of China. Finally, the British and French, he probably had discovered during the conference preliminaries, would not back away from their American ally. Khrushchev, in this short-term sense, had a considerable amount to lose and little to gain from a summit. He wrote in his memoirs, confirming what White House advisers suspected at the time, that he saw an opportunity to exploit the U.S. domestic turmoil as Eisenhower's second term neared its completion.

But Eisenhower, too, bore some responsibility for the failure of he summit. His cold-war strategy was complicated and contained contradictory elements, a reflection of the adversary's *modus operandi*. It entailed firmness—preparations to deter or, if it came anyway, to blunt a surprise attack and a large national security establishment—combined with negotiation. While useful to a President in the thermonuclear age, the U-2 program had diminished in importance. A more careful look at the situation might have revealed Khrushchev's increasingly awkward position. He knew that the Soviets lagged in the arms race, and thus may have found it difficult to believe that the United States had acted out of fear. Khrushchev desired some kind of leverage. Eisenhower was famous for getting excellent intelligence about his adversaries and a variety of expert advice before making decisions. In the case of the U-2 missions, he later admitted, he been "lulled into overconfidence."

Now that things had gone badly for Ike, as is always the case for the person in the White House, his critics saw an opportunity to speak. At first it appeared that damage was not great. The Soviets temporarily withdrew their disarmament delegation from ongoing talks at Geneva, and Khrushchev withdrew his invitation for Eisenhower to visit the Soviet Union. In an NSC meeting Eisenhower pointed out, "by and large the situation is now about the same as it was before the break-up of the summit conference." Visits between high officials of the two governments still were taking place, a moratorium on nuclear testing continued, and in Geneva the two sides negotiated on nuclear testing and disarmament and reduced conventional forces. But in fact the atmosphere had changed. Eisenhower added two carrier task forces to the American arsenal and decided not to disband three air wings. Then nuclear-test suspensions broke down in September of 1961: first the Soviets and then the Americans resumed their programs. At this time, the Soviets detonated a whopping 58-megaton weapon, the largest ever, before or since, to be unleashed into the atmosphere.

What, then, had been Eisenhower's national security record and legacy? Should he have done better? Was his two-track strategy of preparedness and conciliation contradictory, or unsuited to a democracy? The most famous American commander of the century had failed to rein in sufficiently the American defense establishment—the armed forces, arms manufacturers, and intelligence agencies. Events in the last three years of his administration had brought more military spending than was necessary and covert activities that were difficult to control or even stop. Eisenhower's hope of preserving full democratic freedoms at home came up against the fact that in the last analysis, and despite their ongoing communications, the superpowers sought security not in openness, conciliation, and compromise, but in secrecy, hostility, and the development and stockpiling of weapons that were both extremely expensive and dangerous. His foreign policy apparatus—including questionable operations and, in some instances, assassination attempts, by the CIA in such places as Cuba, Guatemala, Iran, Indonesia, Indochina, and the Congo—had demanded his constant activity and review, but he continued to worry about the fate of democracy. At the same time, political opposition based on erroneous charges grew, which by 1960 brought consternation to the Republicans. The Democratic presidential candidate, John F. Kennedy, insisted that neither liberty nor security were on a firm foundation.

By other and perhaps more important measures, however, Eisenhower's foreign policies had been successful. The United States, having finally, after two world wars, accepted the responsibilities of world leadership, was far ahead of every other country economically, technologically, and militarily. Eisenhower had preserved for the first time after a war a U.S. military establishment suited to the tasks at hand, though it was too late for his pet project of universal military training. In 1959 defense spending, emphasizing technology, leveled at $41 billion and included a nuclear retaliatory force of over 2,000 strategic bombers and 14 aircraft carriers. Production programs were underway for both the solid-fueled Minuteman missile as well as liquid-fueled ICBMs and the invulnerable, solid-fueled Polaris submarine-launched IRBM. By 1962 the United States was securely ahead of the Soviet Union in the arms race: the United States had 144 Polaris missiles on 9 submarines to 0 for the Soviets, and 200 ICBMs to less than 100 for the Soviets. The navy proceeded with its supercarrier program and the air force with its B-47 and B-52 bomber programs, reconnaissance flights, and the maintenance of airbases around the Soviet periphery. By the end of Eisenhower's second term, U.S. capacity to fight limited wars included 14 army divisions (with 5 in Europe and 2 in Korea), 4 fleets of naval alert forces, 34 tactical air force wings, and some 200 allied divisions (with air and naval forces). In 1957 the Soviet Union had been the first to put a satellite into Earth's orbit, but by mid-1960 the United States had launched 26 satellites, the Soviets only 8. In the summer of 1960 alone, the United States launched 5 satellites to 1 for the Soviet Union and test fired 12 missiles to the Soviets' 2.

While the cold war remained entrenched, as did partisan debate about it, Eisenhower had taken steps simultaneously to reduce the superpowers' military competition. To cut manpower in all the U.S. armed services from Korean-War levels by about a third, he lowered the total personnel from 3.5 million to 2.75 by 1955, mainly by reducing the army. Perhaps in response, between 1955 and 1961 the Soviet Union reduced its military strength—by some 2.5 million to 3.3 million people. While Eisenhower had not stopped the destructive and wasteful feuding by greedy special-interest groups or Pentagon rivals, he had identified, publicized, and condemned the problem and its contributing parties. With help from his science adviser he had seen that anti-aircraft missiles would render the proposed B-70 bomber obsolete and stopped the costly project before it went into production. After investing a billion dollars, no positive results had come out of the U.S. nuclear-powered aircraft program, something Ike had warned against in 1953, and he abolished it. More important, in 1958 Eisenhower had initiated the nation's first nuclear-test moratorium, eliminating the danger to the world from radioactive fallout for three years and reducing the possibility that either side might launch a surprise attack. Finally, his April 1959 test-ban proposal became the basis for the treaty signed by Khrushchev and Kennedy in 1963, banning atmospheric nuclear tests.

In retrospect, Eisenhower's performance as the first cold-war commander-in-chief, while straining both democracy and economic freedom in its answers to the challenge and mobilization of a viable national-security strategy, was realistic and statesmanlike. He had not, as he had hoped, prevented the Soviet consolidation in Eastern Europe (the Warsaw Pact) or diminished the influence of communism in the Middle East, Southeast Asia, and the Caribbean. His efforts to render Latin America less attractive to the spread of communism, by fostering individual opportunity and respect for human rights, did not keep up with the explosion of the continent's population and the accompanying poverty there and resulted in U.S. support for dictators deemed to be of the "pro-American" variety. Indeed, it was in the Third World, most notably in Vietnam, that the United States by the late 1960s discovered that it had overextended itself.

National security policy during the Eisenhower years nevertheless embodied a sense of the national interest and, by and large, an awareness of attainable goals. It also achieved important results. The Korean War ended with the integrity of democratic South Korea preserved. A chill swept Soviet-American relations with the collapse of the 1960 summit meeting in Paris, but the President by that time had held three meetings with Soviet leaders, corresponded with them, established negotiations in Geneva about ways to eliminate the danger from surprise attack and testing of nuclear weapons, and pursued policies that helped disrupt the alliance between the Soviet Union and the People's Republic of China. Thanks to Eisenhower, NATO included a rearmed West Germany and was a benefactor of a resurgent European economy. The United States had ended the Suez crisis without serious damage to its alliances or the world oil supply, had helped build a strong Japan (which was now tied to the United States by treaties of mutual cooperation and security), and had successfully protected it friends in Taiwan. As leader of the noncommunist world, the United States had sponsored, joined, or supported treaty organizations in Southeast Asia, the Middle East, central Asia, and the Australian subcontinent—a system that interfered with the ambitions of both the Soviet Union and mainland China and provided a barrier behind which noncommunist regimes could grow. A friendly regime existed in Iran, where in 1954 the CIA had helped to overthrow a nationalist-communist government (although they had reinstalled the Shah's oppressive rule). In Latin America, Cuba had become a socialist dictatorship, but the CIA had established a friendly government in Guatemala, and a plan now existed (with $500 million authorized by Congress) for economic assistance to other Latin American countries. And while the Indochinese insurgency supported by the North Vietnamese leader Ho Chi Minh continued, France had withdrawn its forces and hope still existed (an ill-fated one as it turned out) that South Vietnam would remain an independent nation.

In sum, the world was more divided by 1961 than it had been when Eisenhower took office, and some of the U.S. interventions would not in the long run succeed, notably in Vietnam, Iran, and Central America. Nor would they serve democracy. But by 1961 the communist bloc had become, at least for a time, less threatening, and the world was more stable than it had been from the mid-1940s to the mid-1950s. The Eisenhower administration had dispelled much doubt over U.S. interests and intentions in the minds of both the American people and of the world's leaders. Although unable to have its way wherever it wanted, by almost every measure, including the Bretton Woods economic system in which the world's currencies measured their value in U.S. dollars, the United States was the world's dominant nation. And for those fleeing oppression or seeking a better life, it was the most popular place of refuge.

CHAPTER FIVE

The Politics of Moderation

The way of life Eisenhower sought to protect through his domestic policy was, he believed, the most important source of American strength. Its principal element was the system of free enterprise. His administration, accordingly, would establish the cold-war government for the United States, for many of its features became permanent.

The individual who oversaw the executive departments was Sherman Adams, chief of staff and assistant to the President. Eisenhower first noticed Adams, the wiry and hard-bitten former governor of New Hampshire, because of his activities on the general's behalf in the crucial New Hampshire primary of 1952. Adams had demonstrated his political savvy as floor manager during the Republican convention and was the perfect individual to see to it that the White House, like Eisenhower's wartime headquarters, was a no-nonsense operation. To many observers it appeared that the crusty New Englander, who made few friends because of his austere, abrupt, even caustic manner, actually was running the presidency. Eisenhower did nothing to disabuse people of this notion, any more than he did those who believed that Secretary of State Foster Dulles was single-handedly running foreign affairs. However, Adams's actual position was, in addition to his managerial responsibilities, that of special assistant for domestic policy.

The first item on the President's domestic agenda after the inauguration was to address the problem of national disunity. The divisions typical of American political life—federal-state, executive-legislative, racial, sectional, labor-management, and interparty—needed to be subordinated, said the man from Abilene, to the nation's general welfare. In place of an adversarial society that pitted government against the private sector, Eisenhower sought a cooperative or corporate environment in which the federal government, instead of acting as referee and judge, would serve mainly as exhorter, promoter, and coordinator. A large element of the national disunity was of course racial injustice, but it was not something that Eisenhower felt could be addressed immediately, since he considered it to be a long-term and almost intractable problem. Another large element of this disunity (actually a compound one), internal security and the current Red-baiting campaign of Senator Joseph R. McCarthy of Wisconsin, was urgent—sapping morale at home and the country's reputation abroad. Finally, like the American people, the Republican party was confused at this time, its right wing accustomed to criticizing constantly. Another Democratic victory, Eisenhower said when he had decided to run in 1952, could mean the end of the two-party system and the permanent triumph of New Deal principles over those of the Constitution. On the other hand, Ike had felt that a Republican victory would be little better than a Democratic one if it placed Senator Taft in charge of foreign policy. The only solution was a different GOP. "If there is to be a real two-party system in our country, then there should normally be single-party responsibility in the capital city."

In retrospect, one can see that the Eisenhower years both institutionalized important New Deal reforms such as Social Security and labor legislation, and were a foreshadowing of the more conservative politics that began in 1969 with the presidency of Richard M. Nixon. When Eisenhower left the White

House, Taft was gone (he died of cancer in 1953), but the GOP still had the same factions it had when he had arrived. Still, McCarthyism (the senator from Wisconsin, having been censured by the Senate) was in disrepute, and the political atmosphere in the United States was improved. Relations between the races remained strained, but the Supreme Court decision *Brown* v. *Board of Education of Topeka* had become the opening bell of the civil rights movement of the 1960s. In both the controversial areas of civil liberties and civil rights, Eisenhower had obtained cooperation from a Congress dominated by conservative Southern Democrats and conservative Middle Western Republicans. Finally, the U.S. economy had grown enormously, and without inflation or large federal deficits.

What makes all this more remarkable is something that very few people at the time realized, that Eisenhower performed his duties in the Oval Office despite the steadily increasing personal difficulties caused him by cardiovascular disease.

It is now clear that Eisenhower did much to end the influence of the demagogic McCarthy, although it is possible that the President did not act quickly enough. Eisenhower had been alarmed at what was happening as early as 1950, and by early 1954 he was exasperated. The senator, he declared privately, "makes a few extraordinary and outlandish charges in the papers, and the whole United States abandons all consideration of the many grave problems it faces in order to speculate on whether McCarthy has it within his power to 'destroy our system of government' . . . We have side shows and freaks when we ought to be in the main tent with our attention on the chariot race."

A close associate recalled that Eisenhower had "a very well thought out view as to the role of the Presidency and the Congress and the courts." He knew that any public condemnation of McCarthy by the President (especially one with Eisenhower's fame) likely would give the senator more press value and damage both the GOP and the harmony between the executive and legislative branches of the government. Getting any program through Congress would then be even more difficult. Aware always of the constitutional separation of powers and determined to uphold the President's constitutional prerogatives, he moved indirectly to put an end to McCarthy's siege. He looked first to party leaders. Since the senator from Wisconsin controlled votes of perhaps eight senate colleagues (Herman Welker, Pat McCarran, George Malone, H. Styles Bridges, William E. Jenner, Everett McK. Dirksen, William S. Knowland—the latter four being chairmen of committees), there was little hope of enlisting conservative leaders to his cause. In the end, the narrowness of the Republican majority in the 83rd Congress (which it lost in the election of 1954) would make these senators even more cautious. Not even the final vote to censure McCarthy would bring a Republican consensus: GOP senators split 22 to 22.

McCarthy's crusade against communists in government had begun February 6, 1950, at the Women's Republican Club of Wheeling, West Virginia (the senator had held up a piece of scrap paper and said he had in his hand a list of 205 card-carrying communists employed by the State Department). President Roosevelt, he charged, had sold out Eastern Europe at the Yalta conference, and Truman's State Department in 1949 had brought Mao's victory over the Chinese Nationalists. Indeed, McCarthy labeled a communist sympathizer anyone in the State Department who reported accurately on U.S. policy in China. The senator was throwing out a ridiculously wide net. In foreign policy, he and his colleagues wanted nothing less than repudiation of the Yalta agreements, a campaign of some sort to free Eastern Europe from Soviet domination, and a constitutional proviso—the Bricker Amendment—that would ban international executive agreements made without Senate approval, something that would greatly reduce the President's power in the field of foreign policy.

Despite demands by leading newspaper columnists—after McCarthy slandered Eisenhower's mentor General Marshall, the *New York Times* and *Washington Post* particularly were critical—that the President act to stop the McCarthyites' fear-mongering and negativism, Eisenhower determined to take a course that stemmed from his practice since boyhood: he would be careful to control his temper and act on his own timetable. Recalling Truman's inability to stop the Red-baiting, Eisenhower refused to answer the criticism and even allowed Dulles to appoint a McCarthyite, R. W. Scott McLeod, as head of State Department security. This prompted the *Times* and the *Post* to decide that the President was himself a McCarthyite. Though a disaster to the individuals who lost careers and reputations in the foreign service and, alas, damaging to his true purposes, Eisenhower's handling of the matter was nevertheless carefully considered. Support for a policy, he had determined from experience, was seldom advanced by hateful remarks (or feelings, for that matter). Leadership required good will. "To destroy good will it is only necessary to criticize publicly. This creates in the criticized the subconscious desire to 'get even.' Such effects can last for a very long period." Domestic fear and turmoil, he had decided, were more dangerous than any alleged communist subversion. He was going to get "this Republican Party of ours to be progressive or else—and that's that."

He responded first to attempts to reverse foreign policy, supporting among other things a Senate resolution on Yalta that criticized the Soviet Union for violating agreements and "subjugating whole nations," but he did not repudiate the Yalta agreements outright, as desired by the GOP. He then obtained sufficient support in the Senate to stop all attempts to pass the Bricker Amendment. In 1953 the State Department was being investigated by ten different committees of Congress. Moving to distance his administration from McCarthy, Eisenhower said that appointments in that department were the responsibility of Secretary Dulles "and no one else." The McLeod appointment and the firing of numerous foreign service officers, including virtually all the capable individuals who had been involved with formulating U.S. policy in China and Southeast Asia, provided a means of responding to additional accusations. The State Department now had Republicans in the place of Democratic appointees.

Especially upsetting to the President was the unwarranted attention the pugnacious senator received in the press. After he became President, White House aides saw Ike go "up in an utter blaze," his face reddening, over McCarthy's tactics. He privately condemned the senator's "headline-grabbing, his coarse familiarity, his shotgun attacks," which the senator finally levelled at the White House. Why, he wondered, would somebody want to criticize someone who was "working like a dog just to preserve their right to say whatever they choose?" Moderation had been a theme of his campaign in 1952. "There were two roads," he said at a stop in Idaho, "two extreme philosophies of government that were widely divergent—the Reactionary Right and the Radical Left. Both led to tyranny. The problem was to achieve a balance which would assure individual liberty in an orderly society."

Now, as President, Eisenhower was prepared to take his powers to their limit. When McCarthy joined with McCarran and Malone against confirmation of perhaps the foremost State Department specialist on the Soviet Union, Charles E. Bohlen as ambassador to Moscow, Eisenhower quietly sought support from the Senate leadership. But when the senator attacked part of the executive branch—the army—Eisenhower moved directly. In the most sweeping invoking of White House executive privilege in history, he impounded documents relating to the case, prohibited administration officials from testifying, insisting that in this circumstance he could keep conversations in the executive branch from Congress, and helped arrange the televised proceedings that finally exposed the senator for what he was. "It's his army and he doesn't like McCarthy's tactics at all," Hagerty remarked. "My friends tell me," Eisenhower said, "it won't be long in this army stuff before McCarthy starts using my name." The President decided the senator's ultimate goal was the White House, but he said McCarthy was the "last guy in the world who'll ever get there if I have anything to say." Now under attack himself, the senator's days of finger pointing soon were over.

Americans in the postwar era put their standard of living—employment, rates of inflation, taxes—ahead of almost everything. Eisenhower knew this, and the economy was his preoccupation. Maintenance of prosperity, he told Milton, "interests me mightily," and it was something about which he talked incessantly. Indeed, his second cabinet appointment, after that of secretary of state, was Joseph Dodge, president of the Bank of Detroit and former financial advisor for the American occupation of Germany and Japan, to be director of the Bureau of the Budget.

To observers on the political right, Eisenhower's economic program seemed hypocritical. Aspects of it appeared to contradict the anti–New Deal talk of his presidential campaign. But he meant what he had said on the stump. When Dulles expressed doubt that a totally free economy could continue in the face of "the Soviet menace," Eisenhower disagreed. The nation had to be strong "in the source of all our armaments—our productivity," and this could only be under free enterprise. Bureaucracy, he felt, stifled initiative. Excess federal expenditure, so he expected his cabinet officials to know, was a drain on the economy. With annual deficits "we just can't compete." And defense spending—which he singled out to reduce—"doesn't give the right sort of jobs." It produced "sterile, negative things, silent policemen standing around our house all the time." Working with only partial success to rectify this problem, he reorganized the executive branch, streamlining the National Security Council, establishing agencies for war mobilization and disarmament, and revamping the Defense De-

partment. Eisenhower sought to stir private initiative and in-
dividualism while putting an end to federal paternalism, which
he believed the New Deal had established.

The United States, he believed nonetheless, could not afford to allow the so-called laws of supply and demand alone to
determine the nation's destiny. Stories of the Great Depression appeared regularly in communist propaganda, with Soviet leaders insisting that capitalism was doomed. Ike intended
to show the falseness of such beliefs. Working in Washington
in the late 1920s, he had studied the civil requirements for a
successful wartime economy, including the need to plan for
reconversion to a peacetime economy. The economy he desired to build now would be different from that of Presidents
Harding and Coolidge but similar to that of Hoover. Unlike
Hoover, however, he called for government intervention
through regulation of taxes and the providing of loans and
grants, construction, credit insurance, and a level of social security sufficient to prevent depression. In sum, he desired to
retain New Deal reforms while dismantling its remaining re-
lief programs.

The President's economic experts were Gabriel Hauge and
Donald Paarlberg. Working with the chairmen of the Council
of Economic Advisers, first Arthur Burns of George Washington University and then Raymond J. Saulnier of Columbia,
Hauge and Paarlberg set up a program to monitor the budget. They admired the President's economic outlook, and
Eisenhower, in turn, sought their judgment. He enjoyed seeing trends on a chart and during conferences would point
and say, "Now, look here. I'll tell you where housing starts will
be next month."

The President's deep concern with economic issues brought
him the support of members of the Committee for Economic
Development—executives of large corporations (also members of the Business Council) who during the war had become
concerned about what would follow and who had therefore
helped to convince Ike to run for President. They included

Paul Hoffman, Lucius D. Clay, and Sidney J. Weinberg of Goldman, Sachs, the New York investment banking firm. The latter two recruited Eisenhower's cabinet—George M. Humphrey of the M. A. Hanna Company for secretary of the treasury, Charles E. Wilson of General Motors as secretary of defense, Robert T. Stevens of J. P. Stevens Company as secretary of the army, and Marion B. Folsom as undersecretary of the treasury and later as secretary of health, education, and welfare.

The Eisenhower administration's measures to control the economy were numerous. An army or a nation, Eisenhower once said, could do little without a good morale deriving from loyalty, patriotism, discipline, and efficiency. During the post–Korean War recession of 1954, he extended unemployment compensation to 4 million workers and raised the minimum hourly wage from seventy-five cents to one dollar. If unemployment went much above 5 percent, he was prepared to increase spending for soil conservation, dam construction, roads, public buildings, defense procurement, and shipbuilding.

Success was visible by the election of 1956. If a project was economically good, Eisenhower went for it. He obtained the largest appropriation ever granted for road construction, $2 billion, and initiated the Interstate Highway Program. By mid-1955 the economy was growing at 7.6 percent with inflation at 1 percent and unemployment at 4.1 percent. The federal budget showed a surplus of $4.1 billion.

Setbacks came during Eisenhower's second term, however, revealing an inexact understanding of economic forces and the cumbersome institutions required by cold-war policies. Concurrently with a $2.2 billion cut in military spending, 1957 saw a recession caused by the dwindling demand for capital and consumer goods. By 1958 unemployment was up to 7 percent, and corporate profits had declined by 25 percent. Learning of the severity of the recession, the President quipped forlornly of his desire to be able to leave the economy alone for even one week. By the end of his second term, spending for defense was higher than he had desired. Congress, with the support of bureaucrats, further frustrated his efforts to control federal spending, and while Eisenhower valued the participation of businessmen to create a stable economy, he began to warn against the lobbying of military professionals, bureaucrats, researchers, industrialists—people who sought to gain from weapons production. Disarmament, he believed, contrary to assertions by Pentagon officials and defense lobbyists, would allow an overall smaller budget. But his was a continuing struggle with the defense establishment, which seemed to believe that the United States could afford whatever it wanted. After cutting military spending to achieve a $70 billion federal budget, Eisenhower told the cabinet in 1957 that it was not butter and guns but butter *or* guns. If they talk missiles, "throw it in their teeth" about the needs of big cities.

Uncertainty about what the federal budget should contain, however, surrendered the initiative to Congress, which in an effort to embarrass the President approved a budget that was $4 billion lower than the one he had submitted (later restoring the amount in emergency appropriations). In 1958 the Republicans received the blame for the recession, giving the Democrats their largest gains in a congressional election since the New Deal. Eisenhower's approval rating declined from 79 percent to 52 percent, and the federal deficit reached $12 billion in 1959. Therefore, during the Eisenhower administration, the national debt increased from $257 billion to $290. By 1960 the United States also found itself with a balance of payments deficit for the first time in the postwar period.

However, by 1961, Eisenhower accomplished his economic goals. The gross national product went from $365 to $520 billion, an annual increase of 2.4 percent. Household consumption increased from $230 billion to $335 billion, this brought on by an increase in the national income of 44 percent, personal income of 50 percent, and employment by 10 percent (unemployment remained at 5 percent).

Some of this prosperity was the result of federal spending. Congressional appropriations increased money available for research sponsored by the National Science Foundation from $3.5 million to $155 million. When private spending was included, the total increased from $5.2 billion to $12.4 billion. The National Defense Education Act provided $1 billion for math, science, and language programs in colleges and universities. Defense spending, after initial cutbacks, increased (although not exceeding $41 billion, $19 billion lower than the peak year, 1952, of the Korean War). Domestic spending increased from 23 percent of the budget to 38.6 percent but, with a reduction of 250,000 federal employees, did not exceed a total of $10 billion—only a fraction of what was spent by state and local government, which had increased from $25 billion to $50 billion. Old age and survivors' monthly cash benefits under Social Security increased from $1 billion to $10.7 billion, the number of recipients from 3.5 million to 14.8 million. The Department of Health, Education, and Welfare had come into existence, and medical care for the aged had begun. Foreign economic and military aid (resulting in increased purchases at home) was $5 billion a year. Finally, the St. Lawrence Seaway was completed, and two new states were admitted to the union, Alaska and Hawaii.

Economic growth also resulted from the increased foreign trade promoted by the administration. By expanding trade, Hauge said, the President hoped to get nations working together. Long-term American investment overseas reached $49 billion. Eisenhower committed the Republican party to the concept of reciprocal trade and obtained from Congress the power to reduce tariffs by 15 percent in 1955 and by another 20 percent in 1958. Discovering that many countries would never be able to trade with the United States if their economies did not develop, he changed his party's slogan from "trade, not aid" to "trade and aid." As indicated above, during Eisenhower's term in office, U.S. aid began moving toward the developing world. Furthermore, this assistance was no longer purely military but economic and, as in the case of Latin America, was given also to promote international (economic) cooperation.

All this occurred despite the fact that of the four Congresses during Eisenhower's eight years in office, only the 83rd Congress, 1953–54, was Republican. During his administration Congress overrode only two presidential vetoes.

The most serious long-term cause of national disunity and societal weakness during Eisenhower's presidency was of course the problem of racial injustice. Eisenhower's approach, another series of careful and deliberate moves, received criticism from the left and the right. Far from indifferent to the plight of blacks, as some writers have asserted, Eisenhower made no distinction between individuals based on race, sought equality of opportunity for everyone, and took historic steps in behalf of blacks. In addition to the injustice of it, he believed that bigotry was detrimental to the nation's interests abroad, subtracting from the nation's ability to resist communist propaganda by causing the United States to resemble Nazi Germany. During debate in the United Nations on a resolution condemning apartheid in South Africa, he told Secretary Dulles of the shame he felt, that "if we vote for a tough resolution, we may find ourselves red-faced . . . concerning our own Negro problem."

Having lived in the South and having served throughout his career with Southern enlisted men and officers in the army, he had seen racial discrimination and knew how deeply ingrained it was in American society. He did what he could to overcome it. During the Battle of the Bulge in 1944 he had sent blacks to serve alongside whites. As chief of staff he ordered the integration of the U.S. Army. But he did not believe that it was the responsibility of the federal government to end segregation in the South. Forced school integration, he said, could bring "social disintegration."

Without doing everything he could or perhaps should have done to advance civil rights in America, he nevertheless transformed the legal status of blacks. Having declared adherence to equality in his first state-of-the-union address, he appointed a foe of racism, his campaign advisor Herbert Brownell, as Attorney General. To the post of Chief Justice of the Supreme Court he appointed another civil rights advocate, Earl Warren. By executive order he abolished what remained of discrimination in the armed forces and appointed two blacks, E. Frederick Morrow and Lois Leppenan, to the White House staff. J. Ernest Wilkins served as Assistant Secretary of Labor—the first black to attend cabinet meetings in an official capacity. Eisenhower sent to Congress and pushed passage of the Civil Rights Act of 1957—the first such law since Reconstruction. The Truman administration, Brownell recalled, had focused without success on anti-lynching legislation and the repeal of the poll tax. Under Eisenhower the Justice Department determined that "voting rights was by far the most serious civil rights problem faced by the Negroes of the country." In 1956–57 the President had been dismayed that of 900,000 blacks in Mississippi, only 7,000 were registered voters. The right to vote, Brownell said, was "absolutely fundamental to establish equal rights of citizenship." Such legislation, unlike anti-lynching laws, could be enforced because it would allow local majorities to accomplish what "probably would never be possible wholly as a federal thing." The Civil Rights Act created a civil rights commission in the Justice Department, extended jurisdiction of federal district courts to civil rights cases, and allowed the Attorney General to seek injunctions to protect voting. For the first time, substantial federal money was spent on the protection of civil rights. Between 1958 and 1961, under the new law the Justice Department brought to court a hundred discrimination cases and investigated four thousand complaints.

Historians later quoted Eisenhower as saying that the appointment of Warren was the biggest "damn fool mistake I

ever made." Brownell doubted he said it or, if he did, that it
was in reference to Warren's stand on civil rights, because the
President personally revised and strengthened drafts of
Brownell's statement in behalf of *Brown* v. *Board of Education.*
Eisenhower probably was saying that he disliked the Supreme
Court's approach. What bothered him was less the landmark
decision than the difficulty in carrying out its mandate for "all
deliberate speed" in integrating Southern schools. Enforce-
ment, he felt, might prompt Southern whites to close schools
altogether (turning instead to private ones) thereby hurting
low-income people of both races, perhaps requiring even more
drastic federal intervention. The "all deliberate speed" clause
also increased the probability of violence. Still, the Supreme
Court had spoken, and, despite any off-the-cuff remarks,
Eisenhower supported Warren. "There must be respect for
the Constitution," he told a friend, "which means the Supreme
Court's interpretation of the Constitution—or we will have
chaos."

In 1957, after Governor Orville Faubus of Arkansas mobilized his state's National Guard to prevent the desegregation
of Little Rock's Central High School, Eisenhower was forced
to act. Recognizing that the Court's action had caused what
he called "seething in the South," he tried first to influence
the governor by persuasion, inviting him to his vacation residence in Newport, Rhode Island, for a personal meeting, where
he urged the governor not to withdraw the Guard but rather
to change its orders, directing them instead to maintain the
peace and ensure the admittance of the black children to the
high school. Ignoring the admonition, Faubus continued to
use the Guard troops to block the black children as they tried
to approach the school. Then he withdrew the Guard altogether, permitting an ugly white mob to descend upon the
frightened youngsters. The President had hated to intervene
with force, but now he had been pushed too far and would
not allow a "challenge to federal authority to go unnoticed."
"The federal law," he said, "cannot be flouted with impunity
by any individual or any mob of extremists." Swiftly nationaliz-

ing the Guard, Eisenhower sent 1,000 men of the U.S. Army's 101st Airborne Division to the scene. The black children were enrolled in the high school. The lasting (although unintended) importance of the President's action, in this instance to prevent mob violence, was as precedent for federal intervention in the 1960s to enforce school desegregation.

Any evaluation of Eisenhower's record on civil rights must consider that in the end he was successful in walking a tightrope and accomplishing the goals that he had established for the nation in those difficult times. The chief executive's caution with regard to civil rights stemmed from his awareness that he needed the support of Southern congressmen for vital initiatives abroad, another example of the domestic dilemma of the cold war considering the propaganda edge that bigotry gave to the nation's opponents. Congress, including such key Southern Senators as Lyndon B. Johnson of Texas and Richard Russell of Georgia, supported the President on crucial issues of foreign policy, but this had required his continual effort from the day he took office, including private meetings and White House dinners with legislators, appeals to the cabinet, press conferences, and speeches. In the years that followed, social change in the South would occur, as Eisenhower had predicted, through the efforts of local citizens working to uphold the law. In 1955, in the new legal framework, Martin Luther King, Jr., and the National Association for the Advancement of Colored People (NAACP) called for the desegregation of city buses in Montgomery, Alabama, an event that would become the beginning of the great civil rights crusade of the mid-twentieth century.

Attorney General Brownell developed civil rights initiatives systematically, seeking as many views as possible, but he refused to develop a joint program with black groups When Representative Adam Clayton Powell insisted upon attaching desegregation amendments to all sorts of bills, Eisenhower reminded him that this was no way to obtain goals. He predicted correctly that the Senate would not favorably consider *any* legislation so burdened.

Congress weakened the Civil Rights Act of 1957 with a re-
quirement for trials by jury (a body which could, of course,
easily reflect the bigotry of the county in which the incident
occurred), and the widespread opposition to school desegregation effected a reduction of the power of the Civil Rights
Commission. Eisenhower urged Congress to correct this. The
result was the Civil Rights Act of 1960, which authorized federal judges to appoint polling referees to help blacks register,
and set new criminal penalties for bombings (of the homes of
activists and churches) and the obstruction of court orders.
Clearly, civil rights for blacks, as Eisenhower knew and his successors would learn, would require more widespread public
pressure before Congress would truly mandate equal rights.

Interestingly, the President, despite his failure to please civil
rights leaders, increased his support among African Americans, who appreciated the sincerity of his commitment to civil
rights. White House staff member Morrow, a 46-year-old black
attorney, veteran of World War II, and field representative for
the NAACP remarked that his boss's belief in equality of opportunity for all Americans was "wholly without reservation."
In the election of 1956, thirty-five congressional districts outside the South with a black population of 10 percent or more
of the total saw the GOP vote go up from 42 percent in 1952
to 47 percent. Although Adlai Stevenson, who had also proceeded cautiously on the civil rights issue, received more black
votes in 1956 than did Eisenhower, the President received more
than he had in 1952, which included gains in the states of
Alabama, Arkansas, and North Carolina, where black voters
were a substantial portion of the population. He also did better in the black areas of northern cities. His vote in Harlem,
for example, increased by 16.5 percent.

In the final years of the Eisenhower administration the advance of civil rights, although not what blacks had hoped it
would be, was steady and, considering the glacially slow
progress prior to the Truman administration, encouraging.
For more than forty years the NAACP had been working to

reverse *Plessy* v. *Ferguson*, the 1896 case in which the Court ruled that separate railroad cars for blacks were legal so long as they were equal in quality (they never were), the so-called "separate but equal" doctrine that was the foundation for legal segregation, or "Jim Crow" laws. Civil rights proponents wanted Eisenhower, the symbol of victory over racism in Europe, to speak out more, considering gradualism to be the same as opposition. Prosegregationists, on the other hand, criticized Eisenhower because they disliked his statements in behalf of equal opportunity, his appointment of Earl Warren, and the actions taken at his behest in Little Rock. The President offered little consolation for either group but was able to keep the support of both. Such were the politics of moderation.

Perhaps no statute of Eisenhower's administration was more far reaching than the one the President sponsored in 1956 that set up the National System of Interstate and Defense Highways—the nation's 41,000-mile freeway system. As one of the first army officers to write about mechanized warfare, it is not surprising that he promoted a program linked to the American fascination with the internal combustion engine. If any product was a symbol of American life in the 1950s, it was the automobile. An American's car not only brought independence, a new dominion over time and space, it was an expression of status and a source of personal identity and image—be it stylish, staid, or sporty.

Interstate highways were sure to be popular with the public and obviously with U.S. auto producers, shippers, truckers, retailers, and construction companies, most of whom had been debating for years over how to build such a crosscountry highway system. The current, two-lane highway system left much to be desired. Each year tens of thousands of Americans died on these roads in traffic accidents, many of them in head-on collisions. Traffic jams made it clear that if the federal government failed to organize the system, highway building by local governments would only exacerbate the confusion.

Eisenhower, as mentioned, had accompanied the army's slow, transcontinental convoy of 1919, had seen the usefulness of the autobahns of Germany, and was experienced in the logistics required to move hundreds of thousands of people. In the case of enemy attack he now sought a reliable means of moving large numbers of Americans out of major metropolitan areas. And, of course, he knew that a giant public works project in which the states would use private contractors (and then be repaid by user taxes) was certain to stimulate the nation's economy.

To get things started, he asked his closest associate outside government, Lucius Clay, to form a citizen's advisory committee to study methods of financing a federal intercity highway program. "We were facing a possible recession," Clay recalled. "He wanted to have something on the books that would enable us to move quickly if we had to go into public works. And he thought that the highway program was a very important one." The Clay Committee proposed a federal corporation to finance $2.5 billion of annual construction. Unlike such highways as the Pennsylvania Turnpike that charged fees, the corporation would issue bonds to raise $25 billion to finance highway construction. A federal gasoline tax would repay the bonds over thirty years. Eisenhower invited congressional committee members to the White House to discuss the plan.

The idea of central control brought disagreement. Truckers, engineers, labor, state and county officials, and farmers all had their own opinions about the project's finance and demanded local advantage in the project's administration. Eisenhower then abolished the Clay Committee and set up a cabinet committee under Secretary of Commerce Sinclair Weeks. When a highway-construction bill finally came from Congress, Representatives Hale Boggs of Louisiana and George Fallon of Maryland had provided something for everyone without weighing heavily on truckers. There would be standards for finance and construction (including four lanes and limited access) with costs shared by all of the states. A federal

trust funded by taxes on fuels, tires, and the sales of new vehicles would maintain farm, urban, and trunk roads, and provide an additional $25 million annually for moving earth and
pouring concrete. The plan included procedures for condemning land, thereby preventing land owners from extorting outrageous profits on or refusing to sell the necessary land to the
government. The federal government would pay 90 percent
of the cost of the highway system's construction but redistrib-
ute the money earned from the highways according to need, a
formula that favored urban areas.

The project had a variety of benefits. Few individuals at the
time would have believed that within twenty years the average
American family could drive anywhere in the country on expressways complete with rest stops and information booths,
zipping through the largest cities at 65 miles per hour in tun-
nels or on skyways. Likewise, few businesspeople realized that
before too long their products and goods could be shipped
anywhere in the nation by semitrailer. The undertaking of the
immense project enabled Eisenhower to obtain "greater direction over economic movements" by holding some highway
funds for distribution to states during downturns in the
economy. A publicist for the American Automobile Association insisted, with considerable support, that automobiles and
expressways were good in themselves, and that Americans
wanted "better highways now." The President expressed a willingness to sign any bill that had approval of his Secretary of
the Treasury. Since the highway bill proposed no raids on the
national budget and was self-financing, it was acceptable to
Secretary Humphrey and Eisenhower signed it on June 29,
1956. When completed, $60 billion had gone into the inter-
state highway system, enough concrete, as Eisenhower predicted, to "build six sidewalks to the moon."

On the other hand, few Americans could have envisioned
the side effects of the interstate highway system, other than
the welcomed ones of an expanded economy and national
living space. However, ease of travel for those who owned a

car and could drive would contrast sharply with the confinement felt by those Americans who, because of age or disability, could not drive. With the easy accessibility of the interstates and a virtual explosion in the number of private automobiles in the country, mass transit systems withered, which, of course, was also at the expense of poor, inner-city, and disabled people. Inhabitants of industrial cities became accustomed to a new and more intense sort of traffic jam, that in later years was not-so-affectionately called "gridlock." In places where several freeways met, they sometimes became so entangled that one in Chicago was called "the spaghetti bowl," one in Dallas "the mixmaster." Ribbons of heat-absorbing, steel-reinforced concrete even bisected individually held farms and covered much cropland. Certain cities and towns began to decline if interstates passed them by, some becoming ghost towns. Much of the ambience of former crosscountry travel—tourist homes, historical markers, country stores, family-owned gas stations, detours down elm-canopied streets lined with Victorian frame houses—was lost. There was also a new and dangerous phenomenon: the catastrophic, chain-reaction collision on fog- or dust-bound highways. Finally, downtown neighborhoods and commercial buildings were cut off from stores or parks or literally covered by highways on stilts. Poor black Americans, segregated into ethnically homogeneous neighborhoods jammed into the very centers of cities that once had contained business districts, found themselves in tenements or run-down project housing. For a while, as the former inhabitants of big cities flocked to the suburbs, this wave of new inner-city problems bothered no one but those left stranded. Gradually it became clear that the interstates had helped produce ghettoes while making poverty and racism less visible to middle- and upper-income Americans.

Eisenhower, one must note in appraising his domestic policies, was not able to accomplish all that people expected of him and in many cases even failed to accomplish his own purposes. This was as he had feared when he decided to enter politics in 1952. Part of the problem was that his priorities simply could not accommodate everything that needed doing. In other instances, he was constrained by his sources of support. Much of the criticism was that he was insufficiently bold (an echo of the criticism of his strategy against Germany). His indirect method of dealing with McCarthy was effective but another approach might have been less damaging to American civil liberties and to the careers of loyal government officials. Continued Republican squabbling and defeats in the elections of 1954, 1958, and 1960 revealed that Eisenhower had ended the McCarthy era but had failed to build a new GOP.

His view of the power of the federal government to change ethnic and cultural patterns was modest. His concept of leadership as moral suasion and the need for support from the South for his policies inhibited him from pushing desegregation. Aggravating this last problem, of course, was his effort to expand the regional base for the Republican party and his support for states' rights and local, individual initiative. Such conditions and social philosophies left many, perhaps most of the poor, hungry, and homeless outside or with inadequate community support. One particularly distressing example of this was federal Indian policy, which kept Native Americans impoverished and demoralized.

In economic policy a continuing problem was a system that caused agricultural surpluses and falling prices. Eisenhower worked to end federal intervention in agriculture, desiring to eliminate rigid price supports at 90 percent of parity. Unfortunately when he left office the old ineffective system remained, along with newly established Soil Bank payments to farmers who would actually agree to keep their fields out of production.

As Brownell recalled, Eisenhower had expected to do a better job of "strengthening the financial health of the country and approaching a balanced budget." But in retrospect,

Eisenhower's performance was nonetheless remarkable. Achievements were many and resulted from constant hard work. His foreign policy, especially his negotiated armistice in Korea and the period of "peaceful coexistence" following the Geneva summit with Soviet leaders, helped ease domestic tension. In the words of one historian, Eisenhower "robbed the search for security of much of its anger and intensity" and presided over "a dramatic lessening in public anxieties about domestic subversion." Politically damaging recessions nevertheless occurred in 1954 and in 1957–58. A steelworkers' strike lasted a record 116 days, and a balance of payments deficit threatened the international monetary system. In 1960 came another economic downturn. Still, Eisenhower was unrelenting about the need to avoid a budget deficit. At one point he exhorted Vice President Nixon to "take the battleline and fight" for a balanced budget. "If we don't do this and if you come to this chair you will be the unhappiest man in the United States. If we don't begin to pay as we go, we'll be in a terrible spot and have no recourse except to desert liberty as we understand it." His advice was, "fight it out and to hell with the opposition." National strength, Eisenhower believed, was synonymous with balanced economic growth. Assisting adequate production and distribution of the nation's goods and services—both guns and butter, as he put it—took the largest portion of the time he devoted to domestic affairs, and the prosperity of the 1950s resulted at least in part from these efforts.

Some word remains of the elections of 1956 and 1960, which reflected the nation's response to the administration's policies and performance. Along these lines historians recently have discovered important new information about what the public did not know about the President's health and what effect his condition had on his participation in politics. The election of 1956 was in retrospect perhaps one of the strangest in American history because the President who was running for a second term had the previous year suffered a massive heart attack. While the heart attack was well known to the public, they were not informed of its severity, nor the fact that it was probably the President's third coronary in the previous seven years. Despite the attack, Eisenhower irresponsibly considered his prior medical history to be a private matter and, thanks to the cooperation of his doctors (at least of majority of them), was willing to try to serve as the nation's chief executive for another four years.

The election of 1956, as things turned out, was not a difficult contest. Again Eisenhower defeated Governor Adlai Stevenson, this time with an even greater margin of popular votes. As an expression of their satisfaction with their President, the electorate gave him 10 million more votes than his opponent, a huge margin of victory.

Here it is important to pause to consider the new information that bears upon Eisenhower's decision to run for a second term. Eisenhower was running a grave risk. At two points during his tenure it seemed to political observers that he would not be able to remain in office. The first was the aforementioned heart attack in late September 1955, the second a light stroke in November 1957. The severity of both episodes was withheld from the public. It is probable that Eisenhower's attitude toward his physical well being was shaped by his youthful experiences, his severe leg infection, and his knee injury from playing football at West Point. His upbringing and military training had imbued him with the tenet that injuries and illnesses are part of life and, if allowed to, can have a large effect on one's career and possibilities for service: one therefore does one's best to minimize them. Any other approach would fall into the category of taking seriously oneself rather than one's job, a reversal of Conner's famous dictum. In practice, this meant that Eisenhower had no more intention of letting physical problems affect his personal performance as President than he had as supreme commander. Nevertheless, as they had during the campaign in North Africa and later while he was the acting chairman of the Joint Chiefs of Staff, health problems clearly did affect Eisenhower's execution of his duties.

The heart attack of 1955 had come suddenly. In the early morning hours of September 24, 1955, while he and Mamie were vacationing in Denver, Mamie heard her husband stirring and making sounds and assumed that he was having a dream. She called out to him, and he replied that he was all right. But a few minutes later he appeared at her bedroom door (they were sleeping in separate bedrooms during their stay with Mamie's mother) and said, "Mamie, I am having pain in the lower part of my chest." She told him it was probably the indigestion he had complained of earlier, after twenty-six holes of golf and a lunch consisting of a huge hamburger topped off with a slice of Bermuda onion. She gave him a spoonful of Milk of Magnesia. After he returned to bed, Mamie called Major General Howard McC. Snyder, Eisenhower's personal physician since 1946. Snyder arrived at 3:00 A.M. to find the President writhing in pain. The doctor administered amyl nitrate and injected morphine, papaverine, and heparin, and then, for some inexplicable reason, allowed the President of the United States to drift off to sleep for another seven hours. About noon Snyder called the physicians at Fitzsimons General (the nearby army hospital) and shortly thereafter its cardiologist was dispatched to Mrs. Doud's house to see the President. His diagnosis was a serious heart attack. He then arranged for Eisenhower to go by private automobile to the hospital. Snyder publicly announced soon thereafter that the President had suffered a heart attack.

It is clear from a study by his personal cardiologist at Walter Reed General Hospital, Dr. Thomas W. Mattingly, who also was summoned quickly to the scene, that Eisenhower's health was a much larger concern than anyone at the time knew, and in fact that the President and his personal physician were participating in what can only be termed a medical cover-up. General Snyder, in addition to his medical duties, was Eisenhower's friend and confidant. Their relationship had begun a decade earlier when Snyder had treated Mamie for pneumonia. Eisenhower himself had suffered from an assortment of apparently minor ailments that over the years ranged from his knee injury and bursitis in his shoulder to a ringing in the left ear, high blood pressure, chronic susceptibility to colds, and "alarming abdominal disturbances." The latter, after diagnostic efforts over three decades, was finally diagnosed as Crohn's disease, which causes rough food to lodge at the place where the small and large intestine join: it was finally treated surgically in the summer of 1956. A more serious problem was Ike's cardiovascular difficulties, including a blood pressure that tended to go up and down with his temper. His driving ambition and personality, burdens of public service, enjoyment of before-dinner scotches, and, until 1949, his habit of smoking four packs of cigarettes a day, all made Ike a prime candidate for serious health problems.

The heart attack in Denver, generally believed to have been Ike's first, was, as mentioned, probably his third, so evidence now shows. The first had been the cause of the episode in 1949 in the Washington hotel, during Eisenhower's struggle with the Pentagon chiefs to unify the armed forces and produce a cold-war budget. Years later Eisenhower described that episode as a state of "collapse" in which he "was on the edge of a precipice and teetering a bit." Snyder, desiring to maintain his famous patient's viability as a presidential candidate, had reported the incident as a digestive problem. Nearly two months of recuperation, first at President Truman's retreat in Key West and then at the Augusta National, and therapy that included quitting smoking—he never smoked again—restored him. The second, a minor heart attack, said Mattingly, probably came in 1953, the night before his "cross of iron" speech on April 16 to American Society of Newspaper Editors, which Dr. Snyder reported publicly as a "slight attack of food poisoning." (The President later described it as an attack with pain and chills and did not mention food poisoning.)

Therefore the heart attack of 1955, during the presidency, was a serious matter indeed. Dr. Snyder knew it, brought in Mattingly and the nation's leading heart specialist, Dr. Paul Dudley White, and from that moment on monitored and recorded Eisenhower's every vital sign and physical activity: pulse, blood pressure, colds, stomach upsets, golf scores, fishing trips, disputes with Mamie, medications—nothing was too trivial for Snyder's journal. Accordingly, from September 1955 on, the President, already surrounded by family, friends, and assistants, was potentially if not actually a captive of his health and he knew it. Snyder counseled him to "curb his emotional reactions . . . limit his work hours to those in which he is mentally alert and never allow himself to become fatigued or mentally weary." But the very thought of such a life depressed Eisenhower, who did his best to avoid the subject and, despite Snyder's irritation with him, gradually returned to his regimen of administrative duties and daily golf.

In any event, the heart attack brought Eisenhower's political future to the fore. Earlier he had confided to an aide that he did not expect to run in 1956 unless there was some international emergency. After the attack, paradoxically, he had second thoughts. His brush with death gave him a new appreciation of life and his public service. He was pleased with what he had accomplished in his first term. The old ambition returned. In February 1956, White told the press (despite private misgivings and protests from Mattingly) that Ike could lead an active life for from five to ten more years. This was long enough for Ike. He did not believe the Republican party was yet progressive enough. The thinking of the "reactionary fringe," he said, "was completely uncoordinated with the times in which we live." They considered labor a "mere item on cost sheets" and believed the United States "alone could live and prosper in a world gone communist." His goal, he explained to Dulles, was to be move the world toward peace and disarmament. He and Dulles, if he did not run for reelection and win, would be "succeeded by individuals of less experience, lesser prestige, and without ties of acquaintanceships and even friendships" with other world leaders. Never once even alluding to his heart attacks, he announced for reelection on February 29, 1956.

The vice-presidential spot, it is now evident, had an importance that few people realized. Nixon, Eisenhower felt, "just hasn't grown." "People don't like him." Anxious nevertheless to encourage the young politician, he recommended that he take a cabinet post such as the secretaryship of commerce or defense, for administrative experience. The Vice President, he said, "should chart his own course." None of this did any good, for Nixon told Eisenhower he wanted to continue to be Vice President.

The year 1956, as it turned out, was an excellent one for the GOP, the high point of the Eisenhower presidency. The economy was strong, McCarthy had faded from the scene, Khrushchev—after the Geneva summit—gave a speech denouncing Stalin for crimes against the party. With the dawn of the television age, Eisenhower did not even have to go on the travel circuit in order to campaign effectively. Stevenson, his opponent for a second time, attempted to benefit from public discomfort with the arms race and radioactive fallout caused by nuclear testing. But Eisenhower pointed to his summit meeting at Geneva and American strength to deter aggression. He made five nationally televised speeches. With crises in Suez and Hungary in the days immediately preceding, the election revealed huge support for the American President. Thanks to a decision by Stevenson, perhaps even considering what was known at the time, a major blunder, the President's health never became an issue. The vote, another landslide for Ike, was 35,581,003 to 25,738,765, almost double the 6-million-vote margin of 1952 and the largest in history. The President received 53.7 percent of the popular vote and 457 electoral votes. Stevenson carried only seven states, all in the South. But Eisenhower added two southern states to the four he had carried in 1952, splintering apparently once and for all the southern stronghold of the Democrats. As mentioned above, he also increased his vote among blacks.

The key to victory may have been national prosperity, benefiting both Southern whites and Northern working men at the time. As the political scientist Samuel Lubell observed, "The New Deal generation, once so zealous to make America over, devotes its evenings to wrestling with mortgage payments and inculcating a respect for tradition and discipline in overly progressive children." White ethnic Americans, with the assistance of Veterans Administration and Federal Housing Administration loans, moved into the suburbs and "liked Ike."

While Eisenhower's priority of economic growth was well placed, moving the GOP away from its reputation as the party of the Great Depression continued to elude him. Even with his landslide victory he was unable to bring the Republican majorities in both houses of Congress that had accompanied his victory four years earlier. Control of Congress moved back into the hands of the Democrats—only the second time in history that a President won a second term without a majority in either house.

Eisenhower's policy of moderation, while restoring national strength, was insufficient in his second term to sway a majority of Americans to a more conservative stance and to ensure the Republicans a victory in the election of 1960. Eisenhower, everyone knew, was already a lame duck, for he was the first President to fall under the provisions of the Twenty-second Amendment, prohibiting a third term. Southern Democrats had declared war against the civil rights program, and *Sputnik* had provided grist for the avid cold warriors. Finally, Eisenhower's health became a concern, and a scandal involving White House chief of Staff Sherman Adams became an issue, both surfacing inconveniently close to the congressional election of 1958.

What remains unclear at this writing is what effect Eisenhower's cardiovascular condition and the physical debility resulting from it had upon such intangibles as levels of energy and clarity of thought. In other words, could his condition have stifled initiatives that a more robust President might have taken? The incident that brought Eisenhower's health to the fore occurred on November 25, 1957, probably resulting from clotting material—an embolus—that had broken loose from his damaged heart. Eisenhower's secretary, Ann Whitman, found the President sitting at his desk confused and apparently unable to read. When he tried to talk he was incoherent. She immediately called Goodpaster and gave him a note on which she had written "something terrible has happened." The two called General Snyder who realized that the President had suffered a stroke. It was, as it turned out, a slight one, with no permanent damage. "Physically, I have no defects," he told legislative leaders who came to visit him a few days later, "but I don't seem to be articulate. I get the wrong words." He returned to work on December 2 and shortly thereafter flew to Europe to attend a NATO conference. But thereafter his personal staff never knew what might happen. Dr. Snyder stepped up his surveillance, and Eisenhower became ever more attentive to his ailments, even something of a hypochondriac.

Meanwhile, White House chief of staff Adams's brusque manner and the popular misconceptions about his actual authority in the White House had antagonized many in Washington. Information reached the press that the chief of staff had accepted gifts from a New England industrialist at a time in which the latter was being investigated by the Securities and Exchange Commission. No evidence ever surfaced that Adams exchanged favors for the gifts (which included hotel payments and a vicuna coat) but the appearance (and publicity) was sufficiently bad that congressional Republicans determined that Adams was hurting the party, and their chances for re-election. Eisenhower had included Adams on his lists of possible successors. Indeed, the chief of staff was often the first name listed. Eisenhower considered loyalty a prime virtue and attempted to hold the press and senators at bay, but finally, as part of his attempt to break the siege of the White House, he asked his assistant to resign. It was a severe blow.

Nothing Eisenhower did seemed enough. In 1960 he was unable to pass his legacy on to the Republican candidate, his own Vice President. Still, the election was close, so close in fact that historians have tried without much success to say what caused Nixon's defeat. There was the Kennedy charm and wit, the driving cadence of his Harvard accent. Television had become a force in politics, and Kennedy and his wife were wonderfully photogenic people. The Democratic candidate's managers were able to set up a series of televised debates that showed him to advantage and increased the turnout of first-time voters, who cast ballots for Kennedy.

The President attributed Nixon's defeat largely to the *Sputnik* hysteria, and his intuition was no doubt close to the mark. He later recalled that he needed fifteen years to convince people that the Soviets were not ahead, that American security was not in jeopardy, but only had three. Underlying it, he believed, was the selfishness of businessmen. Khrushchev had precipitated the crisis atmosphere, after the Paris summit even saying that he might prefer to deal with the next U.S. government. He then traveled to the UN to meet with Third World leaders, including Nasser and Castro. Events in the Congo, where the Soviet leader threatened intervention, and his support for the anti-American Cuba, made it appear that the Russians were pushing everywhere, that GOP claims of having contained the Soviets and kept the peace were false. Perhaps more important was a domestic issue, the national economy. A recession had occurred in part because of Eisenhower's efforts to reduce inflation and the postwar era's first imbalance of international payments.

Public misunderstanding of the relationship between Eisenhower and Nixon was another factor. In 1952, observers had doubted Eisenhower's support for Nixon, and information had leaked that Eisenhower, as mentioned, had wanted someone else on the ticket in 1956. Furthermore, reporters incorrectly interpreted Eisenhower's response to a question about the decisions Nixon had participated in as meaning he felt the Vice President was incompetent: when asked to name key decisions that Nixon as an individual had helped make, Eisenhower, who never shared decision-making responsibility, responded honestly, "give me some time and I may think of some." This, of course, became grist for the Democrat's campaign propaganda mills.

Finally, there was Nixon's decision, in hindsight regrettable, to distance himself from the President who so many believed had allowed the nation to fall behind in the "space race" and the "missile gap," who had, they thought, put fiscal prudence ahead of national security.

Ike at first did not campaign for Nixon, merely supporting the candidate behind the scenes, helping raise money, and seeing him off at the airport. He gave a few speeches that were described as nonpartisan. When the election appeared to be a close one, he gave addresses in Philadelphia, Pittsburgh, Cleveland, and New York—where he received a huge ticker-tape parade. Rockefeller credited Eisenhower for a surge of 400,000 votes for the GOP in his state. In retrospect, it seems that Nixon might have won had he been able to bring the President into the campaign earlier.

Only a handful of people knew the factor that had prevented this, the President's health. Even participating in moderate campaign activities in October caused Ike's blood pressure to rise and his heart to beat irregularly. Dr. Snyder and Mamie began to worry, and Nixon thoughtfully asked Eisenhower not to make a planned trip to parts of Illinois, Michigan, and back to New York. Considering Eisenhower's popularity, even at the end, and the closeness of the election, this concern for Ike's health may have been decisive in the election's outcome.

The election of 1960 was one of the closest in American history. Kennedy won by just under 119,000 of 69 million votes cast, or 49.7 percent to Nixon's 49.5 percent. The electoral college voted 303 to 219. The Democrats continued with large majorities in both houses.

The news of his party's defeat disturbed the President. On the morning after the election, Dr. Snyder recorded that when the President got up, "he told Mamie that there was only one other occasion in his life when he felt that life was not worth living, and that was the occasion when it was determined that he could not play football any more because of his injured knee." He felt he has been "hit in the solar plexus with a ball bat."

Here it is perhaps important to note in retrospect and in Eisenhower's behalf that the United States by 1961 had the ability to do a great deal more in pursuit of its interests than ever before. Eisenhower had maintained his power as President better than his predecessor, Harry Truman, and better than his successors. It also was satisfying for him to know that had the Constitution allowed a third term, he probably would have been reelected, his personal popularity rating, after all, had averaged 66 percent, and in early 1961 a Gallup poll still registered confidence in him at 59 percent. So well had Eisenhower articulated and conveyed his global strategy that not even John F. Kennedy, his most strident critic, desired a change in its direction, merely insisting that it was insufficiently bold and vigorous. The new President, who Eisenhower considered to have "no idea of the complexity of the job," in fact had little mandate at all. In Richard Nixon, the Republicans, although beginning to lean further toward the right with Goldwater, had in 1960 and eight years later, thanks in large measure to Ike's tutelage, a moderate standard bearer at a time when the Democrats increasingly were split into Southern and Northern branches—liberal versus conservative by religion, attitudes toward race, and federal social programs.

As President, Eisenhower, probably to a fault, had honored Conner's dictum, always to take one's job seriously, never oneself. In late November 1960, he worked with his speech writers on his farewell address. On the evening of January 17, 1961, having sent his State of the Union speech to be entered in the *Congressional Record,* he instead made a televised farewell speech to the American people. He warned against communism, the "hostile ideology—global in scope, atheistic in character, ruthless in purpose, and insidious in method." But he also warned against materialism, the urge to live for today, and against the "unwarranted influence, whether sought or unsought by the military-industrial complex." More important than the threat of communism, he said, were the dangers at home that scientific research would fall under the domination of the federal government and public policy would become captive to a scientific-technological elite. This final speech, as he hoped, would be the best-remembered of the Eisenhower presidency.

CHAPTER SIX

Retirement

Ike and Mamie felt strange as they left the White House on January 20, 1961. It was a cold, wintry day as he drove his own automobile through the iron White House gates, then out by the Catoctin Mountains, the location of Camp David, and finally on to Gettysburg, Pennsylvania, away from the pressure for the first time in twenty years, away from the responsibility he, the oldest man ever to have been President, had left to his successor, the youngest man ever to be elected President (whom Ike called in jest, "little boy blue.") The loss was palpable, but now, finally he could turn to such things as growing hay and barley, raising black Angus cattle—commonplace activities of the rural Pennsylvania that he and Mamie had talked about living in for so long. Still, he was aware that the nation and the way of life he so loved were passing into hands much, much less capable. The new President had been a PT-boat skipper in the Pacific (and not an entirely successful one at that, his boat having been run over by a Japanese destroyer) when he, Eisenhower, had been directing all Western forces to victory against Hitler's Germany. As he stopped at the gate to the Gettysburg farm, getting out into the snow to open it, he realized that retirement in the true sense would not be possible. There would be telephone calls and correspondence to answer, books and articles to write, and trips to make from time to time back to Washington. The pace and choice of activities, he hoped, would at least be of his own making—certainly there now would now be more time to spend with his friends and grandchildren.

Quickly, however, the general, as he liked to be known, in retirement had become a national resource. From everywhere, it seemed, came requests that he do, say, or at least think about something. Republicans sought him for fund-raisers, presidential candidates for advice and support, Boy Scouts for his photograph, tourists for his autograph, archivists and historians for permission to organize and publish his papers, and CBS for his help in the production of televised documentaries about his career. In the single month of October 1961 he turned down "212 urgent requests for some kind of service or help" and was "holding at least 25 for possible restudy." Something, he wrote, "is going to bust around here pretty soon." In the year 1966 he calculated that he received 60,789 letters and postcards and more than a thousand telegrams.

During retirement he did manage to play a great deal of golf, but in the end things did not go as he had hoped, for he could not escape national affairs in Gettysburg any more than he had been able to thirteen years earlier in Morningside Heights, this despite his now uncertain (and soon to be failing) health. He served as an unofficial adviser to the two Democratic Presidents who followed him in office during the difficult times from the early 1960s until he was incapacitated in 1968. He occupied himself with writing and did his best to remain abreast of public affairs. He worried and pondered as the programs of Kennedy and then Johnson failed to head off what became for the United States the most disastrous foreign intervention, triggering the worst domestic unrest, of the century, the Vietnam War. In the process he displayed again, to those observers in a position to know, his great advantage over his successors in his preparation for and understanding of the responsibilities of being the chief executive. And while he knew how little power he now had to influence events, ever the patriot, he never refused to give his advice when asked.

For four full years he kept an active, even tiring schedule but at last, in the autumn of 1965, came another heart attack and other problems as well. In 1968 he was forced to move to Walter Reed General Hospital in Washington, where from his room he watched as Nixon was finally elected President, this time on his own platform of national unity and a "secret plan" for a U.S. withdrawal with honor from South Vietnam.

To live among the hills and fields of southeastern Pennsylvania, next to one of the nation's most historic battlefields, had been a dream of Ike's since he and his friend George Allen first had seen an attractive farm near Gettysburg in 1948. Pennsylvania was the state from whence his father's family had set out for Kansas in the 1870s, so it was something of a return when he and Mamie moved into a new, large, colonial-style, farmhouse (the original house on the farm property, made of logs, was uninhabitable) close to the place where Confederate General Robert E. Lee had ordered General George E. Pickett to send ten thousand men against the impregnable Union positions of General George G. Meade's troops on July 3, 1963. Here the retired general-statesman could immerse himself in the past and write his memoirs, three volumes in all. There were barbecues in the yard just beyond the enclosed back porch, and he enjoyed taking visitors on battlefield tours. Field Marshall Sir Bernard L. Montgomery arrived for a visit. Having lost none of his egotism, Montgomery signed the guest register "Field Marshal Montgomery of Alamein." Best of all, however, Eisenhower could be with his friends from the former years with whom he often had golfed, including, besides Allen: George Humphrey, Barry Leithead, Ellis "Slats" Slater, William Robinson, Freeman Gosden, George Love, and Robert Woodruff. To them he insisted now on his right to be called, "Ike."

He also found ways to enjoy some private activities at the Gettysburg farm, playing bridge games with intimates, recourse once again to his beloved paints and easel, the visits of friends, and enjoying the nearby residence of his son John and family. In a small office at Gettysburg College he worked on two large volumes of White House memoirs entitled *Mandate for Change* and *Waging Peace*, which were published two and four years after he left the presidency. He then undertook a more personal autobiography, of which he published a delightful first portion, under the name *At Ease*, in 1967.

Nationally and internationally, of course, the 1960s were a decade of turmoil. By voting for Kennedy rather than Nixon the nation had rejected Eisenhower's more deliberate approach, at least it soon appeared that way. The new President had charged that Eisenhower had been behind the times on domestic reform and weak in foreign policy. Then, with Kennedy's death in 1963, Lyndon B. Johnson became President and, using the outpouring of grief and outrage, persuaded Congress to pass his predecessor's New Frontier program and also his own more sweeping "war against poverty," the so-called Great Society. To most of these and other Democratic domestic policies, Eisenhower was opposed.

Calling himself a "progressive conservative," Ike became chairman of two organizations dedicated to furthering human freedom and democracy: the Freedom's Foundation of Valley Forge, and the People-to-People Organization of Kansas City. Working with his brother Milton he also set up the Republican Critical Issues Council. He asked Hauge, Burns, Admiral Arleigh Burke, General Lauris Norstad, Robert B. Anderson, Lewis Strauss, James Mitchell, and Marion Folsom to work for a platform and nominee "of the character that would carry forward the basic purposes and principles which I applied between 1953–1960."

His principal political activity during these years of "retirement," as it turned out, may have been encouraging and advising his former Vice President. Eisenhower believed his young associate had come along nicely under his tutelage and decided that Nixon would carry on what he had started. Indeed, after the 1960 election he treated him like a son. Nixon, he said, should maintain contacts with potential political benefactors. He counseled that "a word of thanks can change an intermittent supporter to a permanent one." He invited him to play golf, outings that were a tonic to both men. After one rained-out game, Nixon wrote that he had had a wonderful time nonetheless and "there seems to be a great residue of political fever left in me." Eisenhower encouraged Nixon to run for governor of California in 1962. When reports that Eisenhower was lukewarm about Nixon's presidential ambitions appeared, he responded with a categorical denial. Nixon, he said, was a man for whom he had "the highest personal and official regard" and was one of the "best informed, most capable and most industrious vice presidents in the history of the United States." Considering the ambiguities of their relationship in 1952 and 1956, this was exactly what Nixon needed Ike to say.

Eisenhower's first concern about U.S. foreign policy was Cuba. His hostility to Castro's government, which he saw as part of the Sino-Soviet bloc, helped bring the debacle at the Bay of Pigs in which 1,300 U.S.-trained Cuban exiles went ashore without air cover and were promptly killed or captured. Eisenhower had ordered the CIA to plan a covert undertaking of some sort and told Kennedy that the best policy was to assist Cubans to replace the Castro regime with a "democratic government oriented toward the West and genuinely responsive to Cuba's needs." Open support of anti-Castro Cubans might be necessary. "We cannot let the present government there go on." These plans had not, however, progressed sufficiently to allow their implementation, so Eisenhower had no recommendation about them. Made with the CIA's urging (supported also by the Joint Chiefs), the young President's decision to go ahead brought a fiasco.

The way in which the Bay of Pigs invasion had been managed confirmed the former President's misgivings about Kennedy. Called to Camp David for a briefing, he listened as Kennedy revealed gaps in intelligence and errors in "ship loading, timing, and tactics." Cuban air force T-33s had strafed the beach and sunk the ship carrying the exiles' communications and most of their ammunition. In a futile effort to conceal the hand of the United States, Kennedy refused carrier-based air support for the exiles who had already been dispatched. Fifteen or twenty U.S. jet fighters were over the beach and could have offered support, but, fearing international repercussions of overt assistance, the new administration's ambassador to the United Nations, Adlai Stevenson, persuaded the President to call off the attack. Kennedy seemed to know where he had gone wrong, but his predecessor was dismayed. He saw two major errors. Americans, Eisenhower said, "would never approve direct military intervention by their own forces, except under provocations against us so clear and so serious that everybody will understand the need for the move." As for the operation, "when you go into this kind of thing it must be a success." The Bay of Pigs was a "profile in timidity and indecision," a barbed allusion to the President Kennedy's book, *Profiles in Courage*.

It might possibly be said that Eisenhower had led his youthful successor into the Cuban fiasco. There was some truth in this accusation, often heard at the time and later, for it was true that the training of exiles occurred during the Eisenhower administration, along with an incestuous organizational set up in which the agency that recommended the operation, the CIA, received the orders to carry it out. Yet the decision to invade was Kennedy's. Documents that reveal Eisenhower's thinking make it clear that the general-President had wanted the Castro regime out but also knew that the necessary conditions for a successful coup—including, in addition to an invasion, a strong government in exile, disaffection among the Cuban people, and a good chance that American participation in such an operation would remain secret—did not prevail when he left office. And of course by April 1961, they still did not.

In the months that followed the Bay of Pigs disaster, Kennedy told Eisenhower how much he admired him, explaining that he understood there would be "differences on some matters, especially on domestic issues." But, he said, he felt that in matters of national concern, especially foreign affairs, "we will see eye to eye."

Then, soon after learning that the Soviets had set up launchers in Cuba for medium- and intermediate-range nuclear missiles, Kennedy again sought Eisenhower's advice, using CIA director John McCone as a liaison. On October 17, 1962, Eisenhower told McCone that any military action against Cuba short of the invasion and occupation of the island would be inconclusive—a surprise attack would be good militarily but not politically. Action should be based on knowledge that only the President had of "war plans" and "the most recent diplomatic exchanges with Castro, Khrushchev, and our allies." He went on to advise "a blockade, intense surveillance, and announcing the intention of taking military action" (both air strikes and an invasion) if the Soviets and Cubans refused to remove the launchers. On the morning of October 22, Kennedy called Eisenhower to say he had decided on the blockade. The general reiterated that air strikes alone would be "detrimental" and spoke again of the need for "communications" with the adversary and of the possibility of invasion. The President, it turned out, working with his other advisers, had taken Ike's advice.

Eisenhower saw little cause for celebration when a much-relieved Kennedy, days later, told him that Khrushchev—as a result of an American military buildup, presentations at the UN, and a naval "quarantine"—had agreed to a withdrawal in exchange for an American agreement never to invade Cuba. Eisenhower worried that the President had given up freedom of action. He was not in favor of any promise that would imply anything "more than we actually meant." If Castro should attack the American military base at Guantanamo Bay or send agents to Latin American countries, it might still be necessary for U.S. forces to occupy the island. The United States should "by all means hold the initiative that it had finally seized when it established the blockade."

Eisenhower doubted Kennedy's resolve. In private he quipped that a White House attitude again brought to mind Fox Conner's admonition, "Always take your job seriously, never yourself." These people are just the reverse, he opined. "Take yourself seriously, and to hell with the job." Kennedy sensed the disdain. Robert F. Kennedy recalled that his brother felt (accurately) that Eisenhower was unhappy "that he was so young and that he was elected President."

And there were other worries. Eisenhower had begun negotiations for a nuclear test-ban treaty but was suspicious when in 1963 Khrushchev agreed to a ban on atmospheric nuclear tests. He feared Kremlin intentions, perhaps a plot to keep the People's Republic of China from obtaining nuclear weapons or to place itself ahead of the United States in the arms race by developing an antimissile system. He worried about the difficulties of withdrawing from such an agreement, and he feared a possible linkage between the test-ban treaty and "other issues like Cuba, Laos, and Vietnam where the U.S. would continue to push."

News of Kennedy's assassination reached Eisenhower in New York City, and he immediately canceled his appointments and went to Washington to meet with the new President, Lyndon Baines Johnson. The two former partners in much of the legislation of the 1950s talked about the nation's future. The former President recommended a short speech to a joint session of Congress. The American people, he said, must be reminded about national strength and mobilize "to increase the spiritual, intellectual, and material resources of the nation and to advance her prestige and her capacity for leadership in the world for peace." He recommended government and business cooperation to achieve economic expansion, a tax cut, and a budget for 1965 not in excess of that for 1964. Above all, the new President should be sure to assemble a good staff. Eisenhower recommended his friend, former Secretary of the Treasury Robert B. Anderson, as a good adviser on international finance. Former Special Assistant for National Security

Affairs Gordon Gray and former Staff Secretary Goodpaster, he said, would be excellent appointees because of their "thoroughly studied analyses of important international factors." Recalling the meeting Johnson said, "I was deeply moved that the former President should go into such specific detail and give me his recommendations and his support." Eisenhower, he said, was "a source of solid encouragement and strength." Johnson arranged for Goodpaster to brief Eisenhower regularly on national security problems.

Two days later, Ike and Mamie shared an automobile with former President Truman and his daughter Margaret in attendance at the Kennedy funeral. Afterward the Eisenhowers stopped at Blair House for a visit, and it was there that the two former Presidents, opponents for over a decade, finally buried the hatchet. They were to remain friends for the few years of life that both had left.

Eisenhower turned down President Johnson's invitation to attend his inauguration in 1965, explaining that he and Mamie would be in California and that Mamie did not like to travel by airplane. Kennedy's successor, victor in the presidential election against Goldwater, said he was sorry and hoped Eisenhower would "give him benefit of his advice, counsel" and added, prophetically, that "if he got his tail in a crack, he would come running."

Like Kennedy, the new President had no desire to let it be known that he was open to Eisenhower's advice. He did bring the former President's friend Robert Anderson into his administration, and the latter became for Ike another channel of informal communication. Johnson, Anderson reported, knew "a lot of his votes were votes 'against' Goldwater and not 'for' him." Anytime Eisenhower had advice, Anderson said, Johnson "would be happy to receive it." The President, he said, was a vain man and wanted to go down in history as one who had done the best he could for his country.

Not surprisingly, most of the advice Johnson sought from Eisenhower concerned national security. The result, unhappily, served neither the President nor the nation. In outlook the two men were far apart. On the one side was the ebullient Texan, long a seeker of national power, who at last, almost through a fluke, had achieved it. Kennedy had invited Johnson on the ticket in 1960 so that he, Kennedy, could get the nomination on the first ballot by sewing up the large Texas delegation and the Southern Democratic vote. Johnson surely did not think that he was about to crown his notable Senate career with the presidency of the United States. Then, when assassination brought the great prize, he found the holding of national power exhilarating, and he did his best to push through the (domestic) legislation he had long sought. On the other side of the political fence stood Eisenhower, who also had possessed a program, a series of hopes and purposes quite removed from the New Deal–Fair Deal, now called the Great Society. The former President gradually became more active, supporting appropriations for mutual security, actions to correct the adverse international balance of payments, and a program to inform the world of American purposes and values. He sent a letter to General DeGaulle encouraging him to keep France within NATO. At one point he told Johnson that he was "flatly opposed to many of the things that he had succeeded in having enacted into law" and was "philosophically opposed to the level of expenditures we now have."

Johnson sought Ike's help most often concerning U.S. policy in Southeast Asia. Eisenhower, however, was already beginning to doubt American capacity to influence events in Vietnam. He had opposed Kennedy's decision to increase the number of American "advisers" in South Vietnam beyond the current level of one thousand because he was not prepared to recommend that the United States commit sufficient resources to actually win the war. The problem in the southern half of Vietnam was how to establish a stable, independent, noncommunist regime in the face of corruption and police oppression by the current government and terrorist attacks aimed a village leaders by the northern-supported Vietnamese Communists (Viet Cong). When the U.S.-backed South Vietnamese President, Ngo Dinh Diem, died in a U.S.-condoned coup in 1963,

Eisenhower expressed dismay that Americans would have approved the "cold-blooded killing of a man who had, after all,
shown great courage when he undertook the task some years
ago [1954] of defeating communist attempts to take over his
country." When, in February 1965, the Viet Cong mortared
the flight line at the Marine helicopter base in Pleiku, killing
nine Americans and demolishing five U.S. aircraft, the President asked for Ike's advice. On February 16 the five-star general flew from California to New York, where, to divert public
attention from his trip's real purpose, he met with his son John
and Goodpaster. The next morning he made his way incon-
spicuously to Washington and the White House for a meeting
with the President and his advisers, Secretary of Defense Robert S. McNamara, National Security Adviser McGeorge Bundy,
and Chairman of the Joint Chiefs of Staff General Earle G.
Wheeler.

In the fashion of a professor leading a seminar of graduate
students, the former President evoked lessons from Clausewitz,
Napoleon, and the American Civil War. Eisenhower believed
that not just Vietnam but other countries like Cambodia, Thailand, the Philippines, and Indonesia were threatened by a
militant communism supported by the Soviet Union and the
People's Republic of China. The object, he said, was to prevent the fall of all of Southeast Asia (to communism) by sending adequate assistance, including the necessary military force,
to ensure the region's political and economic stability and good
morale in South Vietnam. The latter factor he said, quoting
Napoleon, was to the "material element in war as three is to
one," only he rated it "higher even than that," especially in a
guerilla war like the one in Vietnam (here he cited Confederate operations in northern Virginia during the Civil War). The
enemy could be successful only as long as he had support of
the population. "People must want to be saved; otherwise nothing can be done." Air strikes, he said, could not stop the infiltration of the communists, from Ho Chi Minh's regime north
of the seventeenth parallel, into rural areas of South Vietnam,
but they could raise morale in the South and hurt it in the

North. The United States should launch them in direct response to the murders of village chiefs in the South. Meanwhile the United States needed to find a Vietnamese leader.
He counseled against negotiation from a point of weakness or
a settlement that would not be verifiable. Ike praised the
Tonkin Gulf resolution, which Congress had passed in August
1964 after a torpedo-boat attack on U.S. destroyers off the coast
of North Vietnam, and which authorized the President to use
"all necessary measures" to counter North Vietnamese aggression. Based on his Formosa Resolution of 1955, Ike felt that
the Tonkin Gulf Resolution provided the President the necessary "discretion and flexibility." In response to Johnson's questions about how to handle an enemy escalation of the war (and
relying upon similar lessons learned in the Korean conflict)
Eisenhower urged the decentralization (meaning leeway to
the U.S. commander in South Vietnam) and unity of command. The President should "back a commander and trust
him," defining his mission broadly. "Once we had committed
ourselves to the war [in Korea]," he said, "he had advised Mr.
Truman that we must use whatever force was needed." Responding to the hypothetical situation, he said that he would
warn the Chinese and then use six to eight divisions if necessary. The United States must be resolute. Letting the enemy
believe that we would go just so far and no further, he said,
would be "the beginning of the end." Prestige was involved.
"Indonesia is now failing. We cannot let the Indo-Chinese peninsula go."

General Wheeler assured Eisenhower that he agreed, and
Johnson did, too. On July 2, the morning that the President
prepared to send U.S. ground forces into South Vietnam,
Eisenhower spoke with him by telephone, expressing agreement. Ground troops were needed, he said, to protect air bases,
but he cautioned that once appealed to, force had to be all-
out. "Do what you have to do to win."

Communication between the former and the current President during the period after the Pleiku incident reveals that
the latter accepted the former's support and was willing to use

force. But Johnson seemed not to hear the advice about circumstances and methods. Eisenhower soon came to see that the two were talking past each other. Goodpaster, serving as Eisenhower's liaison, thought Johnson lacked resolve. He would seem to "appreciate what Eisenhower suggested and he [Johnson] wanted to do it. But then, as he started down the road he would hedge, temper, curtail, and the action would lose its impact." The advice seemed to bring "war within LBJ himself in what he was trying to do. The necessary degree of decisiveness was too much for him." The buildup of U.S. military force in Vietnam went on slowly, not quickly and with resolve as Ike had proposed, and was matched step by step by the enemy; it never was sufficient to beat the North Vietnamese.

In June 1966, seeing stalemate in the situation in Vietnam, the condition that all his professional life he had sought to avoid, Eisenhower began to talk about the United States' disengagement. Johnson, increasingly frustrated, had mentioned the possibility of using the same way out of Vietnam that Eisenhower had used in Korea, alluding to threats to use nuclear weapons. Eisenhower pointed out that the contrast between 1953 and 1965 in numbers of nuclear weapons available to both sides was glaring—no two military or political situations were the same.

By mid-1967, harkening to 1953 in a different sense, Eisenhower turned his attention to the increasing problem of national disunity. His conversations with Goodpaster now concerned racial unrest, urban riots, unemployment, and a lack of education among blacks in America. Peeved at first and then philosophical about an anti–Vietnam War movement that brought a march on the Pentagon, he admitted that perhaps it was better to have these problems out in the open "rather than festering and building up explosive suppressed resentment."

The Tet offensive of January 1968 was the turning point of the Vietnam War. During the Buddhist lunar holiday, the Viet

Cong launched a simultaneous attack on every provincial capital in South Vietnam. They even penetrated the American embassy compound in Saigon, this at a time when President Johnson had been saying that the American-backed South Vietnamese were winning the war. The Americans and their South Vietnamese allies quickly rallied, liberated the capitals, and decimated the Viet Cong (50,000 died). But is was too late. As a result of the surprising show of communist strength, Johnson decided not to seek reelection. This, combined with vastly destructive riots in dozens of the nation's urban ghettos and protests in the streets at the time of the Democratic national convention in Chicago, brought Nixon's election to the presidency on a platform of "peace with honor." In Eisenhower's view, Johnson's decisions gradually to escalate the conflict in Vietnam and then to withdraw from public service at the conflict's height was deplorable, revealing failure both of policy and leadership. Eisenhower even discussed turning the conflict over to the Vietnamese and SEATO nations, perhaps obtaining the diplomatic intervention of the Chinese. He favored this only if the plan were "constructive—not negative," and "fit the conditions of the day." He still held to his belief, in retrospect erroneous, that a strong United States could bring peace by causing the enemy to conclude he was paying too high a price. He took comfort in the fact that a man (Nixon) who had done an apprenticeship of sorts with him, upon whom he had pinned his hopes for the nation, would find a way to end the nation's involvement in the war.

In hindsight it is clear that Eisenhower erred about Vietnam. While his focus was on morale (both in the North and the South), the unconventional nature of the war, the geopolitical context, and the relationship of ends to means was correct, his premises about how they applied to the particular situation were not. He assumed that the South Vietnamese desired to be a free and independent people, that the North Vietnamese dictator Ho Chi Minh at some point would blanche at the American determination to prevent a communist unification of the nation, that U.S. bombing and finally the deployment of American ground troops would create a nation in the South, that the United States would retain its boldness and resolve. Another major mistake was to assume that Johnson, despite his lack of background in military matters, understood the principles of war. He believed that Johnson, as he himself most often had done, would make a decision based on careful and well-conceived strategy. Instead the President had engaged in a gradual escalation of the military involvement. He personally helped to choose the bombing targets and designated safe areas in the north but could do nothing about political corruption in and popular disaffection with the U.S.-backed South Vietnamese government.

Therefore, the last years of retirement revealed Eisenhower as a more pessimistic observer of the national and international scene. In cold war it seemed one could not trust even one's own people. And domestic politics "seem to create the same kind of hysteria as war."

Personally, the retired general-President enjoyed reminiscing, and he reflected on individuals who had provided him opportunity at times when he had thought there was none. They included Conner: "Always take your job . . ." And Marshall: "I can get many brilliant men to analyze and bring to me their problems; few will make their own decisions . . ." And Dulles: "The more ignorant a writer is of international facts the more harshly critical. . . ."

He traveled back to the beaches of Normandy to tape a CBS documentary, "D-day Plus Twenty," this time crossing the Channel on the *Queen Elizabeth*. Back at home on the Gettysburg farm he saw himself on the television screen along with the reporter Walter Cronkite walking through the cemetery where 9,000 American soldiers were buried. "The men in this cemetery were cut off in their prime," he watched himself say, "they were never allowed to fulfill themselves, to have and enjoy their families, to raise their children. That is the full measure of their sacrifice. These men of D-day gave us a chance. They bought time for us, so we could learn to do better than the generations did before. . . ."

And as always, during the final years there were the letters. A midshipman at Annapolis sought advice about a career. Eisenhower spoke of intangibles, of promotions if one "stands high in the estimates of his comrades," working for "wider influence for the good of the service and the nation." His greatest accomplishment, he wrote a former member of his administration, was to have been the leader of an administration "that for eight years preserved the peace without loss of life, territory or of any vital interest of the United States, during which the nation enjoyed real human progress and general prosperity at home." "The secret," he told Nixon, was "adequate and skillful organization."

Then his health began to decline. Most Americans knew he had physical problems but virtually no one besides Mamie, John, Dr. Snyder, and the specialists at Walter Reed knew the severity of his condition, that he in fact, as the saying goes, was "living on borrowed time." In the late spring and autumn he could be found at Augusta National in Georgia, and during winters at El Dorado, a club in Palm Desert, California. In the spring of 1965 while at Palm Desert he had mild congestive heart failure during an attack of asthma-like bronchitis. Nine months later at Augusta he developed chest pain, and doctors diagnosed another (fourth) heart attack. His health now turned sharply downward. He returned to California and to playing golf, but he soon found himself in bed with stomach distress and chest pains. On December 12, 1966, he had gall bladder surgery. The following spring, again in Palm Desert, after a painful journey over the mountains by railroad, there was more angina, respiratory infections, and, in February, another episode of congestive heart failure, followed two months later by yet another stroke. He returned to Gettysburg but on the way experienced abdominal pain. This problem, diagnosed as gastroenteritis, recurred in July, and in October he returned to the hospital. For a time in early 1968 he felt better, good enough in fact to play golf. But in April he suffered another heart attack and congestive failure.

His doctors flew him to Walter Reed on May 14, 1968. Again he recovered slightly; he was able to make a brief televised address from his hospital room to the Republican national convention. Withered and thin—a mere 125 pounds—he waved and smiled to well-wishers and photographers from his hospital window.

As the end neared, Nixon's victory in November brought satisfaction, and on closed-circuit television he enjoyed watching the marriage of his grandson David to the new President's daughter Julie. He greeted Nixon's newly appointed national security adviser, Henry Kissinger, and the cabinet appointees. He was heartened that his ideas seemed again to be in the center of national affairs. Perhaps politics finally had turned toward the progressive Republicanism he desired.

On March 28, 1969, he died.

CONCLUSION

An extraordinary if understandable cycle of interpretation has affected the appraisal of Eisenhower's career. The first articles and books appeared in the late 1950s and portrayed an inept and fumbling man in the White House, an interpretation that, with few exceptions, continued into the 1980s. According to these accounts Ike delegated responsibility to his staff and spent much if not most of his time on the golf course. These critics said this was not surprising. After all, he had remained an army major for sixteen years and never served with troops in battle. He became a hero of course, but this stemmed from a combination of factors, including the brilliance of his superior, General Marshall, the wartime productive capacity of the United States, his expansive personality, and wartime public relations. Fortunately, they asserted, the 1950s were a time unlike the preceding decades, when the President did not have to make important decisions. The American people in the 1950s—a period like an earlier postwar Republican era, that of Presidents Warren G. Harding and Calvin Coolidge—desired little leadership. Ike was their man. A ranking by seventy-five historians in 1961 placed Eisenhower twenty-second best out of thirty-one Presidents, between Chester A. Arthur and Andrew Johnson. According to newspaper caricatures of the time, Eisenhower was an amiable President whose lack of attention to detail was reflected in imprecise answers to reporters' questions. His appointments to the cabinet—"eleven millionaires and a plumber"—betrayed an infatuation with wealth and influence. Eisenhower considered the Tennessee Valley Authority to be a form of "creeping socialism," Chief Justice Warren's appointment to the Supreme Court his biggest mistake, and social security debilitating to the American people.

This initial estimate, it is now clear, was faulty and stemmed partly from the problem of writing contemporary history—an absence of information and perspective. Without access to the documents, pundits and historians wrote of a Republican administration, successor to that of the New Deal–Fair Deal, that was less helpful to ordinary Americans.

Another problem was Eisenhower's identity as a World War II military hero. Combining as they must the qualities of appeal and uniqueness, war heroes elicit both expectation and, because of an antimilitary bias extending back to the time of the American Revolution, when British red coats found themselves facing a hostile population, revulsion. George Washington, Andrew Jackson, and Zachary Taylor overcame the bias, but Americans recalled the less successful presidency of Ulysses S. Grant. And of course a new generation of Americans had reached voting age by the early 1960s. Young Americans, many college-educated, saw the world as sophisticated, abstract, and above all, modern. Eisenhower's prominence had originated in a war—the crusade of 1941–45 now past, its ways rendered obsolete. His scorn for the handsome Kennedy and dislike of rock music (the Beatles in particular) and abstract art represented the generation that had seen two world wars and the Great Depression, who enjoyed Lawrence Welk's polkas and Grandma Moses's American primitive style of art.

The adverse criticism stemmed in part from deliberate myth and folklore that played upon the penchant of the American people (in this case with the cooperation of Ike's wartime publicist) for oversimplification, a love of stereotypes and controversy. Eisenhower's carefully crafted mask of command hid what few besides Conner, MacArthur, Marshall, and such advisers as Bedell Smith and Eisenhower's brother Milton knew about the former supreme commander. His wartime public relations manager, Captain Harry Butcher, portrayed Ike as a genial commander whose background and personality was that of his troops, "soldiers of democracy" who liked to fish, smoke, play cards, and read western novels. This was the General Ike of victory parades, his arms stretched above his head, waving through ticker tape and confetti, eyes radiating innocence. The actual Eisenhower—the teenaged boy who had studied Hannibal's battles, the young officer who had mastered Clausewitz, the ambitious young professional who graduated first in his class at the command and general staff college, the care-worn commander who scanned the North African wilderness near the Kasserine Pass at night just an hour before Rommel broke through—remained hidden.

Criticism also derived from contemporary politics, one of the risks Eisenhower accepted upon entering the partisan arena with his so-called middle way. Criticism came from both the left and the right, neither side desiring to truly understand who Eisenhower was or what he had done. The former included Democrats who had been unhappy because of his decision to run for President on the Republican ticket, and liberals who disliked his budget-balancing, states'-rights approach and his refusal to take strong public positions in support of civil rights. The latter, the conservatives of both parties, disagreed with his defense cuts, refusal to roll back New Deal reforms, and legislation to help African Americans (especially his intervention in Little Rock). The Democrats, generally remaining the majority party in Congress, sought an issue after their defeat in the 1956 presidential election. They found their issue the following year in space and military technology, traditionally an area of American cold-war dominance. In October 1957, *Sputnik* passed into orbit, and a severe economic recession was underway. In the months that followed, Khrushchev laid down an ultimatum on Berlin, Castro took over Cuba, and Soviet air defense forces shot down an American U-2 plane. Many Americans not surprisingly criticized Eisenhower's style and policies. Marquis Childs, a popular columnist, published a book entitled *Eisenhower: Captive Hero*, describing how the President had failed. The pundit drew upon information from such individuals as Emmett John Hughes, formerly of *Time-Life* and an Eisenhower speech writer, author of the 1952 speech promising to go to Korea. Hughes had broken from the administration and during the second term wrote *America the Vincible* and *The Ordeal of Power*, charging Eisenhower with failing to resolve conflicts with the Soviet Union. C. D. Jackson also provided derogatory appraisals. (Jackson was another individual from *Time-Life* and a White House expert on psychological warfare who had resigned after the United States failed to help Hungary during the Red Army's invasion in 1956.)

Finally, in the 1980s came the opening of new records and documents in which Eisenhower was more fully revealed. Clearly, there were some flaws. His unrelenting pace and the resulting toll on his health, especially after the 1955 heart attack, was a problem. In 1957 he confided to his diary that he had underestimated what a second term would "mean to me in the way of a continuous toll upon my strength, patience, and sense of humor." The stroke that year caused him to question his competence. Everything considered, his willingness to ignore his serious medical condition placed him and, considering the lack of a constitutional provision for presidential disability, the nation at risk.

As President, Eisenhower did not deal easily with reporters. The feisty Truman, critics recalled, always seemed relaxed and would "drop in" at the press room and ask for peanuts or join a poker game. The former supreme commander did not do this. Attracting attention wherever he went after his return from Europe in 1945, he believed reporters' desire for "sensation and a ready-made story" led them to "questions that are unseemly and undesirable." Such activity, he thought, brought "depreciation of prestige of the presidential office." His diffidence, as a result, sometimes led reporters to portray him as irresponsible or ignorant. At the first televised White House press conference on January 19, 1955, a live performance, his words tumbled out in fits and starts. He refused questions about the loyalty review program, and he said that he did not know about American troops on the Tachen Islands, then threatened by Chinese invasion. He was not aware of a statement that Dulles reportedly had made but nonetheless said he supported anything Dulles had said. This was, the evidence reveals, purposeful obfuscation. The reporters, not knowing this and looking, as always, for a story portrayed a President who was not fully in command.

Then there was the issue of political leadership in a democracy. As a man who had learned about politics as a military officer and commander and who gained his stature and success in large measure because of his character, innate good sense, diligence in administration, and popularity, it is probable that Eisenhower, though well versed in history, diplomacy, and world politics, lacked the sensitivity that he would have gained by rising through ward and county partisan politics, running for public office and suffering a defeat or two in the process. Among other things he would have learned that in domestic politics, public opinion, no matter how ill-informed, can make all the difference. There was in this sense an innocence about this man, a certain lack of guile that went hand in hand with his ambivalence, even distaste for politicians as a group. Often this served him well, putting him above the fray, and was part of his appeal, his mystique. On the other hand, his lack of the politician's instinct about the trouble that public perceptions, even when false, can bring, especially for a lame-duck President, probably blinded him to the domestic political dangers caused by *Sputnik*.

Finally, as Eisenhower readily admitted, during his administration the cold war increased in destructive potential and costs. A question remains here about the extent to which the general from Abilene was at fault. Critics were justified nonetheless, as they were a generation later during the Reagan years, when they pointed with dismay at the arms race, demanded a world-wide nuclear freeze, and called attention to the danger in relying for security on the fear of surprise nuclear attack. A peace that existed by, as one historian has written, "putting at risk what one was attempting to accomplish" (including tens of millions of one's fellow citizens) raised moral issues. Eisenhower struggled unsuccessfully with the Soviets to move away from this. A concomitant problem was Eisenhower's lack of success in addressing the self-seeking nature of the national security apparatus—the armed services, the CIA, the defense lobbyists, and Congress. Did his experience, the critics asked, create a tendency toward military solutions rather than conciliation and compromise? Adlai Stevenson, they speculated, would have found a better way.

But was there a better way? The American people in choosing Eisenhower twice elected a soldier whose outlook was less that of a warrior than a problem-solver and diplomat, an individual who believed world peace after 1945 would have to be a product of American strength and leadership. Recently, from the newly opened documents and the perspective of time, a more favorable appraisal of Eisenhower emerged. By the 1980s, huge defense spending, high taxes, and unbalanced budgets—Eisenhower's primary worries—had become serious issues. The nuclear arms race moved out of control in the Kennedy years, the result of both Kremlin risk-taking and Washington's decision to increase U.S. missile superiority. Although the assassination of Kennedy produced a martyr for liberal social programs and drove forward Johnson's Great Society, social reform came to a halt with the ill-fated escalation of the U.S. involvement in Vietnam. After Nixon actually increased the stakes in Vietnam, the Watergate scandal brought down his administration, forcing him to resign in shame. The brief administration of Gerald R. Ford and the one-term presidency of James E. Carter caused people to wonder how a U.S. President could be successful. The Reagan years, although extending to two terms, brought Defense Department purchasing scandals, a National Security Council staff that traded arms to Iran for hostages in Lebanon, and a federal deficit grown virtually out of control. In the midst of such problems,

Eisenhower's integrity, insistence on the constitutional separation of powers, three balanced budgets, and warnings about the defense lobby seemed wise, even prophetic.

Eisenhower's administrative method, it was possible to see, was more effective than those of his successors. He delegated authority, never forgetting Marshall's rule that nothing was more important than the "choice of those to be near you." Drawing on his experience as supreme commander, he reversed the practice of most politicians by creating mechanisms to generate good advice, giving credit to subordinates for accomplishments, and, when possible, personally taking the blame for failures. At cabinet meetings he required that reports be prepared in advance and played devil's advocate to ensure full discussion during their presentation. There were "awful fights in front of him," recalled his son, John, a staff member during the second term, but his method brought results.

Historians began to see that Eisenhower understood and moved with the rhythms of history. In the late 1950s, they now realized, his youthful successor had played upon, and for his purposes worked to stimulate, a popular conviction that Eisenhower and his staff had not been in control of events, that the American people lacked energy and were falling behind the Soviet Union in science and weapons. In his inaugural address, Kennedy called grandly for a post-Eisenhower generation to bear any burden necessary to the success of liberty in the world. Historians noticed that the new President failed to mention that he could say such things and receive support because the 1950s had inspired new laws for civil liberties and civil rights, showing a new idealism about what was possible. Indeed, the Republican President with his sunny face, plainspoken, self-effacing personality, and stewardship of American strength had evoked a new sense of possibilities. Senator Joseph R. McCarthy died discredited and an alcoholic. Civil rights leaders such as Martin Luther King, Jr., had ventured forth. "We shall overcome," they said. In the words of one observer, by the time Eisenhower left office Americans had a chance to "survive and perchance to prosper."

Ike's understanding of the nature of his time had much to do with the reappraisal of his contribution to U.S. history. The key circumstances, he knew, were the Red Army's presence in Eastern Europe, Soviet possession of nuclear-warhead-tipped missiles, and the specter of totalitarianism in control of the Eurasian land mass. As he said in 1955, "Truth, honor, justice, consideration for others, liberty for all—the problem is how to preserve them, nurture them, and keep the peace—if the last is possible—when we are opposed by people who scorn to give any validity whatsoever to those values." The American response to the dangers of the post–World War II world was to be strong and provide leadership. The thirty-fourth President of the United States had goals that were long-term and measured power in political, economic, spiritual, as well as military terms; they had everything to do with preserving a way of life. Most important, they were part of a "grand strategy for promoting national security." Eisenhower thus transformed Truman's arrangements for dealing with problems such as a Soviet empire with ambitions in Europe and communist Chinese power in Asia into a U.S. sponsored and supported free world. In constructing and maintaining this system the West— in part because of its superior industrial base and more profound understanding of human affairs, but also because of the quality of its American leadership—proved far more imaginative, dexterous, and resourceful than its Marxist-Leninist opponents. In the end, the result, albeit with many difficulties and large costs, was the collapse of the Soviet empire and then of the Soviet Union itself.

Surely, one must conclude, Eisenhower was correct both to worry about what history would say and to believe that historians some day would speak well of his stewardship of American power.

BIBLIOGRAPHICAL ESSAY

General and Interpretive

As indicated in the Preface, this book is the result of many months of research in the archives of the Eisenhower Library in Abilene, Kansas. Perhaps the best sources available in local libraries on Dwight David Eisenhower are his diary, Robert H. Ferrell, ed., *The Eisenhower Diaries* (New York: Norton, 1981); his last memoirs, Dwight D. Eisenhower, *At Ease: Stories I Tell to Friends* (New York: Doubleday, 1967); and a collection of letters to a childhood friend, Swede Hazlett, with whom he corresponded throughout his life, Robert Griffith, ed., *Ike's Letters to a Friend, 1941–1958* (Lawrence: University Press of Kansas, 1984). The most-interesting and best-illustrated short biography is by Michael R. Beschloss, *Eisenhower: A Centennial Life* (New York: HarperCollins, 1990). The most thorough analysis of his life is the two-volume biography by Stephen E. Ambrose, *Eisenhower: Soldier, General of the Army, President-Elect* (New York: Simon and Schuster, 1983) and *Eisenhower: The President* (New York: Simon and Schuster, 1984). Other sources essential to students of Eisenhower's life and presidency are his White House memoirs, Dwight D. Eisenhower, *Mandate for Change* (Garden City, N.Y.: Doubleday, 1963) and *Waging Peace* (Garden City, N.Y.: Doubleday, 1965); Alfred D. Chandler, Jr., and Louis Galambos, eds., *The Papers of Dwight D. Eisenhower* (Baltimore: Johns Hopkins University Press, 1970–); and the *Public Papers of the Presidents of the United States, Dwight D. Eisenhower*, in 8 vols. (Washington, D.C.: Government Printing Office, 1958–61). Of similar importance are books by Eisenhower's brother (and alter ego) Milton S. Eisenhower and son, John S. D. Eisenhower. The former published a memoir entitled *The President is Calling* (Garden City, N.Y.: Doubleday, 1974) and the latter published his recollections as assistant to the White House staff secretary in *Strictly Personal* (Garden City, N.Y.: Doubleday, 1974). Jean Edward Smith's *Lucius D. Clay: An American Life* (New York: Henry Holt and Company, 1990) is similarly valuable for the light it sheds on Eisenhower's decision to run for President and his management purposes and style. Steve Neal's *The Eisenhowers: Reluctant Dynasty* (Garden City, N.Y.: Doubleday, 1978) gives Ike's family and his Kansas heritage, and Chester J. Pach, Jr.'s complete rewrite of Elmo Richardson's *The Presidency of Dwight D. Eisenhower* (Lawrence, Kans.: University Press of Kansas, 1991) draws upon recent scholarship. Sympathetic treatments of the Eisenhower presidency are Herbert S. Parmet, *Eisenhower and the American Crusades* (New York: The Macmillan Company, 1972) and R. Alton Lee, *Dwight D. Eisenhower: Soldier and Statesman* (Chicago: Nelson–Hall, 1981). More critical are the detailed biography by Peter Lyon, *Eisenhower: Portrait of a Hero* (Boston: Little, Brown and Co., 1974) and the short one by Robert F. Burk entitled, *Dwight D. Eisenhower: Hero and Politician* (Boston: Twayne Publishers, 1986). Piers Brendon in *Ike: His Life and Times* (New York: Harper & Row, 1986) gives little credence to the favorable Eisenhower revisionism. Finally, the most complete bibliographical guide is *Dwight D. Eisenhower: A Bibliography of his Times and Presidency* (Wilmington, Del.: Scholarly Resources, 1991) by R. Alton Lee.

Chapter One: Early Years

The Abilene of Ike's childhood is accessible in Henry B. Jameson, *Heroes by the Dozen: Cattle Days to President Ike* (Abilene, Kansas: Shadinger-Wilson Printers, Inc., 1961) and Bela Kornitzer, *The Great American Heritage: The Story of the Five Eisenhower Brothers* (New York: Farrar, Strauss, 1955). The education of an army officer is discernible in Stephen E. Ambrose, *Duty, Honor, Country: A History of West Point* (Baltimore: Johns

Hopkins University Press, 1966) and in *Howitzer, 1915*, Year-book of the United States Military Academy. Perhaps the best single volume on the great Prussian philosopher of war is Michael Howard and Peter Paret, eds., *Carl von Clausewitz: On War* (Princeton: Princeton University Press, 1976). The background for Eisenhower's experience in the post–World War I U.S. Army and friendship with George Patton is in Martin Blumenson, *The Patton Papers*, vol. I (Boston: Houghton Mifflin Co., 1972) and Samuel P. Huntington, *The Soldier and the State: The Theory and Practice of Civil-Military Relations* (Cambridge, Mass.: Belknap Press, 1957). Dwight D. Eisenhower, "A Tank Discussion," *Infantry Journal* (November 1920) and "War Policies," *Cavalry Journal* (Nov./Dec. 1931) reveal his professional ideas. For Eisenhower in World War II and the years leading to it, one must read Kenneth C. Davis's masterful *Eisenhower: Soldier of Democracy* (Garden City, N.Y.: Doubleday, 1945), written after the author spent time at Eisenhower's headquarters in Europe: the Eisenhower library has a copy with marginalia in the general's handwriting. Harry C. Butcher, *My Three Years with Eisenhower* (New York: Simon and Schuster, 1946) is an almost day-to-day account containing numerous fascinating episodes. Finally, Forest C. Pogue, *George C. Marshall: Education of a General* (New York: The Viking Press, 1963), the first in his definitive four-volume biography of Marshall, and D. Clayton James, *The Years of MacArthur, vol. I, 1880–1941* (Boston: Houghton Mifflin Co., 1970), a similarly excellent multivolume biography of MacArthur, help to explain Eisenhower's quick rise to positions of high command despite his many years of schooling and staff duty in the peacetime army. See also William B. Pickett, "Eisenhower as Student of Clausewitz," *Military Review*, Vol. LXV (July 1985) for a summary of Ike's early years and education.

Chapter Two: War

The first echelon of books on Eisenhower and World War II include Dwight D. Eisenhower, *Crusade in Europe* (New York:

Doubleday, 1948), a best-selling memoir (still in print) that he wrote in 1948 after returning to civilian life but before undertaking his duties as president of Columbia University. Eisenhower's strategy is laid out most clearly by his former chief of staff, Walter Bedell Smith, in a book entitled *Eisenhower's Six Great Decisions: Europe 1944–1945* (New York: Longmans, Green, 1956). Two analyses of Eisenhower as supreme commander are by British writers, a scholar, E. K. G. Sixsmith, *Eisenhower as Military Commander* (New York: Stein and Day, 1972) and Ike's intelligence chief at supreme headquarters, Kenneth Strong, *Intelligence at the Top: The Recollections of a British Intelligence Officer* (Garden City, N.Y.: Doubleday, 1968). Another British scholar, John Keegan, in his book, *The Mask of Command* (New York: Penguin Books, 1987) has provided a useful way to think of Eisenhower, a commander who spanned two ages of warfare. A favorable view of Eisenhower's performance as supreme commander in Europe appears in a book by Martin Blumenson and James L. Stokesbury entitled, *Masters of the Art of Command* (Boston: Houghton Mifflin Co., 1975). Two excellent books are by Eisenhower's son, John S. D. Eisenhower, *Allies: Pearl Harbor to D-Day* (Garden City, N.Y.: Doubleday, 1982) and his grandson, David Eisenhower, *Eisenhower: At War, 1943–1945* (New York: Random House, 1986). See also the comprehensive book by Merle Miller, *Ike the Soldier: As They Knew Him* (New York: G. P. Putnam's Sons, 1987). American strategy in part as organized and implemented by Eisenhower is analyzed by Russell F. Weigley in his book entitled, *The American Way of War: A History of United States Military Strategy and Policy* (Bloomington: Indiana University Press, 1973).

Other valuable accounts include Stephen E. Ambrose, *The Supreme Commander: The War Years of General Dwight D. Eisenhower* (Garden City, N.Y.: Doubleday, 1970); Forrest C. Pogue, *The Supreme Command: The U.S. Army in World War II: The European Theater of Operations* (Washington, D.C.: Office of the Chief of Military History, Department of the Army, 1954); Forrest C.

Pogue, *George C. Marshall: Ordeal and Hope* (New York: Viking, 1966) and *George C. Marshall: Organizer of Victory, 1943–45* (New York: Viking, 1973); and, for the Normandy invasion, see Otto Friedrich, "Every Man was a Hero," *Time*, May 28, 1984. The best account of Eisenhower's leadership in the Normandy campaign is Carlo D'Este, *Decision in Normandy: The Unwritten Story of Montgomery and the Allied Campaign* (London: Collins, 1983) which reveals Montgomery's attempt to cover-up his failure to break out at Caen. See also John Keegan, *Six Armies in Normandy* (New York: Viking Press, 1982). On Eisenhower's favorite U.S. ground commander, Omar Bradley, see the latter's war memoir entitled *A Soldier's Story* (New York: Henry Holt, 1951) and the more reflective and complete book by Omar Bradley and Clay Blair, *A General's Life* (New York: Simon and Schuster, 1983). The President's activities as commander-in-chief appear in James MacGregor Burns, *Roosevelt: Soldier of Freedom* (New York: Harcourt, Brace, 1970) and Eric Larrabee, *Commander in Chief: Franklin Delano Roosevelt, His Lieutenants & Their War* (New York: Harper & Row, 1987). For the effect of the war on Eisenhower's marriage see John S. D. Eisenhower, ed., *Letters to Mamie* (Garden City, N.Y.: Doubleday, 1978). Kay Summersby, Ike's driver and aide in the European theater of operations, wrote a memoir entitled *Eisenhower Was My Boss* (New York: Prentice-Hall, 1948), which contains the recollections of a dedicated and appreciative assistant. For the Summersby issue one can peruse the book by Merle Miller, *Plain Speaking: An Oral Biography of Harry S. Truman* (New York: Berkeley Publishing Corporation, 1974) and Kay Summersby, *Past Forgetting: My Love Affair with Dwight D. Eisenhower* (New York: Simon and Schuster, 1976) which provided grist for the gossip mill. Countering them were the more persuasive accounts by Lester and Irene David, *Ike and Mamie* (New York: G. P. Putnam's Sons, 1981) and John S. D. Eisenhower, above, which reveal an abiding affection between Ike and Mamie. Miller retracted his earlier assertions about a love affair in his biography, *Ike the Soldier,* above. A summary of Summersby's letters from

Eisenhower, revealing only friendship, appeared in Sotheby's catalogue advertising the sale of the letters, "Dwight Eisenhower and Kay Summersby," *Fine Books and Manuscripts Including Important Americana* (New York June 13, 1991), items 161–200.

A good general account of the war with examples of the strategy and tactics of both sides is Keegan's *The Second World War* (New York: Penguin Books, 1989). Theodore Ropp's *War in the Modern World* (New York: Collier Books, 1962) is a standard analysis, containing statistics, context, and interpretation of strategies. A history of the German side and its difficulties despite a long tradition of excellence is T. N. Dupuy, *A Genius for War: The German Army and General Staff, 1807–1945* (Englewood Cliff, N.J.: Prentice-Hall, 1977). H. P. Willmott's *The Great Crusade: A New Complete History of the Second World War* (New York: The Free Press, 1989) is extremely valuable, especially in its treatment of the eastern front.

Chapter Three: The Road to the White House

Eisenhower's decision to enter politics came out of his critique of the Truman presidency and its handling of domestic and especially foreign policies. The best sources on Truman's domestic policy are the following: Robert H. Ferrell's, *Off the Record: The Private Papers of Harry S Truman* (New York: Harper and Row, 1980); and his *Harry S. Truman* (Boston: Little, Brown, 1983); Robert J. Donovan's, *Conflict and Crisis: The Presidency of Harry S Truman, 1945–1948* (New York: Norton, 1977), and his *Tumultuous Years: The Presidency of Harry S Truman, 1949–1953* (New York: Norton, 1982). The rise of the Republican party, with coverage of the Dewey campaign in 1948, appears in Henry Cabot Lodge, *The Storm Has Many Eyes: A Personal Narrative* (New York: Norton, 1973); Richard Norton Smith, *Thomas E. Dewey and His Times* (New York: Simon and Schuster, 1982); and James T. Patterson, *Mr. Republican: A Biography of Senator Robert A. Taft* (Boston: Houghton, Mifflin, 1972). An excellent little survey of the politics of the time is Gary W. Reichard, *Politics as Usual: The Age of Truman and Eisenhower* (Wheeling, Ill.: Harlan Davidson, Inc., 1988). Roger Morris, *Richard Milhous Nixon: Rise of An American Politician* (New York: Henry Holt and Company, 1990) is also useful. The Democratic side of the election of 1952 appears in John Bartlow Martin, *Adlai Stevenson and the World: The Life of Adlai E. Stevenson* (Garden City, N.Y.: Doubleday, 1977).

The activities that gradually led the five-star general into partisan politics included heading the committee on aid to Europe of the Council on Foreign Relations and a familiarity with the reports of economist Howard S. Ellis, author of *The Economics of Freedom: The Progress and Future of Aid to Europe* (New York: Council on Foreign Relations and Harper & Brothers, 1950). At this time Eisenhower was talking with his two closest military advisers and reading their accounts of service in Germany and the Soviet Union. These included Walter Bedell Smith, *My Three Years in Moscow* (Philadelphia: Lippincott, 1950) about his tour as U.S. ambassador to Moscow in 1946, and Lucius Clay, *Decision in Germany* (Garden City, N.Y.: Doubleday, 1950) on his tenure as military governor in occupied Germany and the Berlin blockade. Eisenhower also corresponded with Edward Mead Earle at Princeton during this period and read his edited volume entitled *Makers of Modern Strategy: Military Thought from Machiavelli to Hitler* (Princeton: Princeton University Press, 1952). Theodore H. White, *In Search of History* (New York: Harper and Row, Publishers, 1978) reveals Eisenhower's wartime magic with reporters.

The intellectual origins of the policy of containing Soviet expansion appear in a book by the policy's author, George F. Kennan, *Memoirs, 1925–1950* (Boston: Atlantic—Little, Brown, 1968) and also in Dean Acheson, *Present at the Creation: My Years at the State Department* (New York: Norton, 1969) and Forrest C. Pogue, *George C. Marshall: Statesman, 1945–1959* (New York: Viking, 1987): all three are indispensable books. For many years the standard analysis of the parting of ways of the postwar superpowers has been John Lewis Gaddis, *The United States and the Origins of the Cold War, 1941–1947* (New York: Columbia University Press, 1972). An excellent account drawing on more recent sources is Randall B. Woods & Howard Jones, *Dawning of the Cold War: The United States' Quest for Order* (Athens, Ga.: The University of Georgia Press, 1991). See also the more detailed and critical book by Melvyn P. Leffler entitled, *A Preponderance of Power: National Security, The Truman Administration, and the Cold War* (Stanford, Calif.: Stanford University Press, 1992). The book by Ronald W. Pruessen entitled, *John Foster Dulles: The Road to Power* (New York: The Free Press, 1982) is a good account of the early activities of the individual who would formulate and execute Eisenhower's foreign policy. Blanche Wiesen Cook, *The Declassified Eisenhower: A Startling Reappraisal of the Eisenhower Legacy* (Garden City, N.Y.: Doubleday, 1981) is detailed and useful on Eisenhower's rise and foreign policy as President. A balanced treatment of the literature is the article by Howard Jones and Randall B. Woods, "Origins of the Cold War in Europe and the Near East," *Diplomatic History,* Vol. 17 (Spring 1993). A fine section on the Korean War appears in Allan R. Millett and Peter Maslowski, *For the Common Defense: A Military History of the United States of America* (New York: The Free Press, 1984). See also James L. Stokesbury, *A Short History of the Korean War* (New York: William Morrow, 1988).

Chapter Four: Dilemmas of Power

The urgency of foreign and national security policy during the Eisenhower administration appear most vividly in the memoirs of Robert Cutler, the first special assistant for national security affairs, *No Time for Rest* (Boston: Little, Brown, 1966) and Henry Cabot Lodge's *As it Was: An Inside View of Politics and Power in the '40s and '60s* (New York: Norton, 1976); the latter author had served as Eisenhower's campaign manager, ad hoc political adviser, and ambassador to the United Nations. See also Robert H. Ferrell's edited diary of Eisenhower's press secretary, *The Diary of James C. Hagerty: Eisenhower in Mid-Course, 1954–1955* (Bloomington: Indiana University Press, 1983). Robert J. Donovan, the outsider with the earliest access to classified White House papers, wrote *Eisenhower: The Inside Story* (New York: Harper & Bros., 1956) and *Confidential Secretary: Ann Whitman's 20 Years with Eisenhower and Rockefeller* (New York: E.P. Dutton, 1988), a biography of Ike's personal secretary, one of the most efficient ever to hold the post. A full understanding of the issues of the day is possible only by reading John Lewis Gaddis's, *Strategies of Containment: A Critical Appraisal of Postwar American National Security Policy* (New York: Oxford University Press, 1982) and *The Long Peace: Inquiries into the History of the Cold War* (New York: Oxford University Press, 1987). Articles by John Lewis Gaddis, "The Tragedy of Cold War History," *Diplomatic History*, Vol. 17 (Winter 1993), 1–16; and Stephen G. Rabe, "Eisenhower Revisionism: A Decade of Scholarship," *Diplomatic History*, Vol. 17 (Winter 1993), 97–115, give the two opposing ways—the first favorable, the second critical—in which historians currently view Eisenhower as cold-war President. Robert A. Divine's, *Eisenhower and the Cold War* (New York: Oxford University Press, 1981) is a general account, in the vanguard of the Eisenhower revisionism. A more recent collection is Richard A. Melanson and David Mayers, eds., *Reevaluating Eisenhower: American Foreign Policy in the Fifties* (Urbana, Ill.: University of Illinois Press, 1987). In this volume see especially Kenneth W. Thompson, "The Strengths and Weaknesses of Eisenhower's Leadership," pp. 13–30 and Richard A. Melanson, "The Foundations of Eisenhower's Foreign Policy: Continuity, Community, and Consensus," pp. 31–66. Phillip G. Henderson's book, *Managing the Presidency: The Eisenhower Legacy from Kennedy to Reagan* (Boulder, Colo.: The Westview Press, 1988) scrutinizes Eisenhower's national security apparatus and style and Arthur M. Schlesinger, Jr.'s *The Imperial Presidency* (Boston: Houghton, Mifflin, 1973) provides historical context.

The assumptions and activities of Eisenhower's advisers appear in H. W. Brands, Jr., *Cold Warriors: Eisenhower's Generation and American Foreign Policy* (New York: Columbia University Press, 1988). The best sources on John Foster Dulles as secretary of state are Michael Guhin, *John Foster Dulles: A Statesman and His Times* (New York: Columbia University Press, 1972); and Ronald W. Pruessen, "John Foster Dulles and the Predicaments of Power," Richard W. Immerman, ed., *John Foster Dulles and the Diplomacy of the Cold War* (Princeton: Princeton University Press, 1990).

Among the many studies of Eisenhower's national security policy, several stand out. They include Richard G. Hewlett and Jack M. Holl, *Atoms for Peace and War, 1953–1961: Eisenhower and the Atomic Energy Commission* (Berkeley: University of California Press, 1989), by the Department of Energy's historical program. Eisenhower's two science advisers have written excellent memoirs. They are James R. Killian, Jr., *Sputnik, Scientists, and Eisenhower* (Cambridge, Mass.: MIT Press, 1977) and George Kistiakowsky, *A Scientist at the White House* (Cambridge, Mass.: Harvard University Press, 1976). McGeorge Bundy, President Kennedy's national security adviser, was one of the first, at the end of the Eisenhower years, to see that the U.S. was ahead in the arms race. His *Danger and Survival: Choices about the Bomb in the First Fifty Years* (New York: Random House, 1988) is a superb study of presidential attitudes and American national security concerns. An excellent summary of Eisenhower's approach to the problems of the thermonuclear age appears in Greg Herken, *Cardinal Choices: Presidential Science Advising from the Atomic Bomb to SDI* (New York: Oxford University Press, 1992). The nuclear age as part of the history of science appears in John Ziman, *The Force of Knowledge* (Cambridge: Cambridge University Press, 1976). An account of American secret probing of Soviet borders along with the U2 overflights appears in Douglas Stanglin, et al, "Secrets of the Cold War," *U.S. News and World Report*, March 15, 1993, 30–36.

Four books by historians provide detailed profiles of U.S. policy during this particularly dangerous time: they include Michael R. Beschloss, *Mayday: Eisenhower, Khrushchev, and the U-2 Affair* (New York: Harper & Row, Publishers, 1986); Robert A. Divine, *Blowing on the Wind: The Nuclear Test Ban Debate, 1954–1960* (New York: Oxford University Press, 1978) and *The Sputnik Challenge* (New York: Oxford University Press, 1993); and George F. Kennan, *The Nuclear Delusion: Soviet-American Relations in the Atomic Age* (New York: Pantheon, 1982). The best material on the evolution of American strategy is in Marc Trachtenberg's *History and Strategy* (Princeton: Princeton University Press, 1991). See also David A. Rosenberg, "'A Smoking Radiating Ruin at the End of Two Hours': Documents on American Plans for Nuclear War with the Soviet Union, 1954–1955," *International Security* Vol. 6, No. 3 (Winter 1981–1982) and Henry Kissinger, *Nuclear Weapons and Foreign Policy* (Garden City, N.Y.: Doubleday, 1958), written for Nelson Rockefeller as part of the preparedness debate after the launching of *Sputnik*. Information about plans to move the federal government to safety in the event of nuclear attack appear in Ted Gup, "The Doomsday Blueprints," *Time*, August 10, 1992, 32–39. Finally, Harold Stassen, Eisenhower's arms control official, collaborated with Marshall Houts in publishing *Eisenhower: Turning the World Toward Peace* (St. Paul, Minn.: Merrill/Magnus Publishing Corporation, 1990), a useful memoir.

For Soviet attitudes and policies one should consult Nikita S. Khrushchev, *Khrushchev Remembers* (New York: Bantam Books, 1971), and the book by Soviet defector Oleg Penkovskiy, *The Penkovskiy Papers* (New York: Ballantine Reprint, 1982). Scrutiny by Western historians appears in Carl A. Linden, *Khrushchev and the Soviet Leadership, 1957–1964* (Baltimore: The Johns Hopkins University Press, 1966) and, from Harvard Soviet scholar Adam Ulam, *Expansion and Coexistence* (New York: Praeger, 1974). See also the excellent paper by Jim Marchio entitled "From Revolution to Evolution: The Eisenhower Administration and Eastern Europe," (conference paper, Society for Historians of American Foreign Relations, June, 1993). Two papers that draw upon recently opened Soviet archives include Vladislav M. Zubok, "Khrushchev and the Berlin Crisis (1958–1962)" (Washington, D.C.: The Woodrow Wilson Center for Scholars, May, 1993) and Hope M. Harrison, "Ulbricht and the Concrete 'Rose'" (Washington, D.C.: The Woodrow Wilson Center for Scholars, May, 1993).

Balanced surveys of these issues include Ralph B. Levering, *The Cold War: A Post–Cold War History* (Wheeling, Ill.: Harlan Davidson, Inc., 1994) and Charles R. Morris, *Iron Destinies, Lost Opportunities: The Arms Race Between the U.S.A. and the U.S.S.R., 1945–1987* (New York: Harper & Row, Publishers, 1988). H. W. Brands, Jr., "The Age of Vulnerability: Eisenhower and the National Insecurity State," *American Historical Review* 94 (October 1989) is a critical account. A provocative book that claims that no major wars occurred after 1945 because war had shown itself to be too terrible to accrue any benefits and was therefore obsolete (something that Eisenhower seemed to sense) is John Mueller's, *Retreat from Doomsday: The Obsolescence of Major War* (New York: Basic Books, 1989).

The bases of Soviet policy appear in Nikita S. Khrushchev, *Khrushchev Remembers: The Last Testament* (Boston: Little, Brown, 1974) and Andrei Sakharov, *Memoirs* (New York: Alfred A. Knopf, 1990). See also the more recent revelations in Serge Schmemann, "Soviet Archives Provide Missing Pieces of History's Puzzles," *New York Times*, February 8, 1993, A6.

The documents showing the development of Eisenhower's strategy became available to researchers in 1985. Articles written with the new information in mind are William B. Pickett, "The Eisenhower Solarium Notes," The Society for Historians of American Foreign Relations *Newsletter* Vol. 16, No. 2, June 1985, and "Eisenhower, Clausewitz, and American Power," The Society for Historians of American Foreign Relations *Newsletter*, Vol. 23, December 1991.

One can find a general account of Eisenhower's use of clandestine activities in Stephen E. Ambrose, *Ike's Spies: Eisenhower and the Espionage Establishment* (Garden City, N.Y.: Doubleday, 1981); John Prados, *Presidents' Secret Wars: CIA and Pentagon Covert Operations since World War II* (New York: William Morrow and Company, Inc., 1986); and in the large book by John Ranelagh, *The Agency: The Rise and Decline of the CIA from Wild Bill Donovan to William Casey* (New York: Simon and Schuster, 1986). Rhodri Jeffreys-Jones, *The CIA and American Democracy* (New Haven: Yale University Press, 1989) also is excellent.

For the Korean armistice see Edward C. Keefer, "President Dwight D. Eisenhower and the End of the Korean War," *Diplomatic History* Vol. 10, No. 3 (Summer 1986) and Roger Dingman, "Atomic Diplomacy During the Korean War," *International Security* (Winter 1988–1989).

The decision not to intervene in Indochina in 1954 to help the French is the topic of Richard H. Immerman's article entitled "Between the Unattainable and the Unacceptable: Eisenhower and Dienbienphu," in Richard A. Melanson and David Mayers, above, pp. 120–54. See also the more recent, well-considered account by John P. Burke and Fred I. Greenstein, *How Presidents Test Reality: Decisions on Vietnam, 1954 and 1965* (New York: Russell Sage Foundation, 1989) and that of Melanie Billings-Yun, *Decision Against War: Eisenhower and Dien Bien Phu, 1954* (New York: Columbia University Press, 1988). Furthermore, one will find a favorable interpretation of Eisenhower's policy in George C. Herring's, *America's Longest War: The United States and Vietnam, 1950–1975*, Second Edition (New York: Alfred A. Knopf, 1986) while David L. Anderson's entitled *Trapped by Success: The Eisenhower Administration and Vietnam, 1953–1961* (New York: Columbia University Press, 1991) provides an interpretation that is a critical one.

The best analysis of the Suez crisis is Donald Neff, *Warriors at Suez: Eisenhower Takes America into the Middle East* (New York: The Linden Press, Simon & Schuster, 1981).

For an understanding of Eisenhower's policy toward Latin America (and by implication, the Third World) one should consult a book by the President's closest adviser on the subject, Milton S. Eisenhower, *The Wine is Bitter: The United States and Latin America* (Garden City, N.Y.: Doubleday, 1963), then see Burton I. Kaufman, *Trade and Aid: Eisenhower's Foreign Economic Policy, 1953–1961* (Baltimore: Johns Hopkins University Press, 1982) and Richard H. Immerman, *The CIA in Guatemala: The Foreign Policy of Intervention* (Austin: The University of Texas Press, 1982). Blanche Wiesen Cook, above, and Stephen G. Rabe, in his *Eisenhower and Latin America: The Foreign Policy of Anticommunism* (Chapel Hill: The University of North Carolina Press, 1988) criticize Eisenhower's policies. H. W. Brands, Jr., in *The Specter of Neutralism: The United States and the Emergence of the Third World, 1947–1960* (New York: Columbia University Press, 1989) says that the Eisenhower administration pursued not moralism as historians had thought but geopolitics in places like Yugoslavia, India, and Egypt.

Chapter Five: The Politics of Moderation

Books by individuals closest to the man in the Oval Office are Sherman Adams's, *Firsthand Report* (New York: Harper & Bros., 1961), memoirs by Eisenhower's White House chief of staff; and Milton S. Eisenhower's, *The President is Calling* (Garden City, N.Y.: Doubleday, 1974). Arthur Larson, author of *The President Nobody Knew* (New York: Charles Scribners, 1968), helped formulate Modern Republicanism as an Eisenhower staff member. The revisionist Eisenhower scholarship became prominent with Fred I. Greenstein's book entitled *The Hidden-Hand Presidency: Eisenhower as Leader* (New York: Basic Books, 1982). It bolstered those who believed that the earlier view of Eisenhower was superficial at best. He continued his reappraisal in his article "Dwight D. Eisenhower: Leadership Theorist in the White House," in Fred I. Greenstein, ed., *Leadership in the Modern Presidency* (Cambridge, Mass.: Harvard University Press, 1988). Richard Rovere's, "Eisenhower Revisited: A Political Genius? A Brilliant Man? *New York Times Magazine*, February 7, 1971, and William Bragg Ewald, Jr.'s *Eisenhower the President: Crucial Days: 1951–1960* (Englewood Cliffs, N.J.; Prentice-Hall, Inc., 1981) were in a similar vein. Rovere was an astute journalist and Ewald an assistant to Eisenhower. Political scientist Samuel Lubell's *The Future of American Politics* (New York: Harper, 1954) was a book Eisenhower read at the time.

Three excellent histories of the United States during the Truman and Eisenhower presidencies are Gary W. Reichard, *Politics as Usual: The Age of Truman and Eisenhower* (Wheeling, Ill.: Harlan Davidson, Inc., 1988); William L. O'Neill, *American High: The Years of Confidence, 1945–1960* (New York: Free Press, 1986); and John Patrick Diggins, *The Proud Decades: America in War and in Peace, 1941–1960* (New York: Norton, 1988). Two studies of liberalism in postwar America are William E. Leuchtenburg, *In the Shadow of FDR: From Harry Truman to Ronald Reagan* (Ithaca, N.Y.: Cornell University Press, 1983) and Alonzo L. Hamby, *Liberalism and Its Challengers: From FDR to Bush*, second edition (New York: Oxford University Press, 1992). Larger surveys are James MacGregor Burns, *The Crosswinds of Freedom: From Roosevelt to Reagan—America in the Last Half Century* (New York: Vintage, 1989), richly detailed and important for perspective, and John Edward Wilz, *Democracy Challenged: The United States since World War II* (New York: Harper & Row, 1990), a fine overview.

For the political economy of the 1950s the best treatment is also the only book dealing solely with the administration's fiscal policy as part of the political economy. It is Iwan W. Morgan, *Eisenhower versus "the Spenders": The Eisenhower Administration, the Democrats and the Budget, 1953–60* (New York: St. Martin's Press, 1990). One also should consult Robert Griffith, "Dwight D. Eisenhower and The Corporate Commonwealth," *American Historical Review* 87 (February 1982); Gary Reichard, *The Reaffirmation of Republicanism* (Knoxville: The University of Tennessee Press, 1975); and Harry W. Schreiber, Harold G.

Vatter, and Harold U. Faulkner, *American Economic History* (New York: Harper & Row, Publishers, 1976). Two older accounts are James L. Sundquist, *Politics and Policy: The Eisenhower, Kennedy, and Johnson Years* (Washington, D.C.: Brookings Institution, 1968) and Charles Alexander, *Holding the Line: The Eisenhower Era* (Bloomington: Indiana University Press, 1975). Eisenhower's sway with Senate Republicans appears in William B. Pickett, *Homer E. Capehart: A Senator's Life, 1897–1979* (Indianapolis: Indiana Historical Society, 1990). See also Stephen E. Ambrose, *Nixon: The Education of a Politician, 1913–1962* (New York: Simon and Schuster, 1987).

The causes and effects of the Red scare appear in David W. Reinhard, *The Republican Right Since 1945* (Lexington: University of Kentucky Press, 1985); Richard Gid Powers, *Secrecy and Power: The Life of J. Edgar Hoover* (New York: The Free Press, 1987); and David M. Oshinsky, *A Conspiracy So Immense: The World of Joe McCarthy* (New York: Free Press, 1983). For the demise of the feared senator from Wisconsin and the army-McCarthy hearings see John G. Adams, *Without Precedent: The Story of the Death of McCarthyism* (New York: W. W. Norton & Company, 1983). Jeff Broadwater, *Eisenhower and the Anti-communist Crusade* (Chapel Hill: The University of North Carolina Press, 1992) is a recent analysis that measures Eisenhower's sensitivity to civil liberties.

Earlier analyses brought up to date include Robert Griffith, *The Politics of Fear: Joseph R. McCarthy and the Senate*, second edition (Amherst: University of Massachusetts Press, 1987) and Richard Fried, *Nightmare in Red: The McCarthy Era in Perspective* (New York: Oxford University Press, 1990).

The problem of civil rights in the 1950s appears in books by James C. Duram, *A Moderate Among Extremists: Dwight D. Eisenhower and the School Desegregation Crisis* (Chicago: Nelson-Hall, 1981) and Robert F. Burk, *The Eisenhower Administration and Black Civil Rights* (Knoxville: University of Tennessee Press, 1984). Numan V. Bartley, *The Rise of Massive Resistance: Race and Politics in the South during the 1950s* (Baton Rouge: Louisiana State University Press, 1969) documents white southern resistance to integration. Juan Williams's full and excellent treatment, *Eyes on the Prize: America's Civil Rights Years, 1954–1965* (1987) provides context.

The urban, beltway nation tied together with interstate highways is the subject of Mark H. Rose, *Interstate: Express Highway Politics, 1941–1956* (Lawrence: Regents Press of Kansas, 1979); Richard O. Davies, *The Age of Asphalt: The Automobile, the Freeway, and the Condition of Metropolitan America* (Philadelphia: Lippincott, 1975); and Mark I. Gelfand, *A Nation of Cities: The Federal Government and Urban America, 1933–1965* (New York: Oxford University Press, 1975). For women, children, and homelife in the 1950s, see Elaine Tyler May *Homeward Bound: American Families in the Cold War Era* (New York: Basic Books, 1988)

Robert H. Ferrell has written an excellent and startling book on presidential health and disability, five of the eight chapters of which shed new light on Eisenhower. It is entitled, *Ill-Advised: Presidential Health and the Public Trust* (Columbia, Mo.: University of Missouri Press, 1992).

Robert A. Divine, in his book entitled *Foreign Policy and U.S. Presidential Elections, 1952–1960* (New York: New Viewpoints, 1974), appraises the elections of 1956 and 1960. Theodore H. White's *The Making of the President, 1960* (1961) was the first in his superb series on American presidential elections. See also Divine's book on *Sputnik* mentioned above and Ambrose, *Nixon: The Education*; Parmet, *Eisenhower*; and Reichard, *Politics and Usual*, also above.

Chapter Six: Retirement

The best accounts of the Kennedy presidency, including the Bay of Pigs and the Cuban missile crisis are the following: Herbert S. Parmet, *JFK: The Presidency of John F. Kennedy* (New York: The Dial Press, 1983); Michael Beschloss, *The Crisis Years: Kennedy and Khrushchev, 1960–1963* (New York: Harper Collins,

1991); and Trumbull Higgins, *The Perfect Failure: Kennedy, Eisenhower, and the CIA at the Bay of Pigs* (New York: Norton, 1987), which finds the CIA unprepared for a Cuban invasion as Eisenhower left office. See also Gary Wills, *The Kennedy Imprisonment: A Meditation on Power* (Boston: Little, Brown, 1981) and the book by Kennedy White House historian, Arthur M. Schlesinger, Jr., entitled *Robert Kennedy and His Times* (Boston: Houghton Mifflin Co., 1978).

For Eisenhower as adviser to the Johnson presidency one should see Lyndon B. Johnson, *Vantage Point: Perspectives of the Presidency, 1963–1969* (New York: Popular Library, 1971); John P. Burke and Fred I. Greenstein, *How Presidents Test Reality: Decisions on Vietnam, 1954 and 1965* (New York: Russell Sage Foundation, 1989); Larry Berman, *Planning a Tragedy: The Americanization of the War in Vietnam* (New York: Norton, 1982); Herbert Schandler, *The Unmaking of a President: Lyndon Johnson and Vietnam* (Princeton: Princeton University Press, 1977); H. W. Brands, Jr., "Johnson and Eisenhower: The President, the Former President, and the War in Vietnam," *Presidential Studies Quarterly* 15 (1985); Doris Kearns, *Lyndon Johnson and the American Dream* (New York: Harper & Row, 1976); and Richard Nixon, *R. N.: The Memoirs of Richard Nixon* (New York: Grosset & Dunlap, 1978). See also Mary S. McAuliffe, ed. *CIA Documents on the Cuban Missile Crisis, 1962* (Washington, D.C.: C.I.A., 1992).

Conclusion

An appraisal of Eisenhower entails looking first at the initial evaluation, which is included in the following books: Marquis Childs, *Eisenhower: Captive Hero* (New York: Harcourt, Brace, 1958); Emmet John Hughes, *America the Vincible* (Garden City, N.Y.: Doubleday & Company, Inc., 1959) and *The Ordeal of Power: A Political Memoir of the Eisenhower Years* (New York: Atheneum, 1963); Richard Neustadt, *Presidential Power* (New York: John Wiley, 1960); and Richard Hofstadter, *Anti-Intellectualism*

in American Life (New York: Alfred A. Knopf, 1963). For simi-
lar interpretations of Eisenhower in college textbooks see
James T. Patterson, *America in the Twentieth Century*, Part Two,
A History Since 1939 (New York: Harcourt Brace Jovanovich,
Inc., 1976). The revision of the history of Eisenhower and his
administration began years earlier but first appeared promi-
nently in Robert H. Ferrell's *The Eisenhower Diaries* and Fred
Greenstein's *The Hidden Hand Presidency*, above. Steve Neal's
article entitled "Why We Were Right to Like Ike," *American
Heritage*, Vol. 37, number 1 (December 1985), p. 53, contin-
ued the revisionist view, as did the article by William E.
Leuchtenburg, "Presidents: Each One Makes History," *Life*
(Special Issue, Fall, 1990), 69–71. Both articles drew upon the
findings of Robert K. Murray and Tim H. Blessing, "The Presi-
dential Performance Study: A Progress Report," *Journal of
American History* 70 (December 1983), 535–537. Other analyses of the phenomenon include William Howard Moore, "Do
We 'Like Ike'?: Historians and the Eisenhower Presidency,"
Kansas History (Spring 1990), 192, 196; Alan Brinkley, "A President for Certain Seasons," *The Wilson Quarterly* (Spring 1990),
113–114; Robert F. Burk, "Eisenhower Revisionism Revisited:
Reflections on Eisenhower Scholarship," *The Historian*, Vol. L
(February 1988); and Richard E. Neustadt, *Presidential Power
and the Modern Presidents: The Politics of Leadership from Roosevelt
to Reagan* (New York: The Free Press, 1990), in which he substantially revises his 1960 estimate of Eisenhower. While critical of Ike for not achieving detente, Neustadt mentions Ike's
health as a possible extenuating circumstance and praises him
as a master of decision making and the conservation of presidential power.

For more recent efforts to come to grips with the new
Eisenhower see Richard H. Immerman, "Confessions of an
Eisenhower Revisionist: An Agonizing Reappraisal," *Diplomatic
History* Vol. 14 (Summer 1990), and Anthony James Joe,
"Eisenhower Revisionism and American Politics," in Joann P.
Krieg, ed., *Dwight Eisenhower: Soldier, President, Statesman* (Green-

wood Press, 1987). Arthur M. Schlesinger, Jr., in his interpre-
tive book, *The Cycles of American History* (Boston: Houghton
Mifflin Co., 1986) refuses to countenance an ex post facto re-
habilitation of Eisenhower. But John Lewis Gaddis has placed
the Eisenhower years favorably in historical context. His appraisal appears in "The Unexpected John Foster Dulles: Nuclear
Weapons, Communism, and the Russians," Richard H.
Immerman, ed., *John Foster Dulles and the Diplomacy of the Cold
War* (Princeton: Princeton University Press, 1990) and in his
collection of essays entitled *The United States and the End of the
Cold War* (New York: Oxford University Press, 1992).

INDEX

Dwight David Eisenhower and American Power
Developmental editor, Andrew J. Davidson
Production editor, Lucy Herz
Cartographer, James Bier
Typesetter, Robin Stearns
Printer, McNaughton & Gunn, Inc.
Book designer, Roger Eggers

About the Author: William B. Pickett, born in Crawfordsville, Indiana, received a B.A. from Carleton College and a Ph.D. from Indiana University; he is currently Professor of History at Rose-Hulman Institute of Technology. Professor Pickett's other writings include two books, *Technology at the Turning Point* (1977) and *Homer E. Capehart: A Senator's Life* (1990), and numerous articles on recent U.S. political, diplomatic, and military history. He was a Fulbright lecturer in Japan and is past president of the Indiana Association of Historians.